Spelling Workout

Phillip K. Trocki

Modern Curriculum Press
is an imprint of

PEARSON

Boston, Massachusetts

Chandler, Arizona

Glenview, Illinois

Upper Saddle River, New Jersey

COVER DESIGN: Pronk & Associates

ILLUSTRATIONS: Chris Knowles. 189: Jim Steck.

PHOTOGRAPHS: All photos © Pearson Learning unless otherwise noted.

Cover: Artbase Inc.
5: © Stephen Coburn/Fotolia.com. 8: NASA Marshall Space Flight Center Collection. 9: © Olga Lyubkina/Fotolia.com. 17: © Wally Stemberger/Fotolia.com. 21: © kelleyjoy/Fotolia.com. 24: Photo by the Waterman Co., Chicago, IL/Library of Congress, Prints and Photographs Division, LC-USZ62-50927. 29: © Underwood & Underwood/Library of Congress, Prints and Photographs Division, LC-USZ62-112825. 32: © Comstock Images/Thinkstock. 33: © Digital Vision. 35: © Brand X Pictures. 37: Spacesuit and Spacewalk History Image Gallery/NASA. 40: NASA Johnson Space Center Collection. 41: © James Phelps Jr/Fotolia.com. 44: © Michael/Fotolia.com. 48: © Daniel Bujack/Fotolia.com. 53: © Kenneth Man/Fotolia.com. 56: © Photos.com/Thinkstock. 57: © Laurence Gough/Fotolia.com. 61: © Andres Rodriguez/Fotolia.com. 63: © silver-john/Fotolia.com. 64: © Thomas Northcut/Thinkstock. 65: © PhotoDisc, Inc. 68: © Jupiterimages/Thinkstock. 72: © Chris White/Fotolia.com. 77: © Marcus/Fotolia.com. 80: © Paul Katz/Thinkstock. 81: © Steve Allen/Thinkstock. 84: © Sebastian Corneanu/Fotolia.com. 85: © Helmut Niklas/Fotolia.com. 88: © Jupiterimages/Thinkstock. 89: © Comstock/Thinkstock. 90: © Jupiterimages/Thinkstock. 93: © Jupiterimages/Thinkstock. 94: © Comstock/Thinkstock. 97: © Richard E. Doty/Fotolia.com. 99: © Pearson Education. 101: © Stockbyte/Thinkstock. 104: © Brand X Pictures/Thinkstock. 105: © Stockbyte/Thinkstock. 108: © Jupiterimages/Thinkstock. 109: © Comstock/Thinkstock. 110: © Wild Geese/Fotolia.com. 112: © Kim Steele/Thinkstock. 113: © Ablestock.com/Thinkstock. 116: © Digital Vision. 117: © Jupiterimages/Thinkstock. 120: © Jack Hollingsworth/Thinkstock. 125: © Ablestock.com/Thinkstock. 126: © Dave King/Dorling Kindersley. 128: © Thinkstock Images. 129: © Siri Stafford/Thinkstock. 132: © Lsantilli/Fotolia.com. 133: © Alex_Mac/Fotolia.com. 136: © Jen Siska/Getty Images. 137: © Jupiterimages/Thinkstock. 140: © Romanchuck/Fotolia.com. 141: © Robert Hackett/Fotolia.com. 144: © Matthias Falke/Fotolia.com.

Acknowledgments
ZB font Method Copyright © 1996 Zaner-Bloser.

Some content in this product is based upon WEBSTER'S NEW WORLD DICTIONARY, 4/E. Copyright ©2013 by Houghton Mifflin Harcourt Publishing Company. Reprinted by permission of Houghton Mifflin Harcourt Publishing Company. All rights reserved.

NOTE: Every effort has been made to locate the copyright owner of material reprinted in this book. Omissions brought to our attention will be corrected in subsequent editions.

Modern Curriculum Press
is an imprint of

ISBN–13: 978-0-7652-2494-1
ISBN–10:   0-7652-2494-1

17 V036 18 17 16 15

Table of Contents

Spelling Workout–Our Philosophy

Integration of Spelling with Writing

Spelling Workout provides for the integration of writing and spelling. In each lesson, students are asked to write about a topic related to the list words using various forms, such as poems, reports, advertisements, editorials, and letters.

The study of spelling should not be limited to a specific time in the school day. Use opportunities throughout the day to reinforce and maintain spelling skills by integrating spelling with other curriculum areas. Point out spelling words in books, texts, and the students' own writing. Encourage students to write, as they practice spelling through writing. Provide opportunities for writing with a purpose.

Across the Curriculum with Spelling Words

Each lesson of Spelling Workout contains a list of bonus words. These words were drawn from many subject areas including science, social studies, health, language arts, music, and art. Other bonus words feature terms related to more recent changes in technology.

Instructional Design

Spelling Workout takes a solid phonetic and structural approach to encoding. In each list of twenty words, all relate to the organizing principle or relationship that is the focus of the lesson. Of those list words, at least half are words that the student should be familiar with at that particular grade level. The remaining words introduce new vocabulary with emphasis on meaning, usage, and etymology.

Lessons have been organized as efficiently as possible with the degree of spelling difficulty in mind, and with as much diversity as possible. In addition to lessons based on phonetic and structural analysis, lessons containing challenging words, content words, and words adopted from other languages have been included in order to vary the focus from lesson to lesson.

Research-Based Teaching Strategies

Spelling Workout utilizes a test-study-test method of teaching spelling. The student first takes a pretest of words that have not yet been introduced. Under the direction of the teacher, the student then corrects the test, rewriting correctly any word that has been missed. This approach not only provides an opportunity to determine how many words a student can already spell but also allows students to analyze spelling mistakes. In the process, students also discover patterns that make it easier to spell list words.

High-Utility List Words

Word lists for each lesson have been chosen with the following criteria in mind:

- Frequently misspelled words

- Application to students' academic experiences

- Introduction to new or unfamiliar vocabulary

- Visible structural similarity (consonant and vowel patterns)

- Relationship groupings (prefixes, roots, subject areas, and so on)

Word lists have been compiled from the following:

Columbia University, N.Y. Bureau of Publications. *Spelling Difficulties in 3,876 Words*

Dolch. *2,000 Commonest Words for Spelling*

Florida Department of Education. *Lists for Assessment of Spelling*

Fry, Fountokidis, and Polk. *The New Reading Teacher's Book of Lists*

Green. *The New Iowa Spelling Scale*

Hanna. *Phoneme-Grapheme Correspondence as Cues to Spelling Improvement*

Smith and Ingersoll. *Written Vocabulary of Elementary School Pupils, Ages 6–14*

S.C. Dept. of Education. *South Carolina Word List, Grades 1–12*

Thomas. *Canadian Word Lists and Instructional Techniques*

University of Iowa. *The List of 1,000 Words Most Commonly Misspelled*

A Format That Results in Success

Spelling Workout furnishes an intensive review of spelling skills previously taught and introduces the students to more sophisticated words and concepts. Lesson emphasis is on spelling strategies, developing vocabulary, practicing correct word usage, and understanding word derivations.

Sample Core Lesson

- The **Tip** explains the spelling rules or patterns, providing a focus for the lesson.

- The **List Words** box contains the spelling words for each lesson. Words were selected on the basis of meaning, usage, and origin.

- Each lesson begins with activities centering on vocabulary development, dictionary skills, and word analysis.

- **Did You Know?** exposes students to word origins and word histories while increasing vocabulary. An etymology is found in each lesson.

- **Spelling Practice** exercises give students an opportunity to practice the list words, focusing on their structure and meaning.

Words from Sports — Lesson 32

TIP

Sports and physical fitness are an important part of our daily lives and language.
Them are words that refer to specific sports.
  soccer   skiing   acrobatics
There are words that refer to people in sports.
  sportscaster   goalkeeper
Some sports words name athletic equipment.
  kayak
Some words name specific athletic events.
  Olympics
All the **list** words are from sports. Study the words carefully. Words like *aerobics* and *decathlon* are often misspelled.

Vocabulary Development

Write the **list word** that matches each definition.

1. practice between two teams — scrimmage
2. sport played on ice — hockey
3. a short-distance runner — sprinter
4. exercises that give the body oxygen — aerobics
5. participant in athletic event — contestant
6. moving with quickness and ease — agile
7. a judge in a football game — referee
8. a person who oversees a baseball game — umpire
9. an athletic contest consisting of ten events — decathlon
10. a type of canoe — kayak

Dictionary Skills

Rewrite each of the following **list words** to show how they are divided into syllables.

1. acrobatics — ac/ro/bat/ics
2. gymnastics — gym/nas/tics
3. sportscaster — sports/cast/er
4. Olympics — O/lym/pics
5. goalkeeper — goal/keep/er
6. skiing — ski/ing
7. soccer — soc/cer
8. ankle — an/kle
9. archery — arch/er/y
10. toboggan — to/bog/gan

LIST WORDS

1. acrobatics
2. toboggan
3. archery
4. Olympics
5. sportscaster
6. aerobics
7. contestant
8. goalkeeper
9. referee
10. sprinter
11. agile
12. decathlon
13. gymnastics
14. skiing
15. umpire
16. ankle
17. scrimmage
18. kayak
19. soccer
20. hockey

129

DID YOU KNOW?
Hockey may have come from an old French or Dutch word meaning "hook" or "crook." Long ago, the game was probably played with a ball of wood or cork and curved sticks cut from the branches of willow trees.

Spelling Practice

Word Analysis

Write **list words** to answer the following questions.

Which words end with **ics**?
1. acrobatics
2. Olympics
3. aerobics
4. gymnastics

Which words contain these double consonants?
5. mm — scrimmage
6. gg — toboggan
7. cc — soccer

Which words contain these double vowels?
8. ii — skiing
9. ee — goalkeeper
10. ee — referee

Which words are compound words?
11. sportscaster
12. goalkeeper

Analogies

Write a **list word** to complete each analogy.

1. Nimble is to lively as — agile — is to flexible.
2. Five is to pentathlon as ten is to — decathlon
3. Wrist is to hand as — ankle — is to foot.
4. Sedan is to car as — kayak — is to canoe.
5. Judge is to courtroom as — umpire — is to ballgame.
6. Baseball is to catcher as — hockey — is to goalie.
7. Basket is to basketball as target is to — archery
8. Movie reviewer is to film as — sportscaster — is to athletic event.

Word Application

Underline the **list word** in each sentence that is used incorrectly. Write the correct **list word** on the line.

1. People who take part in a contest are called referes. — contestants
2. The goalkeeper sprained his ankle running to the finish line. — sprinter
3. He trained to be an umpire in the youth soccer league. — referee

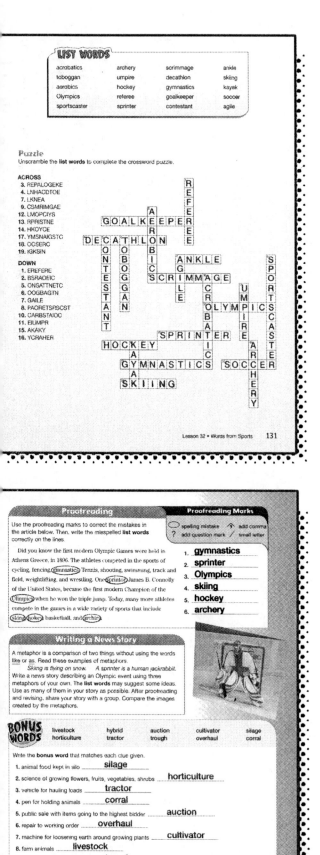

• Activities such as crossword puzzles, riddles, and games help motivate students by making learning fun.

• **Spelling and Writing** reinforces the connection between spelling and everyday writing and encourages students to apply the list words in different contexts.

• **Proofreading** practice builds proofreading proficiency and encourages students to check their own writing.

• **Writing** activities provide opportunities for students to write their spelling words in a variety of writing forms and genres.

• **Bonus Words** offer more challenging words drawn from various curriculum areas. Many of the activities in the *Teacher's Edition* give students the opportunity to practice the words with classmates.

Sample Review Lesson

- The **Review** lesson allows students to practice what they've learned.

- The spelling patterns used in the previous five lessons are reviewed at the beginning of the lesson.

- A variety of activities provide practice and review of selected list words from the previous lessons.

Lessons 31-35 · Review

TIPS

- Recognizing and understanding Latin roots and Latin and Greek prefixes can help you spell and understand unfamiliar words. Some Latin roots and their meanings include **ver** ("turn") as in extrovert ("outgoing") and **viv, vit** ("live") as in revive ("return to life").
- Some Latin and Greek prefixes include **pan** ("all") as in panorama ("sweeping view") and **multi** ("many") as in multicolored ("many colors").
- Some English words are associated with one specific topic. These words are from sports.
  acrobatics   umpire   scrimmage
- There are numerous spelling rules that can help you figure out how to spell a difficult word. When spelling a compound word, think about the way the individual words that make up the compound word are spelled. Some compound words are spelled with a hyphen dividing the two words.
  throughout   two-thousandths
- Remember to divide compound words into syllables between the words that form the compound word.
  book/keeper
- Some words do not follow ordinary spelling rules. Memorize and practice spelling these challenging words.
  numerous   martyr   similar

Lesson 31

List Words

vivid
illusion
ludicrous
versatile
tempest
extemporaneous
vitamin
spectacular
temporary
carnivorous

Write **list words** to answer the questions.

Which **list words** contain the Latin root **temp** that means "time"?
1. tempest   3. temporary
2. extemporaneous

Which **list word** contains the Latin root **vor** that means "eat"?
4. carnivorous

Which **list word** contains the Latin root **spect** that means "see"?
5. spectacular

Which **list words** contain the Latin roots **viv** or **vit** that mean "life"?
6. vitamin   7. vivid

Which **list words** contain the Latin roots **lus** or **lud** that mean "play"?
8. illusion   9. ludicrous

Which **list word** contains the Latin root **ver** that means "turn"?
10. versatile

145

- **Show What You Know** is a cumulative review of the words in the five previous lessons using a standardized-test format.

Show What You Know

Lessons 31-35 · Review

One word is misspelled in each set of **list words**. Fill in the circle next to the **list word** that is spelled incorrectly.

1.	○ carnivorous	○ aerobics	● two-thousanths	○ multiple
2.	○ quarterback	○ illusion	○ equinox	● contesient
3.	○ goalkeeper	○ polyester	○ ludicrous	● bookeeper
4.	○ audio-visual	● referree	○ copyright	○ suspect
5.	○ sprinter	● polysylabic	○ nine-hundredths	○ versatile
6.	○ three-fourths	○ agile	● ellude	○ equidistant
7.	● decathelon	○ polygamy	○ beneficial	○ illusion
8.	● ilminate	○ retrospect	○ omnipotent	○ gymnastics
9.	○ tempest	● pantomine	○ numerous	○ restaurant
10.	○ equilibrium	○ vitality	○ tradition	● sking
11.	○ umpire	● hypocrit	○ extemporaneous	○ polygon
12.	● intravert	○ ankle	○ pandemonium	○ extravagant
13.	○ throughout	● priviledge	○ revive	○ scrimmage
14.	○ similar	○ kayak	● handelbars	○ temporal
15.	○ motorcycle	○ vitamin	○ soccer	● trmendous
16.	○ extrovert	● critisism	○ absent-minded	○ hockey
17.	● twentynine	○ hyperbole	○ inverse	○ luxury
18.	○ omniscient	○ spacecraft	○ prominent	● spectaculer
19.	○ temporary	○ eyewitness	○ hyperactive	● sincerly
20.	○ yacht	○ vivid	● selfsacrifice	○ part-time
21.	● abl-bodied	○ multimedia	○ acrobatics	○ educational
22.	○ multicolored	● marteyr	○ omnipresent	○ toboggan
23.	○ archery	○ panorama	● probabaly	○ vineyard
24.	● suseptible	○ Olympics	○ air-conditioned	○ polytheism
25.	○ multitude	○ loose-leaf	● suddeness	○ sportscaster

148   Lesson 36 · Review

10

Spelling Workout in the Classroom

Classroom Management

Spelling Workout is designed as a flexible instructional program. The following plans are two ways the program can be taught.

The 5-day Plan

Day 1 – Pretest/Spelling Strategy

Days 2 and 3 – Spelling Practice

Day 4 – Spelling and Writing

Day 5 – Final Test

The 3-day Plan

Day 1 – Pretest/Spelling Strategy/
    Spelling Practice

Day 2 – Spelling Practice/Spelling and Writing

Day 3 – Final Test

Testing

Testing is accomplished in several ways. The **Pretest** is administered before beginning the **Spelling Strategy**, and the **Final Test** is administered at the end of each lesson. Dictation sentences for each **Pretest** and **Final Test** are provided.

Research suggests that students benefit from correcting their own **Pretests**. After the test has been administered, have students self-correct their tests in the following manner. As you read each letter of the list word, ask students to point to each letter and circle any incorrect letters. Then, have students rewrite each misspelled word correctly.

Dictation sentences for the bonus words are also furnished for teachers desiring to include these words in weekly tests.

Tests for review lessons are provided as reproducibles in the back of the Teacher's Edition. These tests provide not only an evaluation tool for teachers, but also added practice in taking standardized tests for students.

Individualizing Instruction

Bonus Words are included in every lesson as a challenge for better spellers and to provide extension and enrichment for all students.

Review lessons reinforce the correct spelling of difficult words from previous lessons.

The **Review** lessons also provide for individual needs. Each has space for students to add words from previous lessons that they found especially difficult.

The **Spelling Notebook** allows each student to analyze their own spelling errors and practice writing their troublesome words independently. Notebook pages appear as reproducibles in the Teacher's Edition and as pages at the back of the student book.

A reproducible individual **Student Record Chart** provided in the Teacher's Edition allows students to record their test scores.

Ideas for meeting the needs of ESL students are provided on pages 14–15.

Dictionary

In the back of each student book is a comprehensive dictionary with definitions of all the list words and bonus words. Students will have this resource at their fingertips for any assignment.

The Teacher's Edition —Everything You Need!

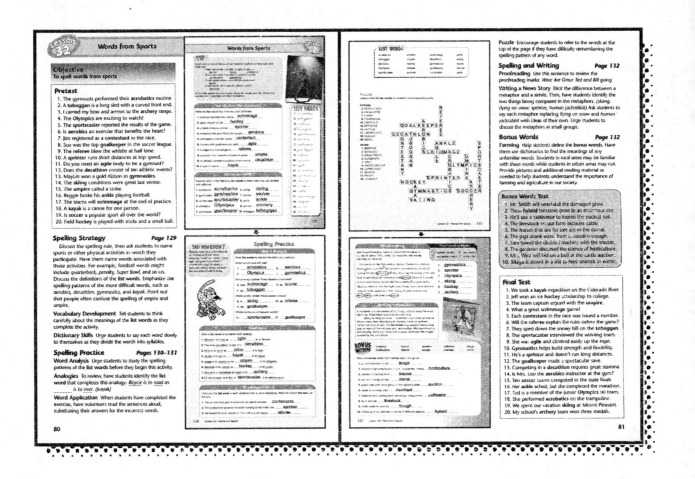

- The **Objective** clearly states the goals of each core lesson.

- A **Pretest** is administered before the start of each lesson. Dictation sentences are provided.

- **Spelling Strategy** provides start-up activities that offer suggestions for introducing the spelling principles.

- Concise teaching notes give guidance for working through the lesson.

- **Spelling Practice** activities provide additional support for reinforcing and analyzing spelling patterns.

- **Spelling and Writing** includes suggestions for helping students use proofreading marks to correct their work. Suggestions for using the writing process to complete the writing activity are also offered.

- Activities for using the bonus words listed in the student books are provided in the **Bonus Words** section.

- Dictation sentences are provided for testing the bonus words.

- A **Final Test** is administered at the end of the lesson. Dictation sentences are provided.

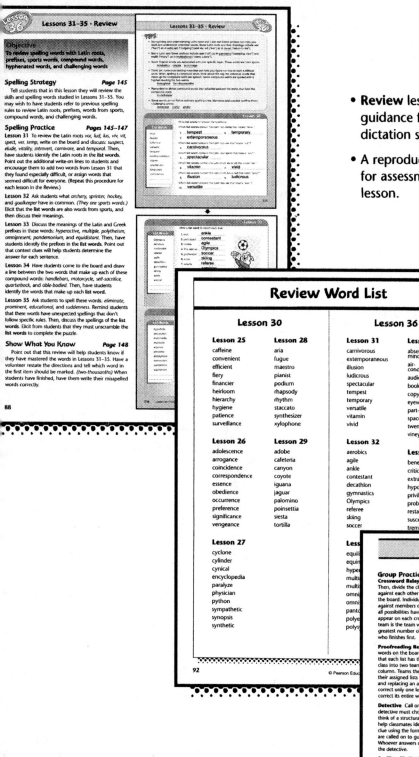

- **Review** lessons review spelling objectives, give guidance for further practice of list words, and provide dictation sentences for a **Final Test**.

- A reproducible two-page standardized test is supplied for assessment purposes for use after each **Review** lesson.

Reproducible study sheets of **Review** lesson words are included in the *Teacher's Edition* to help prepare students for test taking.

Suggested games and group activities make spelling more fun.

Ideas for meeting the needs of **ESL** students are provided on pages 14–15.

Meeting the Needs of Your ESL Students

Spelling Strategies for Your ESL Students

You may want to try some of these suggestions to help you promote successful language learning for ESL students.

• Prompt the use of spelling words by showing pictures or objects that relate to the topic of the lesson, the proofreading piece, or the words themselves. Invite students to discuss the picture or object.

• Demonstrate actions or act out words. Encourage students to do the same.

• Read each Tip and proofreading selection aloud before asking students to read them independently.

• Define words in context and allow students to offer their own meanings of words.

• Make the meanings of words concrete by naming objects or pictures, role-playing, or pantomiming.

Spelling is the relationship between sounds and letters. Learning to spell words in English is an interesting challenge for English First Language speakers as well as English as a Second Language speakers. You may want to adapt some of the following activities to accommodate the needs of your students—both native and non-English speakers.

Rhymes and Songs

Use rhymes, songs, poems, or chants to introduce new letter sounds and spelling words. Repeat the rhyme or song several times during the day or week, having students listen to you first, then repeat back to you line by line. To enhance learning for visual learners in your classroom and provide opportunities for pointing out letter combinations and their sounds, you may want to write the rhyme, song, poem, or chant on the board. As you examine the words, students can easily see similarities and differences among them. Encourage volunteers to select and recite a rhyme or sing a song for the class.

Student Dictation

To take advantage of individual students' known vocabulary, suggest that students build their own sentences incorporating the list words. For example:

> The contestant was agile.
>
> The contestant was agile in gymnastics.
>
> The contestant was agile in gymnastics and acrobatics.

Sentence building can expand students' knowledge of how to spell words and of how to notice language patterns, learn descriptive words, and so on.

Words in Context

Using words in context sentences will aid students' mastery of new vocabulary.

• Say several sentences using the list words in context and have students repeat after you. Encourage more proficient students to make up sentences using list words that you suggest.

• Write cloze sentences on the board and have students help you complete them with the list words.

Point out the spelling patterns in the words, using colored chalk or markers to underline or circle the elements.

Oral Drills

Use oral drills to help students make associations among sounds and the letters that represent them. You might use oral drills at listening stations to reinforce the language, allowing ESL students to listen to the drills at their own pace.

Spelling Aloud Say each list word and have students repeat the word. Next, write it on the board as you name each letter, then say the word again as you track the letters and sound by sweeping your hand under the word. Call attention to spelling changes for words to which endings or suffixes were added. For words with more than one syllable, emphasize each syllable as you write, encouraging students to clap out the syllables. Ask volunteers to repeat the procedure.

Variant Spellings For a group of words that contain the same root, but variant spellings, write an example on the board, say the word, and then present other words in that word family (*district: restrict, constrict*). Point out the root and the letter(s) that make up the root. Then, add words to the list that have similar roots (*conflict, consist, desist*). Say pairs of words (*restrict, consist*) as you point to them, and identify the roots and the different letters that represent the roots (*strict, sist*). Ask volunteers to select a different pair of words and repeat the procedure.

Vary this activity by drawing a chart on the board that shows the variant spellings for different roots. Invite students to add words under the correct spelling pattern. Provide a list of words for students to choose from to help those ESL students with limited vocabularies.

tegorizing To help students discriminate among
nsonant sounds and spellings, have them help you
egorize words with single consonant sounds,
nsonant blends or digraphs, and prefixes. For
mple, ask students to close their eyes so that they
focus solely on the sounds in the words, and then
nounce *premier, prejudice, protrude,* and *protocol.*
xt, pronounce the words as you write them on the
ard. After spelling each word, create two columns—
e for *pre,* one for *pro.* Have volunteers pronounce
h word, decide which column it fits under, and write
word in the correct column. Encourage students to
d to the columns any other words they know that
ve those sounds.

focus on initial, medial, or final consonant sounds,
nt out the position of the consonants, consonant
nds, or digraphs in the words. Have students find
d list the words under columns labeled *Beginning,*
ddle, and *End.*

pe Recording Encourage students to work with a
rtner or their group to practice their spelling words. If
ape recorder is available, students can practice at
eir own pace by taking turns recording the words,
ying back the tape, and writing each word they hear.
udents can then help each other check their spelling
ainst their *Spelling Workout* books. Observe as needed
be sure students are spelling the words correctly.

mparing/Contrasting To help students focus on
ord parts, write list words with prefixes or suffixes on
e board and have volunteers circle, underline, or draw
ine between the prefix or suffix and its base word or
ot. Review the meaning of each base word/root, then
ite students to work with their group to write two
ntences: one using just the base word/root; the other
ing the base word/root with its prefix or suffix. For
ample: *The weather news you heard yesterday was
curate. The weather news today is inaccurate!* Have
dents contrast the two sentences, encouraging them
tell how the prefix or suffix changed the meaning of
e base word/root.

uestions/Answers Write list words on the board
d ask pairs of students to brainstorm questions or
swers about the words, such as "Which word means
ot active'? How do you know?" (*inactive,* the prefix *in*
eans "no") or, "Which word means 'a main station of
railroad or bus line'? How do you know?" (*terminal*
mes from the root word *term,* which means "end"
"limit")

Games

You may want to invite students to participate in these
activities.

Picture Clues Students can work with a partner to
draw pictures or cut pictures out of magazines that
represent the list words, then trade papers and label
each other's pictures. Encourage students to check each
other's spelling against their *Spelling Workout* books.

If desired, you can present magazine cutouts or items
that picture the list words. As you display each picture
or item, say the word clearly and then write it on the
board as you spell it aloud. Non-English speakers may
wish to know the translation of the word in their native
languages so that they can mentally connect the new
word with a familiar one. Students may also find
similarities in the spellings of the words.

Letter Cards Have students create letter cards for
vowels, vowel digraphs, consonants, consonant blends,
consonant digraphs, and so on. Then, say a list word
and have students show the card that has the letters
representing the sound for the vowels or consonants in
that word as they repeat and spell the word after you.
Students can use their cards independently as they work
with their group.

Charades/Pantomime Students can use gestures
and actions to act out the list words. To receive credit
for a correctly guessed word, players must spell the
word correctly. Such activities can be played in pairs so
that beginning English speakers will not feel pressured.
If necessary, translate the words into students' native
languages so that they understand the meanings of the
words before attempting to act them out.

Change or No Change Have students make flash cards
for base words/roots and endings/suffixes. One student
holds up a base word or root; another holds up an
ending or suffix. The class says "Change" or "No
Change" to describe what happens when the base
word/root and ending/suffix are combined. Encourage
students to spell the word with its ending or suffix added.

Scope and Sequence for MCP Spelling Workout

Skills	Level A	Level B	Level C	Level D	Level E	Level F	Level G	Level H
Consonants	1–12	1–2	1–2	1	1	1, 7, 9	RC	3
Short Vowels	14–18	3–5	3	2	RC	RC	RC	RC
Long Vowels	20–23	7–11, 15	4–5, 7–8	3	RC	RC	RC	RC
Consonant Blends/Clusters	26–28	13–14	9–10, 17	5, 7	RC	RC	RC	RC
y as a Vowel	30	16	11–13	RC	RC	RC	27	RC
Consonant Digraphs—th, ch, sh, wh, ck	32–33	19–21	14–16	9	RC	RC	RC	RC
Vowel Digraphs		33	6–7, 9	19–21, 23	8–10	11, 14–17	25	RC
Vowel Pairs	29		26	20, 22	7–8, 10	14	25	
r-Controlled Vowels		22, 25	19–20	8	RC	RC	RC	4
Diphthongs	24	32	31	22–23	11	17	RC	RC
Silent Consonants			8	11	4	8–9	RC	RC
Hard and Soft c and g		21	2	4	2	2	RC	
Plurals			21–22	25–27, 29	33–34	33	RC	RC
Prefixes		34	32–33	31–32	13–17	20–23, 25	7–8, 33	7–11, 19–20
Suffixes/Endings	34–35	26–28	21–23, 25, 33	13–17	25–29, 31–32	26–29, 31–32	5, 9, 13–14, 16, 26	5, 25–27
Contractions		23	34	28	20	RC	RC	RC
Possessives				28–29	20	RC	RC	RC
Compound Words				33	19	RC	34	RC
Synonyms/Antonyms				34	RC	RC	RC	RC
Homonyms		35	35	35	RC	34	RC	RC
Spellings of /f/: f, ff, ph, gh				10	3	3	RC	RC
Syllables					21–23	RC	RC	1
Commonly Misspelled Words					35	34	17, 35	17, 29, 35
Abbreviations						35	RC	RC
Latin Roots							11, 15, 31	13–16

Skills	Level A	Level B	Level C	Level D	Level E	Level F	Level G	Level H
Words with French and Spanish Derivations							10, 29	RC 28
Words of Latin/French/Greek Origin								21–23, 28
List Words Related to Specific Curriculum Areas							31–34, 28, 32	
Vocabulary Development	•	•	•	•	•	•	•	•
Dictionary	•	•	•	•	•	•	•	•
Writing	•	•	•	•	•	•	•	•
Proofreading	•	•	•	•	•	•	•	•
Reading Selections	•	•	•	•	•	•	•	•
Bonus Words		•	•	•	•	•	•	•
Review Tests in Standardized Format	•	•	•	•	•	•	•	•
Spelling Through Writing								
Poetry	•	•	•	•	•	•	•	•
Narrative Writings	•	•	•	•	•	•	•	•
Descriptive Writings	•	•	•	•	•	•	•	•
Expository Writings	•	•	•		•	•	•	•
Persuasive Writings			•	•	•	•	•	•
Notes/Letters	•	•	•		•	•	•	
Riddles/Jokes	•	•	•					
Recipes/Menus	•	•	•			•	•	
News Stories		•	•	•	•	•	•	•
Conversations/Dialogues	•	•		•	•	•		•
Stories	•		•		•		•	•
Interviews/Surveys		•			•	•	•	•
Logs/Journals	•	•	•	•	•	•	•	
Ads/Brochures		•	•	•	•	•	•	•
Reports					•	•	•	•
Literary Devices							•	•
Scripts		•					•	•
Speeches					•	•		•
Directions/Instructions	•	•		•				•

Numbers in chart indicate lesson numbers

RC = reinforced in other contexts

• = found throughout

Lesson 1 — Vowel a

Objective
To spell words with the vowel a

Pretest
1. Your **abdomen** is in the middle of your body.
2. The farmer fed the animals corn and **alfalfa**.
3. New foods taste **alien** the first time you try them.
4. Is your brother still a **bachelor** at thirty?
5. What a sweet and juicy **tangerine**!
6. The store can make a print from that **transparency**.
7. Each morning, we pledge **allegiance** to the flag.
8. Friday is my brother's fifth wedding **anniversary**.
9. Draw a circle six inches in **diameter**.
10. Write down your estimate and then the **actual** cost.
11. This job offers opportunities for **advancement**.
12. Juan is an **amateur** skater, not a professional.
13. We belong to a business **association**.
14. Proofread your **manuscript** for any spelling errors.
15. Which **adhesive** works best with vinyl wallpaper?
16. What kind of **fabric** is that dress made from?
17. You have no **basis** for your opinion, except rumor.
18. My mother is taking a course in **astronomy**.
19. The tenant will **vacate** the apartment on Friday.
20. Your drive will take **approximately** six hours.

Spelling Strategy   *Page 5*
Use these words to discuss the different sounds *a* can spell: *card, careful, among, start.* Have students find **list words** in which *a* has the same sound. Point out that in some words, such as *allegiance, a* may sound like a different vowel entirely. Then, make sure that students understand the meanings of **list words**, having them refer to dictionaries when necessary.

Vocabulary Development Write the words *big* and *large* on the board and ask how they are alike. (*They have the same meaning.*) Point out that such words are synonyms, and have volunteers suggest other synonyms.

Dictionary Skills Ask students if the word *ago* has the long or short *a* sound or another sound. (*the schwa sound*) Explain that the dictionary sound-spelling uses the schwa symbol for the *a* in *ago*. Ask volunteers to name **list words** that also contain the schwa sound for *a*.

Spelling Practice   *Pages 6–7*
Word Analysis Point out that many words contain unusual letter combinations or roots. For example, the first three letters in *alfalfa* are repeated. Then, discuss other spelling patterns that students notice in **list words**.

Word Application Encourage students to use context clues to find the missing word in each sentence. To extend the activity, have students make up sentences for other **list words** that classmates can solve.

18

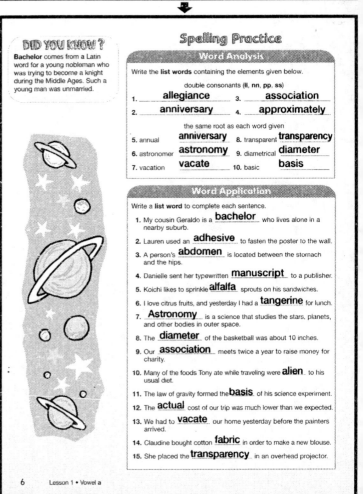

Vowel a

TIP
The vowel *a* can spell many different sounds. Read each word below, and notice the sound that *a* makes in each word.

alien   vacate   fabric   allegiance

In *alien* and *vacate*, you hear the long *a* sound. In *fabric*, you hear the short *a* sound. In *allegiance*, *a* has the schwa sound.

Vocabulary Development
Write the **list word** that matches each synonym.

1. foreign — alien
2. foundation — basis
3. belly — abdomen
4. leave — vacate
5. single male — bachelor
6. fruit — tangerine
7. book — manuscript
8. width — diameter
9. glue — adhesive
10. genuine — actual
11. promotion — advancement
12. beginner — amateur

Dictionary Skills
Write **list words** in which the letter *a* stands for the schwa sound at least once. Use the dictionary to check your answers.

1. alfalfa
2. bachelor
3. tangerine
4. allegiance
5. actual
6. amateur
7. association
8. astronomy

LIST WORDS
1. abdomen
2. alfalfa
3. alien
4. bachelor
5. tangerine
6. transparency
7. allegiance
8. anniversary
9. diameter
10. actual
11. advancement
12. amateur
13. association
14. manuscript
15. adhesive
16. fabric
17. basis
18. astronomy
19. vacate
20. approximately

5

DID YOU KNOW?
Bachelor comes from a Latin word for a young nobleman who was trying to become a knight during the Middle Ages. Such a young man was unmarried.

Spelling Practice
Word Analysis
Write the **list words** containing the elements given below.

double consonants (ll, nn, pp, ss)
1. allegiance   3. association
2. anniversary   4. approximately

the same root as each word given
5. annual — anniversary   8. transparent — transparency
6. astronomer — astronomy   9. diametrical — diameter
7. vacation — vacate   10. basic — basis

Word Application
Write a **list word** to complete each sentence.
1. My cousin Geraldo is a **bachelor** who lives alone in a nearby suburb.
2. Lauren used an **adhesive** to fasten the poster to the wall.
3. A person's **abdomen** is located between the stomach and the hips.
4. Danielle sent her typewritten **manuscript** to a publisher.
5. Koichi likes to sprinkle **alfalfa** sprouts on his sandwiches.
6. I love citrus fruits, and yesterday I had a **tangerine** for lunch.
7. **Astronomy** is a science that studies the stars, planets, and other bodies in outer space.
8. The **diameter** of the basketball was about 10 inches.
9. Our **association** meets twice a year to raise money for charity.
10. Many of the foods Tony ate while traveling were **alien** to his usual diet.
11. The law of gravity formed the **basis** of his science experiment.
12. The **actual** cost of our trip was much lower than we expected.
13. We had to **vacate** our home yesterday before the painters arrived.
14. Claudine bought cotton **fabric** in order to make a new blouse.
15. She placed the **transparency** in an overhead projector.

6   Lesson 1 • Vowel a

Puzzle
Use the **list words** to complete the crossword puzzle.

ACROSS
1. contains the stomach
3. strange or foreign
4. unmarried man
6. photographic slide
8. moving forward
11. cloth
13. nearly correct
17. loyalty or devotion
19. a sticky substance

DOWN
2. a line passing through the center of a circle
3. nonprofessional
5. typewritten book
7. the study of stars and planets
9. once-a-year date
10. group of people joined in some way
12. citrus fruit
14. to make vacant
15. food for cattle
16. as it really is
18. foundation

Lesson 1 • Vowel a   7

Proofreading

Proofreading Marks
- spelling mistake
- add apostrophe
- capital letter
- add period

Use the proofreading marks to correct the mistakes in the paragraph below. Then, write the misspelled **list words** correctly on the lines.

In the early 1600s, Galileo Galilei turned a new invention, the telescope, upon the night sky, and a great advancment was made in the science of astromony Galileo was the first scientist to view alein worlds in more detail than was possible with the naked eye. He saw that the moon's surface was not smooth, but that it had what looked like mountains. Even more important, he discovered approximatley four small bodies orbiting around the planet jupiter. Galileos discovery destroyed the bases for the belief that all bodies in the solar system revolved around Earth

1. advancement
2. astronomy
3. alien
4. approximately
5. basis

Writing a Description

Imagine that you are an astronomer who has discovered a new planet in another solar system using a space- or Earth-based telescope. Write a description of your observations, using as many of the **list words** as you can. Proofread and revise your description and fix any mistakes. Then, share your writing with the class.

BONUS WORDS

utensils	luncheon	buffet	blanch	marinate
beverage	perishable	casserole	microwave	garnish

Write the **bonus word** that matches each clue given.

1. scald or boil — blanch
2. something to drink — beverage
3. decorate — garnish
4. can spoil — perishable
5. tools — utensils
6. baking dish — casserole
7. midday meal — luncheon
8. soak in liquid — marinate
9. kind of oven — microwave
10. place to set out food — buffet

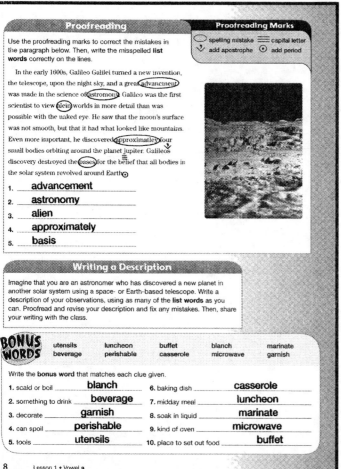

Puzzle Discuss crossword puzzle strategies with students. Remind them to print neatly and to first fill in all the answers that they know. These will help them figure out the other answers.

Spelling and Writing   Page 8

Proofreading Write *moms freinds name is joan* on the board and use it to demonstrate the proofreading marks for spelling mistakes, capital letters, adding periods, and missing apostrophes.

Writing a Description To help students prepare to write, discuss what kinds of things they might observe when studying a new planet through a telescope. As students suggest ideas, write them on the board. Encourage students to use these ideas as they write.

Bonus Words   Page 8

Culinary Terms Point out that the **bonus words** are used by those who prepare or serve food. Through discussion and dictionary use, help students understand the words' meanings. Then, have them complete the **bonus words** activity.

Bonus Words Test
1. Store **perishable** foods carefully.
2. Make sure that all your **utensils** are clean.
3. Potatoes will bake quickly in a **microwave** oven.
4. Parsley makes a pretty **garnish** for fish.
5. The waiter took their **beverage** orders first.
6. Put all the ingredients into an uncovered **casserole**.
7. Eat a light **luncheon** before you leave on your hike.
8. I like how you've arranged everything on the **buffet**.
9. Tough meat will be more tender if you **marinate** it.
10. First, **blanch** the almonds in boiling water.

Final Test
1. The editor reviewed the **manuscript** that Jill wrote.
2. A liter is **approximately** the same size as a quart.
3. Jan made a dress from the **fabric** that she bought.
4. On the **basis** of these facts, I'll agree with you.
5. Is a **bachelor** an unmarried man?
6. You must **vacate** the premises now!
7. The teacher showed a **transparency** of Africa.
8. A circle's **diameter** is twice its radius.
9. My favorite fruit is a **tangerine**.
10. Are those plants with the purple flowers **alfalfa**?
11. The **actual** cost was less than I had imagined.
12. The **amateur** golfer out-scored the professional.
13. An ant's largest body segment is its **abdomen**.
14. My **astronomy** club is building a telescope.
15. The **adhesive** held the lamp together.
16. We joined an **association** of nature photographers.
17. Did your parents go to dinner on their **anniversary**?
18. Marco swore **allegiance** to his new country.
19. The new school was very **alien** to Greta.
20. I'm proud of my sister's professional **advancement**.

Lesson 2

Vowel e

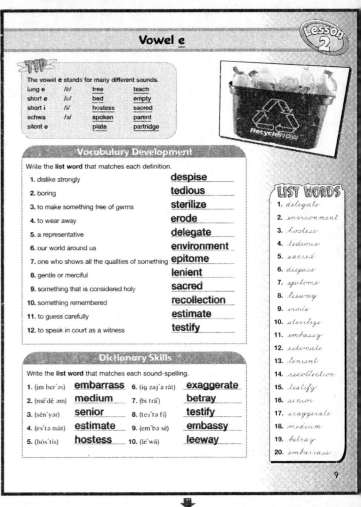

Vowel e

Lesson 2
Vowel e

TIP

The vowel e stands for many different sounds.

long e	/ē/	tree	teach
short e	/e/	bed	empty
short i	/i/	hostess	sacred
schwa	/ə/	spoken	parent
silent e		plate	partridge

Vocabulary Development

Write the **list word** that matches each definition.

1. dislike strongly — **despise**
2. boring — **tedious**
3. to make something free of germs — **sterilize**
4. to wear away — **erode**
5. a representative — **delegate**
6. our world around us — **environment**
7. one who shows all the qualities of something — **epitome**
8. gentle or merciful — **lenient**
9. something that is considered holy — **sacred**
10. something remembered — **recollection**
11. to guess carefully — **estimate**
12. to speak in court as a witness — **testify**

Dictionary Skills

Write the **list word** that matches each sound-spelling.

1. (im ber'əs) **embarrass**
2. (mē'dē əm) **medium**
3. (sēn'yər) **senior**
4. (es'tə māt) **estimate**
5. (hōs'tis) **hostess**
6. (ig zaj'ə rāt) **exaggerate**
7. (bi trā') **betray**
8. (tes'tə fī) **testify**
9. (em'bə sē) **embassy**
10. (lē'wā) **leeway**

LIST WORDS

1. delegate
2. environment
3. hostess
4. tedious
5. sacred
6. despise
7. epitome
8. leeway
9. erode
10. sterilize
11. embassy
12. estimate
13. lenient
14. recollection
15. testify
16. senior
17. exaggerate
18. medium
19. betray
20. embarrass

9

Objective
To spell words with the vowel e

Pretest

1. Who will serve as our **delegate** at the convention?
2. Acid rain can harm the **environment**.
3. The **hostess** served a buffet luncheon.
4. Painting a long fence can become **tedious**.
5. Those artifacts are **sacred** to the Hawaiian people.
6. I absolutely **despise** spicy foods!
7. The ballerina was the **epitome** of grace.
8. Open-minded people have **leeway** in their ideas.
9. The rocks along the shore will **erode** in time.
10. **Sterilize** the jars before you fill them with pickles.
11. The king will appear at the **embassy** party tonight.
12. I **estimate** that 80,000 people were in the stadium.
13. The sympathetic judge was **lenient** in his ruling.
14. In my **recollection**, 1987 was a wonderful year.
15. Dr. Lee was asked to **testify** as an expert witness.
16. Is your sister a **senior** at Wittenberg University?
17. I can't **exaggerate** the importance of seat belts.
18. These gloves come in small, **medium**, and large.
19. A loyal dog would never **betray** its owner.
20. Please don't **embarrass** me by asking me to sing.

Spelling Strategy
Page 9

Discuss the spelling rule. Use these words for further examples of the sounds that the vowel e often stands for: /ē/: *freedom, theme, beat*; /e/: *head, pencil*; /i/: *actress*; /ə/: *towel, spotted*; /-/ [silent e]: *phone, discharge*. If desired, have students name other examples. Then, work with students to define each **list word**, and call on volunteers to use each one in an oral sentence.

Vocabulary Development Before the exercise, have students name **list words** to match these definitions: "to overstate" (*exaggerate*); "a female host" (*hostess*).

Dictionary Skills Use examples from a dictionary to review sound-spellings. Then, have students look up the sound-spellings of the **list words** *delegate*, *lenient*, and *sacred*, and write them on the board.

Spelling Practice
Pages 10–11

Word Analysis Have students analyze the **list words** on page 11 to help them complete this exercise.

Word Meaning Begin by writing on the board, *Uncle John's tendency to delegate his stories made us hesitant to believe him.* Have students use context clues to replace the underlined word with the **list word** that makes sense in the sentence. (*exaggerate*)

Spelling Practice

DID YOU KNOW?

Exaggerate comes from a Latin word meaning "to heap up." Heaping something up into a tall pile tends to make it look larger.

Word Analysis

Write **list words** to answer the following questions.

Which words contain silent e?
1. **delegate**   3. **erode**   5. **estimate**
2. **despise**   4. **sterilize**   6. **exaggerate**

Which words contain these double consonants?
7. rr **embarrass**   8. gg **exaggerate**   9. ll **recollection**

Which words contain the double consonants ss?
10. **hostess**   11. **embassy**   12. **embarrass**

Which words contain four syllables?
13. **environment**   15. **recollection**
14. **epitome**   16. **exaggerate**

Word Meaning

Each underlined **list word** in the sentences below must be moved to a different sentence to make sense. Write the correct **list word** in the blank.

1. Our senior came up with wonderful party favors last night. **hostess**
2. Pat stood up in the courtroom and prepared to despise. **testify**
3. We visited many old hostess sites in Japan. **sacred**
4. Carrie is a sacred at Central High School, and she will graduate next year. **senior**
5. The foundation of the old house had started to testify. **erode**
6. The nurse has begun to wash and erode the instruments. **sterilize**
7. I absolutely embarrass shoveling snow in the winter. **despise**
8. I would never sterilize your trust in me. **betray**
9. The trains are running late, so allow plenty of lenient to arrive on time. **leeway**
10. The bus ride to the game was delegate due to all the traffic. **tedious**
11. The embassy the plumber gave us for repairs was reasonable. **estimate**
12. He is a leeway teacher and usually accepts late papers. **lenient**
13. People sometimes blush when situations estimate them. **embarrass**
14. You elect a betray to represent you at student council meetings. **delegate**
15. Great Britain has an office, or tedious, located in Washington, D.C. **embassy**

10   Lesson 2 • Vowel e

Puzzle

Use the **list words** to complete the crossword puzzle.

ACROSS
1. representative
3. to make free of germs
7. something that has typical qualities
9. approximate count
11. to cause self-consciousness
12. to rot; wear away
13. foreign office
14. middle-sized
16. female host
17. deserving respect
18. setting or surroundings
19. older; of highest rank

DOWN
1. to hate
2. something remembered
4. margin; extra room
5. to give as proof; state facts
6. to deceive or desert
8. tiresome; boring
10. to make larger than reality
15. mild; merciful

```
    D E L E G A T E           R
    E       B         S T E R I L I Z E
T   S       E                 E       C
E S T I M A T E     E P I T O M E     O
S   I   S   R   E               D     L
T   F   E   A   X             W       L
I   Y   M B A R R A S S       A       E
F       I   Y   G     E R O D E       C
Y           S   G                     T
                G E M B A S S Y   M E D I U M
            L   E                     O
H O S T E S S   S A C R E D           N
      E     N
E N V I R O N M E N T
      I     E
    S E N I O R
      N     T
      T
```

Proofreading

Use the proofreading marks to correct the mistakes in the paragraph below. Then, write the misspelled **list words** correctly on the lines.

Experts estimate that soon almost all newspapers and phone books will be printed on Recycled paper. This will help the envirment Many communities no longer offer any leway to polluters who disobey laws that protect our natural resources. Newspaper recycling began decades ago, but recycling other kinds of paper is just now becoming common. following a few simple rules need not be tediuos The key is to collect clean, well-sorted, and dry paper. Then, it is important to separate the paper, such as putting heavy paper like cardboard and mideum weight paper like writing paper in different bundles.

Proofreading Marks

- ◯ spelling mistake
- ⁄ small letter
- ≡ capital letter
- ⌗ add space
- ⌿ delete word

1. **estimate**
2. **environment**
3. **leeway**
4. **tedious**
5. **medium**

Writing a Letter to the Editor

Recycling can help to preserve the quality of our natural resources by making use of materials that would otherwise collect in landfills and eventually pollute our land and water. Write a letter to the editor in which you try to persuade your community about the importance of recycling. Try to use as many **list words** as you can. Remember to proofread and revise your writing. Then, read aloud your letter to classmates.

Acid Rain Threatens Forests

Vehicle Exhaust
Fumes Harm
Air Quality

Oil Spills
in Ocean
Hurt Wildlife

Industrial Wastes Pollute Rivers

BONUS WORDS

lobbyist	conservative	federal	sovereign	coalition
diplomatic	amendment	arbitrate	proponent	assembly

Write **bonus words** to answer the questions.

Which two nouns mean "group"? 1. **coalition**   2. **assembly**

Which two nouns mean "one who supports a certain position"?
3. **proponent**   4. **lobbyist**

Write the **bonus word** that matches each definition clue.

5. not liberal   **conservative**   8. tactful or fair   **diplomatic**
6. national   **federal**   9. to settle a dispute   **arbitrate**
7. supreme or royal   **sovereign**   10. a revision or addition   **amendment**

Puzzle Review the process for solving crossword puzzles, explaining the relationship between the numbers preceding the clues and those in the puzzle grid.

Spelling and Writing   Page 12

Proofreading Write on the board: *Davidwent too the the Store on friday.* Use the sentence to demonstrate the proofreading marks in this lesson.

Writing a Letter to the Editor Display and discuss actual news stories and editorials on environmental issues. Point out that news stories contain facts that students can use to strengthen their arguments and add support to their letters. When finished writing, provide time for volunteers to read their work aloud. Students may enjoy submitting their letters to the school paper.

Bonus Words   Page 12

Social Studies Call on volunteers to look up the **bonus words** in dictionaries and read the definitions aloud. Have other students use the words in oral sentences. Relate the words to the writing project topics, as well as current social studies readings and recent news.

Bonus Words Test

1. The king is **sovereign** ruler.
2. Mr. Garcia will **arbitrate** the labor dispute.
3. My uncle is a **lobbyist** for the dairy industry.
4. Susan hopes to work in the **diplomatic** corps.
5. The **conservative** politicians worked for tax reform.
6. A **federal** law mandates equal job opportunities.
7. An **amendment** gives voting rights to women.
8. Senator Ames is a **proponent** for lower taxes.
9. The president will address the **assembly** at noon.
10. Members of the **coalition** spoke for world peace.

Final Test

1. We visited the **sacred** burial ground of an old tribe.
2. Sarita will **testify** in court tomorrow morning.
3. The chemist will **sterilize** the jars in boiling water.
4. Stop, or you will **embarrass** me!
5. Your **recollection** of the story differs from mine.
6. Seawater will cause the embankment to **erode**.
7. Jan enjoyed the lecture, but Jeff found it **tedious**.
8. Traitors are people who **betray** their countries.
9. Is Jim's brother a **senior** in high school?
10. The foreign minister arrives at the **embassy** today.
11. The committee sent a **delegate** to the conference.
12. Homeowners **despise** floods and termites.
13. Everyone benefits from a safe **environment**.
14. I **estimate** that the Jets will win about ten games.
15. I **exaggerate** when I say I could eat a horse.
16. The judge was the **epitome** of wisdom and justice.
17. In bad weather, give other cars plenty of **leeway**.
18. After dinner, the **hostess** introduced the speaker.
19. The sweater labeled **medium** was actually small.
20. Is a trainer **lenient** with a dog that bites?

Vowel i

Objective
To spell words with the vowel i

Pretest

1. Is that fence too low to be a real **barrier**?
2. Add a little **cinnamon** to the applesauce.
3. The error was due to an accident, not **ignorance**.
4. This project will **involve** the entire class.
5. The mechanic will **align** the car's wheels.
6. This is a real **bristle** brush, not a plastic one.
7. In the corner of the room was a **circular** staircase.
8. The writer wanted an **illustration** for each chapter.
9. Try to **isolate** anyone who has a bad cold.
10. The judge and jury heard each person's **testimony**.
11. The latest **bulletin** gave the most recent news.
12. My club does not **prohibit** anyone from joining.
13. Our car **insurance** paid for the repairs.
14. The mayor wore a white **orchid** on her jacket.
15. Do you get bored when you are **idle** too long?
16. This pitcher has a two-quart **capacity**.
17. That's a strange cure for **hiccups**!
18. The contestants all wore formal **attire**.
19. Is a **peninsula** surrounded by water on all sides?
20. In the play, Manuel played the **villain**.

Spelling Strategy   Page 13

Discuss the spelling rule. Use these words as further examples of the different sounds i can spell: *icicle, again, vanity, scarier,* and *first*. Have students find **list words** in which i has the same sounds. Point out that in words such as *barrier*, i may sound like a different vowel entirely. Urge students to find other words in which i has an unexpected spelling. Make sure that students understand the meanings of the **list words,** having them refer to dictionaries as needed.

Vocabulary Development To start, write *not busy* on the board and ask which **list word** matches it. (*idle*)

Dictionary Skills Write *illustration* on the board as one word and also divided into syllables: *il/lus/tra/tion*. Discuss the rules of syllabication, giving students other examples as needed.

Spelling Practice   Pages 14–15

Word Analysis Remind students that some words contain distinctive word parts or spellings, which can help them remember how to spell the words, such as the silent *t* in *bristle*. Discuss other spelling patterns in the **list words** as needed.

Word Application Remind students that their answers must be spelled correctly and make sense in each sentence. Afterward have students discuss the clues that revealed the answers.

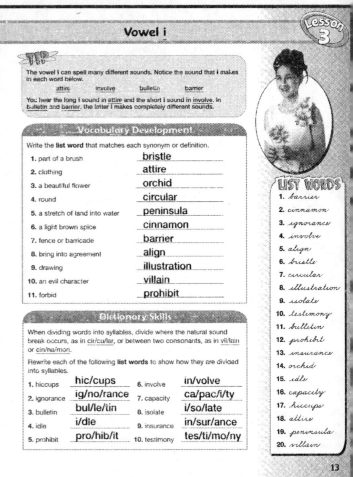

Vowel i

TIP
The vowel i can spell many different sounds. Notice the sound that i makes in each word below.

attire   involve   bulletin   barrier

You hear the long i sound in attire and the short i sound in involve. In bulletin and barrier, the letter i makes completely different sounds.

Vocabulary Development
Write the **list word** that matches each synonym or definition.

1. part of a brush — **bristle**
2. clothing — **attire**
3. a beautiful flower — **orchid**
4. round — **circular**
5. a stretch of land into water — **peninsula**
6. a light brown spice — **cinnamon**
7. fence or barricade — **barrier**
8. bring into agreement — **align**
9. drawing — **illustration**
10. an evil character — **villain**
11. forbid — **prohibit**

Dictionary Skills
When dividing words into syllables, divide where the natural sound break occurs, as in cir/cu/lar, or between two consonants, as in vil/lain or cin/na/mon.

Rewrite each of the following **list words** to show how they are divided into syllables.

1. hiccups — **hic/cups**
2. ignorance — **ig/no/rance**
3. bulletin — **bul/le/tin**
4. idle — **i/dle**
5. prohibit — **pro/hib/it**
6. involve — **in/volve**
7. capacity — **ca/pac/i/ty**
8. isolate — **i/so/late**
9. insurance — **in/sur/ance**
10. testimony — **tes/ti/mo/ny**

LIST WORDS
1. barrier
2. cinnamon
3. ignorance
4. involve
5. align
6. bristle
7. circular
8. illustration
9. isolate
10. testimony
11. bulletin
12. prohibit
13. insurance
14. orchid
15. idle
16. capacity
17. hiccups
18. attire
19. peninsula
20. villain

Spelling Practice

DID YOU KNOW?
Peninsula comes from Latin words that mean "almost an island." A peninsula would be an island if it were completely surrounded by water.

Word Analysis
Write the **list words** containing the elements given below.

the prefixes ig, il, or in
1. **ignorance**   3. **involve**
2. **illustration**   4. **insurance**

the long i sound
5. **align**   7. **idle**
6. **isolate**   8. **attire**

double consonants
9. **barrier**   13. **hiccups**
10. **cinnamon**   14. **attire**
11. **illustration**   15. **villain**
12. **bulletin**

Word Application
Write a **list word** to complete each sentence.

1. That witness's **testimony** convinced the jury of the accused's guilt.
2. Get the paint off every **bristle** of the paintbrush when you clean it.
3. Florida is a **peninsula** that extends into the Atlantic Ocean.
4. Every **illustration** was drawn by the artist with great care.
5. Most states require that drivers buy auto **insurance**.
6. My hard-working parents are almost never **idle**.
7. Our **ignorance** of local customs led to many misunderstandings.
8. A planet's orbit is not completely **circular** in shape.
9. Our greenhouse has many exotic plants for sale, including a rare **orchid**.
10. The Majestic Theater has a seating **capacity** of 1,500.
11. His **attire** was much too casual for such a fancy restaurant.
12. Please **align** the desks in the classroom into neat rows.
13. **Cinnamon** is a great spice to use in apple pies and cookies.
14. The scientists will try to **isolate** the new virus before more people become sick.

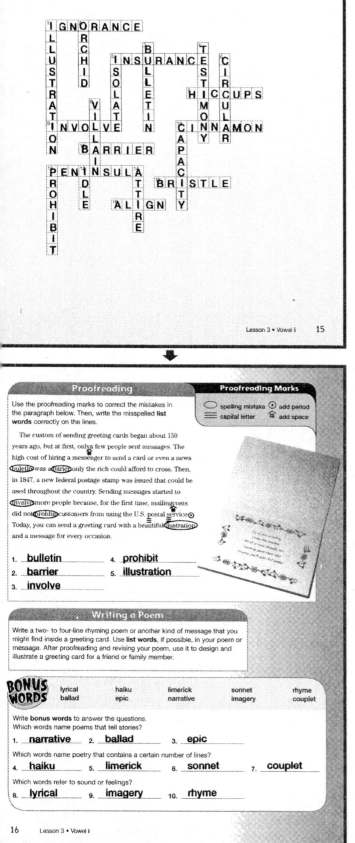

LIST WORDS

attire	ignorance	bulletin	capacity
idle	circular	prohibit	hiccups
bristle	illustration	insurance	barrier
involve	peninsula	orchid	isolate
align	testimony	cinnamon	villain

Puzzle
This is a crossword puzzle without clues. Use the length and the spelling of each **list word** to complete the puzzle.

Proofreading

Use the proofreading marks to correct the mistakes in the paragraph below. Then, write the misspelled **list words** correctly on the lines.

Proofreading Marks
- ⌒ spelling mistake
- ≡ capital letter
- ⊙ add period
- ⌖ add space

The custom of sending greeting cards began about 150 years ago, but at first, onlya few people sent messages. The high cost of hiring a messenger to send a card or even a news bulletin was aquartei only the rich could afford to cross. Then, in 1847, a new federal postage stamp was issued that could be used throughout the country. Sending messages started to involve more people because, for the first time, mailingcosts did not prohibit customers from using the U.S. postal service⊙ Today, you can send a greeting card with a beautiful ilustration and a message for every occasion.

1. bulletin
2. barrier
3. involve
4. prohibit
5. illustration

Writing a Poem

Write a two- to four-line rhyming poem or another kind of message that you might find inside a greeting card. Use **list words**, if possible, in your poem or message. After proofreading and revising your poem, use it to design and illustrate a greeting card for a friend or family member.

BONUS WORDS

lyrical	haiku	limerick	sonnet	rhyme
ballad	epic	narrative	imagery	couplet

Write **bonus words** to answer the questions.
Which words name poems that tell stories?
1. narrative   2. ballad   3. epic

Which words name poetry that contains a certain number of lines?
4. haiku   5. limerick   6. sonnet   7. couplet

Which words refer to sound or feelings?
8. lyrical   9. imagery   10. rhyme

Puzzle Discuss with students how they might go about completing the crossword puzzle. Remind them to print neatly, and suggest that they first fill in known answers.

Spelling and Writing   Page 16

Proofreading Write *Todayis kristi's berthday* on the board and use it to demonstrate the proofreading marks in this lesson. Point out that students will use these marks to correct the paragraph.

Writing a Poem Have students discuss various types of greeting cards and messages. After students have written their poems, you may wish to encourage them to illustrate their poems and use them as actual cards to be sent to family members or friends.

Bonus Words   Page 16

Poetry Point out that the **bonus words** are related to poetry. If possible, try to find poems or words that exemplify each term, using poetry anthologies as sources. Help students understand each word's meaning, and then have them complete the **bonus words** activity.

Bonus Words Test
1. Try to find a word that will **rhyme** with my name.
2. That **limerick** is very silly!
3. We read a **lyrical** poem about nature's beauties.
4. The **haiku** is a Japanese verse form.
5. Those two lines form a famous **couplet**.
6. An **epic** poem is often about a national hero.
7. The poet's **imagery** creates pictures in your mind.
8. A **narrative** poem tells some kind of story.
9. A **ballad** might be a poem or a song.
10. This **sonnet** was written by William Shakespeare.

Final Test
1. At the end of the story, the **villain** is punished.
2. Will the new law **prohibit** left turns at that corner?
3. The house on the **peninsula** has ocean views.
4. You should always wear warm **attire** in the winter.
5. I love the smell of **cinnamon**!
6. Every parent should have life **insurance**.
7. Jan's **hiccups** vanished after she held her breath.
8. This plan will **involve** the entire teaching staff.
9. Although he appeared **idle**, Juan was thinking.
10. First, **align** the window with its frame.
11. My **ignorance** was obvious when I failed the test.
12. This baking pan has a two-quart **capacity**.
13. The **barrier** keeps the dog out of the living room.
14. Try to **isolate** the sick birds from the healthy ones.
15. Don't wash a **bristle** brush in water.
16. In what climate will an **orchid** grow best?
17. A clerk wrote down every word of **testimony**.
18. This **illustration** shows the floor plan of the house.
19. The shape of the room is **circular**, not square.
20. Did the weather **bulletin** predict rain today?

Lesson 4 — Vowel o

Objective
To spell words with the vowel o

Pretest

1. Was Ramón nervous in **anticipation** of his speech?
2. A **blockade** across the harbor kept ships out.
3. The finest racers signed up for the **competition**.
4. This **continuous** rainfall will flood the streets!
5. Saluting the flag is a **patriotic** gesture.
6. At the **armory** museum, we saw suits of armor.
7. The funds were given by a generous **donor**.
8. I saw that actor in a **commercial** for cereal.
9. At the **conclusion** of the play, they find the gold.
10. The company's **policy** is to satisfy its customers.
11. Speak into the **microphone** so we can hear you.
12. The cereal's advertising **slogan** is "Vote for Oats!"
13. Gail worked to solve the **complicated** problem.
14. The secretary took **copious** notes of the meeting.
15. The **prospector** was searching for gold.
16. Photographers need models who are **photogenic**.
17. The controls of a plane are in the **cockpit**.
18. Is the **continent** of Australia a large island?
19. Dark, **ominous** clouds preceded the thunderstorm.
20. Who will be Jason's **opponent** in the tennis match?

Spelling Strategy
Page 17

Discuss the spelling rule. Use these words for further examples of the common sounds of the vowel o: /ō/: *total, road*; /ô/: *pork, court*; /ä/: *lock, hospital*; /u/: *tongue, son*; /oo/: *hook, hood*; /o͞o/: *soon, broom*; /ou/: *loud, out*; /ə/: *actor, committee*. Then, discuss the **list words**. Work with students to define each word.

Vocabulary Development Call on volunteers to identify **list words** that match these definitions: "someone who gives" (*donor*); "a large land mass" (*continent*).

Dictionary Skills Review syllabication by having students identify the number of syllables in *anticipation* (5), *photogenic* (4), and *patriotic* (4).

Spelling Practice
Pages 18–19

Word Analysis To extend the activity, have students identify other words with the same o vowel sounds as the **list words**.

Analogies Review analogies by writing on the board: *movie, television, radio*. Then, read this example aloud and have students select the word that best completes it: *Vision is to books as hearing is to _____*. (*radio*)

Word Application Urge students to use context clues to find the missing **list word** for each sentence. To extend, have students make up similar context-clue sentences for other **list words** that classmates can solve.

24

Vowel o — Lesson 4

TIP
The vowel o stands for many different sounds. Here are some of the most common o sounds.

/ō/ phone	hostess	/oo/ book	wolf
/ô/ horn	orchestra	/o͞o/ spool	room
/ä/ block	prospect	/ou/ shout	crowd
/u/ sponge	ton	/ə/ continue	armory

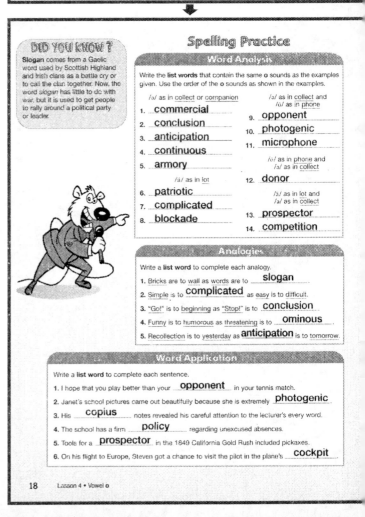

Vocabulary Development

Write the **list word** that matches each definition.

1. proud of one's country — patriotic
2. very threatening — ominous
3. without a stop or break — continuous
4. a contest or rivalry — competition
5. the act of looking forward to something — anticipation
6. the end — conclusion
7. difficult to understand — complicated
8. a device for augmenting voices — microphone
9. attractive in photographs — photogenic
10. a place to store weapons — armory

LIST WORDS
1. anticipation
2. blockade
3. competition
4. continuous
5. patriotic
6. armory
7. donor
8. commercial
9. conclusion
10. policy
11. microphone
12. slogan
13. complicated
14. copious
15. prospector
16. photogenic
17. cockpit
18. continent
19. ominous
20. opponent

Dictionary Skills

Write the **list words** that contain two syllables.

1. blockade
2. donor
3. slogan
4. cockpit

Write the **list words** that contain three syllables.

5. armory
6. commercial
7. conclusion
8. policy
9. microphone
10. copious
11. prospector
12. continent
13. ominous
14. opponent

17

DID YOU KNOW?
Slogan comes from a Gaelic word used by Scottish Highland and Irish clans as a battle cry or to call the clan together. Now, the word *slogan* has little to do with war, but it is used to get people to rally around a political party or leader.

Spelling Practice

Word Analysis

Write the **list words** that contain the same o sounds as the examples given. Use the order of the o sounds as shown in the examples.

/ə/ as in collect or companion
1. commercial
2. conclusion
3. anticipation
4. continuous
5. armory

/ə/ as in collect and /ō/ as in phone
9. opponent
10. photogenic
11. microphone

/ä/ as in lot
6. patriotic
7. complicated
8. blockade

/ō/ as in phone and /ə/ as in collect
12. donor

/ä/ as in lot and /ə/ as in collect
13. prospector
14. competition

Analogies

Write a **list word** to complete each analogy.

1. Bricks are to wall as words are to slogan
2. Simple is to complicated as easy is to difficult.
3. "Go!" is to beginning as "Stop!" is to conclusion
4. Funny is to humorous as threatening is to ominous
5. Recollection is to yesterday as anticipation is to tomorrow.

Word Application

Write a **list word** to complete each sentence.

1. I hope that you play better than your opponent in your tennis match.
2. Janet's school pictures came out beautifully because she is extremely photogenic
3. His copius notes revealed his careful attention to the lecturer's every word.
4. The school has a firm policy regarding unexcused absences.
5. Tools for a prospector in the 1849 California Gold Rush included pickaxes.
6. On his flight to Europe, Steven got a chance to visit the pilot in the plane's cockpit

18   Lesson 4 • Vowel o

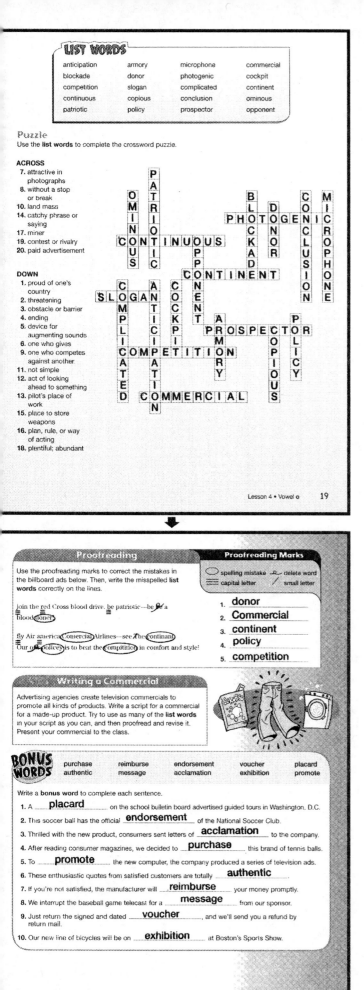

LIST WORDS

anticipation	armory	microphone	commercial
blockade	donor	photogenic	cockpit
competition	slogan	complicated	continent
continuous	copious	conclusion	ominous
patriotic	policy	prospector	opponent

Puzzle
Use the **list words** to complete the crossword puzzle.

ACROSS
7. attractive in photographs
8. without a stop or break
10. land mass
14. catchy phrase or saying
17. miner
19. contest or rivalry
20. paid advertisement

DOWN
1. proud of one's country
2. threatening
3. obstacle or barrier
4. ending
5. device for augmenting sounds
6. one who gives
9. one who competes against another
11. not simple
12. act of looking ahead to something
13. pilot's place of work
15. place to store weapons
16. plan, rule, or way of acting
18. plentiful; abundant

Lesson 4 • Vowel o   19

Proofreading
Use the proofreading marks to correct the mistakes in the billboard ads below. Then, write the misspelled **list words** correctly on the lines.

Proofreading Marks
◯ spelling mistake   ϱ delete word
≡ capital letter   ⁄ small letter

join the red Cross blood drive. be patriotic—be a blood doner.

fly Air america Comercial Airlines—see the continant

Our old policys is to beat the compitition in comfort and style!

1. donor
2. Commercial
3. continent
4. policy
5. competition

Writing a Commercial
Advertising agencies create television commercials to promote all kinds of products. Write a script for a commercial for a made-up product. Try to use as many of the **list words** in your script as you can, and then proofread and revise it. Present your commercial to the class.

BONUS WORDS

purchase	reimburse	endorsement	voucher	placard
authentic	message	acclamation	exhibition	promote

Write a **bonus word** to complete each sentence.

1. A **placard** on the school bulletin board advertised guided tours in Washington, D.C.
2. This soccer ball has the official **endorsement** of the National Soccer Club.
3. Thrilled with the new product, consumers sent letters of **acclamation** to the company.
4. After reading consumer magazines, we decided to **purchase** this brand of tennis balls.
5. To **promote** the new computer, the company produced a series of television ads.
6. These enthusiastic quotes from satisfied customers are totally **authentic**.
7. If you're not satisfied, the manufacturer will **reimburse** your money promptly.
8. We interrupt the baseball game telecast for a **message** from our sponsor.
9. Just return the signed and dated **voucher**, and we'll send you a refund by return mail.
10. Our new line of bicycles will be on **exhibition** at Boston's Sports Show.

20   Lesson 4 • Vowel o

Puzzle Review, if needed, the relationship between the clue numbers and the numbers in the puzzle grid.

Spelling and Writing   Page 20
Proofreading Demonstrate the proofreading marks in this lesson with this sentence: *what a a Great Slogen!*

Writing a Commercial Ask students to describe television ads that they feel are effective, and have them support their opinions with reasons. Brainstorm "fantastic" products that might be popular to consumers, such as robots that do homework or cars that can be programmed to travel to certain places. Urge students to take notes before they begin to write. When finished writing, provide time for students to give oral presentations or dramatizations of their ads.

Bonus Words   Page 20
Advertising Discuss the **bonus words**, having students define those that are familiar and calling on volunteers to read dictionary definitions for those that are not. Urge students to relate the words to their experiences as consumers.

Bonus Words Test
1. I saw an **exhibition** of new computers.
2. The athlete was paid for his **endorsement**.
3. We decided to **purchase** a new carpet for the hall.
4. I will **reimburse** you if you're not satisfied.
5. Listen to a **message** from our sponsor.
6. The play was greeted by critical **acclamation**.
7. The clerk gave me a **voucher** marked "Paid in full."
8. This advertising **placard** was designed by Raul.
9. The company uses radio ads to **promote** its product.
10. The claims in ads are not always **authentic** facts.

Final Test
1. The band played a medley of **patriotic** marches.
2. The **prospector** examined the rocks for gold.
3. The politician will debate her **opponent** on TV.
4. The restaurant's **policy** is to accept credit cards.
5. I went to bed early in **anticipation** of a busy day.
6. Shields and swords were on display at the **armory**.
7. A fashion model must be **photogenic**.
8. When making a tape, speak into the **microphone**.
9. A dam was built to **blockade** the river.
10. A **donor** provided funds for the new gymnasium.
11. The pilot and navigator sit in the **cockpit**.
12. My campaign **slogan** is "Kate's Great!"
13. The cat food **commercial** featured dancing cats.
14. Did you find the computer manual **complicated**?
15. Asia is the largest **continent**.
16. The school has a poetry writing **competition**.
17. The **continuous** noise was making me nervous.
18. George took **copious** notes during the lecture.
19. The picnic was cancelled due to **ominous** clouds.
20. Will this question mark the **conclusion** of the test?

Lesson 5

Vowel u

Objective
To spell words with the vowel u

Pretest

1. Kindness is her most outstanding **attribute**.
2. Will new students be given a map of the **campus**?
3. The actor showed only **subtle** changes in emotion.
4. What a beautiful **lullaby** that is!
5. Like many medicines, this **serum** saves lives.
6. One radioactive element is called **uranium**.
7. The horses ran the **circumference** of the corral.
8. I want to plant a **geranium** near the front door.
9. You will find nail scissors in the **manicure** kit.
10. The **smudge** on Kim's shirt wouldn't come off.
11. One of your chores is to **vacuum** the carpet.
12. Our chorus sounds good because of its **unity**.
13. One **industrious** worker can paint the wall in a day.
14. Will regular exercise improve **muscular** strength?
15. Pigment is the **substance** that gives paint its color.
16. For **amusement**, we can play a game.
17. To learn about a country's **culture**, try visiting it.
18. The **linoleum** covered an old wooden floor.
19. You will have to pay a **premium** for front-row seats.
20. Wear your **suspenders** instead of a belt.

Spelling Strategy   *Page 21*

Discuss the different sounds the letter *u* can spell. Use these words as further examples, if needed: *blush, flute,* and *focus.* Have students find the **list words** in which *u* has the same sound. Explain that in words such as *tutor, u* may sound like a different vowel entirely. Make sure that students understand the meanings of the **list words**, having them refer to dictionaries when necessary. You may wish to have students use the words in oral sentences.

Vocabulary Development Write *level* and *flat* on the board, explaining that they are synonyms. Then, have students give other examples of synonym pairs.

Dictionary Skills Write *industrious* on the board as one word and also divided into syllables: *in/dus/tri/ous.* Discuss the rules of syllabication, giving students other examples if necessary.

Spelling Practice   *Pages 22-23*

Word Analysis Discuss with students different ways to remember word spellings. Point out, for example, that the words *unity* and *unify* are spelled alike except for one letter.

Word Application Encourage students to use context clues to find the missing word for each sentence. To extend, you may wish to have students create similar sentences using other **list words** for classmates to solve.

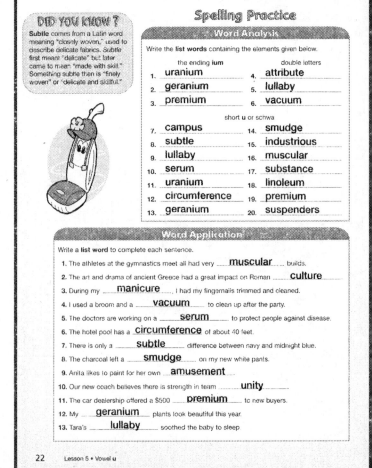

Vowel u — Lesson 5 (Student page 21)

TIP The vowel u can spell many different sounds. Listen for the sound of u in each word below.

smudge   attribute   campus

You hear the sound of short u in smudge and the sound of long u in attribute. In campus, the letter u stands for the schwa sound.

Vocabulary Development

Write the **list word** that matches each synonym.

1. flooring	linoleum	
2. schoolyard	campus	
3. smear	smudge	
4. flower	geranium	
5. medicine	serum	
6. hardworking	industrious	
7. strong	muscular	
8. characteristic	attribute	
9. perimeter	circumference	
10. void	vacuum	
11. entertainment	amusement	
12. matter	substance	

LIST WORDS

1. attribute
2. campus
3. subtle
4. lullaby
5. serum
6. uranium
7. circumference
8. geranium
9. manicure
10. smudge
11. vacuum
12. unity
13. industrious
14. muscular
15. substance
16. amusement
17. culture
18. linoleum
19. premium
20. suspenders

Dictionary Skills

Rewrite each of the following **list words** to show how they are divided into syllables.

1. lullaby — lull/a/by
2. uranium — u/ra/ni/um
3. premium — pre/mi/um
4. suspenders — sus/pen/ders
5. culture — cul/ture
6. campus — cam/pus
7. manicure — man/i/cure
8. substance — sub/stance
9. unity — u/ni/ty
10. amusement — a/muse/ment
11. subtle — sub/tle
12. attribute — at/trib/ute

21

DID YOU KNOW?

Subtle comes from a Latin word meaning "closely woven," used to describe delicate fabrics. *Subtle* first meant "delicate" but later came to mean "made with skill." Something subtle then is "finely woven" or "delicate and skillful."

Spelling Practice

Word Analysis

Write the **list words** containing the elements given below.

the ending **ium**
1. uranium
2. geranium
3. premium

double letters
4. attribute
5. lullaby
6. vacuum

short u or schwa
7. campus
8. subtle
9. lullaby
10. serum
11. uranium
12. circumference
13. geranium
14. smudge
15. industrious
16. muscular
17. substance
18. linoleum
19. premium
20. suspenders

Word Application

Write a **list word** to complete each sentence.

1. The athletes at the gymnastics meet all had very **muscular** builds.
2. The art and drama of ancient Greece had a great impact on Roman **culture**.
3. During my **manicure** I had my fingernails trimmed and cleaned.
4. I used a broom and a **vacuum** to clean up after the party.
5. The doctors are working on a **serum** to protect people against disease.
6. The hotel pool has a **circumference** of about 40 feet.
7. There is only a **subtle** difference between navy and midnight blue.
8. The charcoal left a **smudge** on my new white pants.
9. Anita likes to paint for her own **amusement**.
10. Our new coach believes there is strength in team **unity**.
11. The car dealership offered a $500 **premium** to new buyers.
12. My **geranium** plants look beautiful this year.
13. Tara's **lullaby** soothed the baby to sleep.

22   Lesson 5 • Vowel u

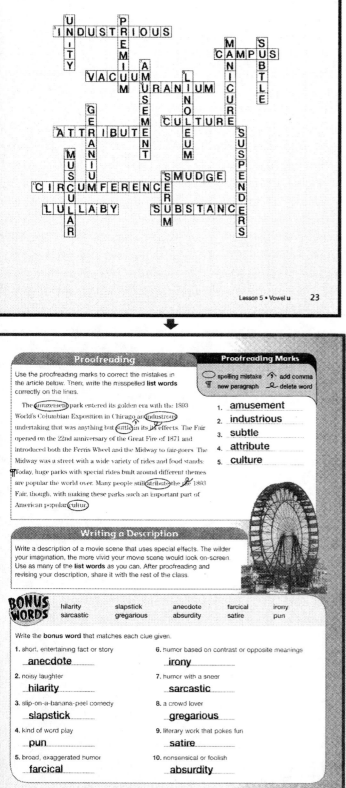

attribute	uranium	suspenders	muscular
campus	linoleum	circumference	culture
subtle	geranium	industrious	unity
lullaby	manicure	amusement	premium
serum	smudge	substance	vacuum

Puzzle

This is a crossword puzzle without clues. Use the length and the spelling of each **list word** to complete the puzzle.

Lesson 5 • Vowel **u**   23

Proofreading

Use the proofreading marks to correct the mistakes in the article below. Then, write the misspelled **list words** correctly on the lines.

The amuzement park entered its golden era with the 1893 World's Columbian Exposition in Chicago an industrous undertaking that was anything but suttle in its its effects. The Fair opened on the 22nd anniversary of the Great Fire of 1871 and introduced both the Ferris Wheel and the Midway to fair-goers. The Midway was a street with a wide variety of rides and food stands. Today, huge parks with special rides built around different themes are popular the world over. Many people still atribute the the 1893 Fair, though, with making these parks such an important part of American popular cultur.

Proofreading Marks

- ◯ spelling mistake
- ⫟ new paragraph
- ⋏ add comma
- ⸋ delete word

1. amusement
2. industrious
3. subtle
4. attribute
5. culture

Writing a Description

Write a description of a movie scene that uses special effects. The wilder your imagination, the more vivid your movie scene would look on-screen. Use as many of the **list words** as you can. After proofreading and revising your description, share it with the rest of the class.

BONUS WORDS

hilarity	slapstick	anecdote	farcical	irony
sarcastic	gregarious	absurdity	satire	pun

Write the **bonus word** that matches each clue given.

1. short, entertaining fact or story
   anecdote
2. noisy laughter
   hilarity
3. slip-on-a-banana-peel comedy
   slapstick
4. kind of word play
   pun
5. broad, exaggerated humor
   farcical
6. humor based on contrast or opposite meanings
   irony
7. humor with a sneer
   sarcastic
8. a crowd lover
   gregarious
9. literary work that pokes fun
   satire
10. nonsensical or foolish
    absurdity

Puzzle Discuss how the boldfaced letters and the length of the **list words** can help students complete the puzzle. Remind them to first fill in answers they know.

Spelling and Writing   Page 24

Proofreading Write on the board: *Nancy sliped on the the ice.* Use the sentence to show the proofreading marks. Ask students to provide examples demonstrating the "add comma" and "new paragraph" marks.

Writing a Description Ask students to name movie scenes that use special effects. Discuss how special effects artists often draw storyboards before creating a scene. Students may enjoy drawing a series of sketches with captions to use as visual outlines to help them write their descriptions.

Bonus Words   Page 24

Humor Point out that the **bonus words** are related to humor. Have students suggest situations or examples to clarify the words' meanings. Through discussion and dictionary use, help students understand each word's meaning.

Bonus Words Test

1. A **pun** depends on a word's multiple meanings.
2. A joke is one type of **anecdote**.
3. The **hilarity** was caused by the comedy.
4. The **farcical** uniforms barely resembled real ones.
5. **Irony** relies on the audience knowing the truth.
6. Most **slapstick** comedy has lots of physical action.
7. That **sarcastic** tone of voice sounds unkind.
8. A **gregarious** person is rarely alone.
9. We laughed at the **absurdity** of the situation.
10. The play is a **satire** about the politics of the time.

Final Test

1. The **lullaby** soon put the baby to sleep.
2. A **manicure** will improve your fingernails.
3. Look how **muscular** that horse is!
4. The bank is offering a **premium** to new investors.
5. I noticed the **suspenders** under his jacket.
6. The **substance** can be a gas or a solid.
7. You can see the **smudge** that the eraser left.
8. That **serum** will save thousands of lives!
9. List each **attribute** that a candidate should have.
10. **Uranium** is named in honor of the planet Uranus.
11. That artist uses only **subtle** colors in her works.
12. Sue's classroom is all the way across the **campus**.
13. Did you measure the **circumference** of the circle?
14. Can a **geranium** be grown indoors and outdoors?
15. Beavers are very **industrious** animals.
16. A **vacuum** is a completely empty space.
17. Team **unity** is more important than the score.
18. An old **linoleum** floor requires waxing to shine.
19. Every country has its own distinctive **culture**.
20. Dave likes to skate for **amusement**.

Lessons 1–5 · Review

Objective
To review spelling words with different vowel sounds

Spelling Strategy
Page 25

Tell students that in this lesson they will review the spelling patterns of words they studied in Lessons 1–5. Read and discuss the spelling rules with students, having them name each vowel and the sounds it stands for in the example words. Have students give other examples of words containing similar sounds.

Spelling Practice
Pages 25–27

Lesson 1 Write these words on the board: *alfalfa, basis, car,* and *ago* and use them to discuss the sounds that the vowel *a* can stand for. Then, have students identify the sound that *a* stands for in each **list word**. Point out the additional write-on lines and encourage students to add two words from Lesson 1 that they found especially difficult, or select and assign certain words that seemed difficult for everyone. (Repeat this procedure for each lesson in the Review.)

Lesson 2 Use these words to review the sounds that *e* can stand for: *epitome, senior, plated, token,* and *erode.* Then, have students identify the sounds *e* stands for in the **list words**. If needed, have students identify other words that contain these sounds.

Lesson 3 Write *circus, orchid, prohibit,* and *high* on the board. Use the words to review the different sounds that the vowel *i* can stand for. Then, have students identify the same sounds in the **list words**. Work through the first item with students, asking why *capacity* is the correct answer. (*It makes sense in the sentence.*)

Lesson 4 Use these words to review different sounds that the vowel *o* can stand for: *flock, corn, stone, son, hook, pool, found,* and *conspire.* Then, have students identify the sounds that *o* stands for in the **list words**. To extend the activity, students could provide clues for other **list words** from Lesson 4 and from Lessons 1–3 as well.

Lesson 5 Write the words *uranium, put, sure,* and *custom* on the board. Use the words to discuss the sounds that *u* can stand for. Before students begin the puzzle, elicit from them the steps involved to solve it.

Show What You Know
Page 28

Point out to students that this review will help them know if they have mastered the words in Lessons 1–5. Have a volunteer restate the directions and tell which word in the first item should be marked. (*antisapation*) When students have finished the exercise, have them write their misspelled words correctly.

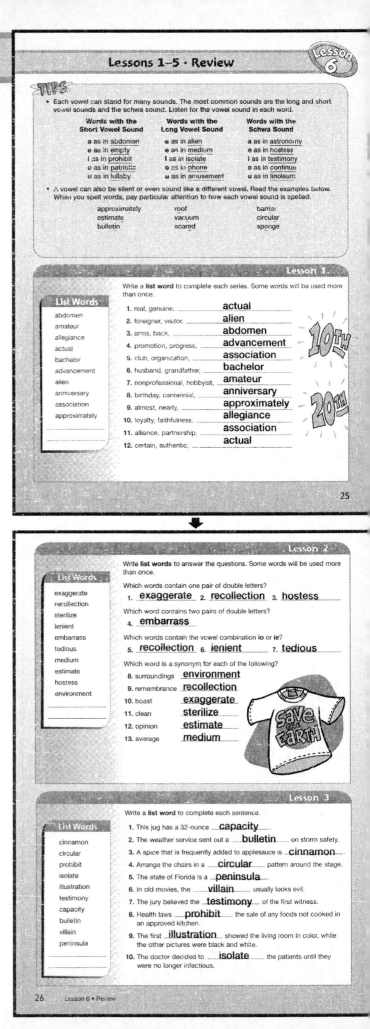

Lessons 1–5 · Review

TIPS
- Each vowel can stand for many sounds. The most common sounds are the long and short vowel sounds and the schwa sound. Listen for the vowel sound in each word.

Words with the Short Vowel Sound	Words with the Long Vowel Sound	Words with the Schwa Sound
a as in abdomen	a as in alien	a as in astronomy
e as in empty	e as in medium	e as in hostess
i as in prohibit	i as in isolate	i as in testimony
o as in patriotic	o as in phone	o as in continue
u as in lullaby	u as in amusement	u as in linoleum

- A vowel can also be silent or even sound like a different vowel. Read the examples below. When you spell words, pay particular attention to how each vowel sound is spelled.

approximately	roof	barrier
estimate	vacuum	circular
bulletin	scared	sponge

Lesson 1

List Words
abdomen
amateur
allegiance
actual
bachelor
advancement
alien
anniversary
association
approximately

Write a **list word** to complete each series. Some words will be used more than once.

1. real, genuine, __actual__
2. foreigner, visitor, __alien__
3. arms, back, __abdomen__
4. promotion, progress, __advancement__
5. club, organization, __association__
6. husband, grandfather, __bachelor__
7. nonprofessional, hobbyist, __amateur__
8. birthday, centennial, __anniversary__
9. almost, nearly, __approximately__
10. loyalty, faithfulness, __allegiance__
11. alliance, partnership, __association__
12. certain, authentic, __actual__

25

Lesson 2

List Words
exaggerate
recollection
sterilize
lenient
embarrass
tedious
medium
estimate
hostess
environment

Write **list words** to answer the questions. Some words will be used more than once.

Which words contain one pair of double letters?
1. __exaggerate__ 2. __recollection__ 3. __hostess__

Which word contains two pairs of double letters?
4. __embarrass__

Which words contain the vowel combination io or ie?
5. __recollection__ 6. __lenient__ 7. __tedious__

Which word is a synonym for each of the following?
8. surroundings __environment__
9. remembrance __recollection__
10. boast __exaggerate__
11. clean __sterilize__
12. opinion __estimate__
13. average __medium__

Lesson 3

List Words
cinnamon
circular
prohibit
isolate
illustration
testimony
capacity
bulletin
villain
peninsula

Write a **list word** to complete each sentence.

1. This jug has a 32-ounce __capacity__
2. The weather service sent out a __bulletin__ on storm safety.
3. A spice that is frequently added to applesauce is __cinnamon__
4. Arrange the chairs in a __circular__ pattern around the stage.
5. The state of Florida is a __peninsula__
6. In old movies, the __villain__ usually looks evil.
7. The jury believed the __testimony__ of the first witness.
8. Health laws __prohibit__ the sale of any foods not cooked in an approved kitchen.
9. The first __illustration__ showed the living room in color, while the other pictures were black and white.
10. The doctor decided to __isolate__ the patients until they were no longer infectious.

26   Lesson 6 • Review

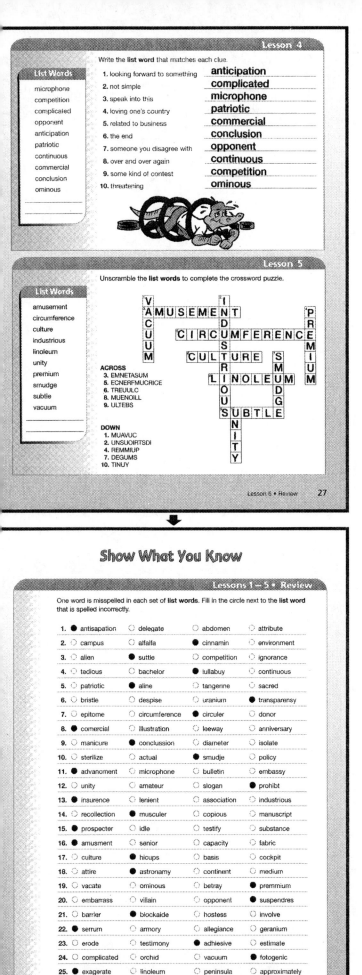

Lesson 4

List Words: microphone, competition, complicated, opponent, anticipation, patriotic, continuous, commercial, conclusion, ominous

Write the **list word** that matches each clue.

1. looking forward to something — anticipation
2. not simple — complicated
3. speak into this — microphone
4. loving one's country — patriotic
5. related to business — commercial
6. the end — conclusion
7. someone you disagree with — opponent
8. over and over again — continuous
9. some kind of contest — competition
10. threatening — ominous

Lesson 5

List Words: amusement, circumference, culture, industrious, linoleum, unity, premium, smudge, subtle, vacuum

Unscramble the **list words** to complete the crossword puzzle.

ACROSS
3. EMNETASUM
5. ECNERFMUCRICE
6. TREUULC
8. MUENOILL
9. ULTEBS

DOWN
1. MUAVUC
2. UNSUOIRTSDI
4. REMMIUP
7. DEGUMS
10. TINUY

Lesson 6 • Review   27

Show What You Know

Lessons 1 – 5 • Review

One word is misspelled in each set of **list words**. Fill in the circle next to the **list word** that is spelled incorrectly.

1. ● antisapation ○ delegate ○ abdomen ○ attribute
2. ○ campus ○ alfalfa ● cinnamin ○ environment
3. ○ alien ● suttle ○ competition ○ ignorance
4. ○ tedious ○ bachelor ● lullabuy ○ continuous
5. ○ patriotic ● aline ○ tangerine ○ sacred
6. ○ bristle ○ despise ○ uranium ● transparensy
7. ○ epitome ○ circumference ● circuler ○ donor
8. ● comercial ○ illustration ○ leeway ○ anniversary
9. ○ manicure ● conclusion ○ diameter ○ isolate
10. ○ sterilize ○ actual ● smudje ○ policy
11. ● advancment ○ microphone ○ bulletin ○ embassy
12. ○ unity ○ amateur ○ slogan ● prohibt
13. ● insurence ○ lenient ○ association ○ industrious
14. ○ recollection ● musculer ○ copious ○ manuscript
15. ● prospecter ○ idle ○ testify ○ substance
16. ● amusment ○ senior ○ capacity ○ fabric
17. ○ culture ● hicups ○ basis ○ cockpit
18. ○ attire ● astronamy ○ continent ○ medium
19. ○ vacate ○ ominous ○ betray ● premmium
20. ○ embarrass ○ villain ○ opponent ● suspendres
21. ○ barrier ● blockaide ○ hostess ○ involve
22. ● serrum ○ armory ○ allegiance ○ geranium
23. ○ erode ○ testimony ● adhiesive ○ estimate
24. ○ complicated ○ orchid ○ vacuum ● fotogenic
25. ● exagerate ○ linoleum ○ peninsula ○ approximately

28   Lesson 6 • Review

Final Test

1. Sara is an **amateur** chef, not a professional.
2. The settlers felt homesick in the **alien** land.
3. This party is to celebrate our wedding **anniversary**.
4. The **actual** cost was a bit more than the estimate.
5. Each shelf is **approximately** two feet long.
6. Stop! Please don't **embarrass** me.
7. Carol had a **recollection** of buying shoes that day.
8. Dr. Farnum asked the nurse to **sterilize** the tools.
9. Is the punishment for a first offense **lenient**?
10. My little brother may **exaggerate**, but he won't lie.
11. One person's **testimony** changed the trial.
12. Is the **capacity** of this box large enough?
13. Don't miss the emergency weather **bulletin**!
14. The real **villain** was not who readers expected.
15. Jon's cottage is out on the end of a **peninsula**.
16. What **ominous** black clouds those are!
17. We all applauded at the **conclusion** of the speech.
18. What a hilarious cereal **commercial**!
19. A **continuous** stream of visitors filled the halls.
20. Beneath the flag were portraits of **patriotic** people.
21. Our baseball team plays well because it has **unity**.
22. Are **premium** peaches the most expensive?
23. The **smudge** came out when the tie was cleaned.
24. There are **subtle** differences between the colors.
25. Is vacuum short for **vacuum** cleaner?
26. My uncle was a **bachelor** until he was thirty-five.
27. Is the Chamber of Commerce an **association**?
28. Citizens must promise **allegiance** to our country.
29. Ana's **advancement** in her profession was steady.
30. Dr. Tsao gently tapped the patient's **abdomen**.
31. I'll be glad when this **tedious** job is done.
32. Use a **medium**-sized hammer for this job.
33. Did the plumber give you an **estimate** of the cost?
34. Our **hostess** is the woman wearing the red skirt.
35. Help keep the **environment** clean!
36. Each **illustration** is a genuine work of art.
37. Try to **isolate** the dangerous virus from the others.
38. The club will **prohibit** guests from loitering.
39. This clock has a **circular** face, not a square one.
40. Did you put a dash of **cinnamon** in the apple pie?
41. Try to speak directly into the **microphone**.
42. That was a fierce **competition** between the teams!
43. Break a **complicated** problem into several steps.
44. My **opponent** refused to debate with me anymore.
45. Patrick cleaned the room in **anticipation** of guests.
46. Watch out! The **linoleum** floor was just waxed.
47. On Saturday, Dad took us to an **amusement** park.
48. Can you measure the **circumference** of a circle?
49. What an incredible **culture** the Romans had!
50. An **industrious** worker can finish this job quickly.

29

Lesson 7 — Words Beginning with <u>ap</u>, <u>as</u>

Objective
To spell words beginning with *ap* or *as*

Pretest

1. A leg is an **appendage** to the body.
2. The crowd cheered to show their **appreciation**.
3. Jeremy is a cashier in a men's **apparel** shop.
4. Cocker spaniels have great **appeal** as pets.
5. Does the store offer a large **assortment** of shoes?
6. Vote "YES" to show your **approval** of the issue.
7. The realtor will **appraise** the value of the house.
8. Try to **appease** Rowena with a gracious apology.
9. The citizens paid for new firefighting **apparatus**.
10. Speak clearly to **assert** your opinion.
11. The crowd stood to **applaud** the singer.
12. What a delicious **appetizer** this is!
13. Granddad was an electrician's **apprentice**.
14. Abraham Lincoln was killed by an **assassin**.
15. Was the **assault** on the castle successful?
16. Are the charts in the **appendix** of the report?
17. A swimsuit is not **appropriate** dress for a prom.
18. We bought a new stove at the **appliance** store.
19. He gave me his **assurance** that he'd fix my car.
20. A good education is a valuable personal **asset**.

Spelling Strategy — Page 29

Discuss the spelling rules with students. For further examples of words in which *ap* and *as* are prefixes, use: *appear*, *appoint*, *assign*, and *associate*. For examples of words in which they are not prefixes, use: *apple*, *appaloosa*, *asparagus*, and *asphalt*. Then, have students use dictionaries to find the meanings and etymologies of all the **list words**.

Vocabulary Development Before the exercise, have students name **list words** to match these definitions: "proper" (*appropriate*); "to quiet or satisfy" (*appease*).

Dictionary Skills Use these words to review alphabetization to the sixth letter: *transform*, *transaction*, *transport*, and *transition*.

Spelling Practice — Pages 30–31

Word Analysis To extend the activity, have students separate the words into syllables, then use dictionaries to check their work.

Analogies Ask students to explain what an analogy is, and have them give examples. Work through the first item together and discuss why *approval* is the correct answer.

Word Application To extend the activity, have students make up similar sentences for the remaining **list words** that classmates can solve.

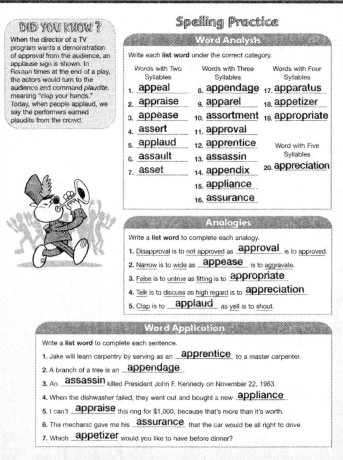

Words Beginning with <u>ap</u>, <u>as</u> — Lesson 7

TIP

Sometimes, the prefixes **ap** or **as** are added to Latin roots to form nouns or verbs. Both prefixes mean "motion toward," "addition to," or "nearness to." The prefix **ap** is added to roots beginning with **p**. The prefix **as** is added to roots beginning with **s**.

Latin Root	Meaning	English Word with Prefix	New Meaning
proprius	"one's own"	appropriate (v.)	"to take for one's own use"
serere	"to claim"	assert (v.)	"to state or declare"

Other words beginning with **ap** or **as** are derived directly from foreign roots. *Appetizer* comes from the French word *appetit*. *Assault* comes from the Latin word *assaltus*.

Vocabulary Development

Write the **list word** that matches each synonym or definition.

1. clothes — apparel
2. variety — assortment
3. equipment — apparatus
4. clap — applaud
5. machine — appliance
6. to evaluate — appraise
7. student worker — apprentice
8. gratitude or thanks — appreciation
9. first course of meal — appetizer
10. valuable possession — asset

LIST WORDS
1. appendage
2. appreciation
3. apparel
4. appeal
5. assortment
6. approval
7. appraise
8. appease
9. apparatus
10. assert
11. applaud
12. appetizer
13. apprentice
14. assassin
15. assault
16. appendix
17. appropriate
18. appliance
19. assurance
20. asset

Dictionary Skills

Write the **list words** that begin with **ap** in alphabetical order.

1. apparatus
2. apparel
3. appeal
4. appease
5. appendage
6. appendix
7. appetizer
8. applaud
9. appliance
10. appraise
11. appreciation
12. apprentice
13. appropriate
14. approval

Write the **list words** that begin with **as** in alphabetical order.

15. assassin
16. assault
17. assert
18. asset
19. assortment
20. assurance

29

DID YOU KNOW?
When the director of a TV program wants a demonstration of approval from the audience, an applause sign is shown. In Roman times at the end of a play, the actors would turn to the audience and command *plaudite*, meaning "clap your hands." Today, when people applaud, we say the performers earned *plaudits* from the crowd.

Spelling Practice

Word Analysis

Write each **list word** under the correct category.

Words with Two Syllables
1. appeal
2. appraise
3. appease
4. assert
5. applaud
6. assault
7. asset

Words with Three Syllables
8. appendage
9. apparel
10. assortment
11. approval
12. apprentice
13. assassin
14. appendix
15. appliance
16. assurance

Words with Four Syllables
17. apparatus
18. appetizer
19. appropriate

Word with Five Syllables
20. appreciation

Analogies

Write a **list word** to complete each analogy.

1. Disapproval is to not approved as **approval** is to approved.
2. Narrow is to wide as **appease** is to aggravate.
3. False is to untrue as fitting is to **appropriate**.
4. Talk is to discuss as high regard is to **appreciation**.
5. Clap is to **applaud** as yell is to shout.

Word Application

Write a **list word** to complete each sentence.

1. Jake will learn carpentry by serving as an **apprentice** to a master carpenter.
2. A branch of a tree is an **appendage**.
3. An **assassin** killed President John F. Kennedy on November 22, 1963.
4. When the dishwasher failed, they went out and bought a new **appliance**.
5. I can't **appraise** this ring for $1,000, because that's more than it's worth.
6. The mechanic gave me his **assurance** that the car would be all right to drive.
7. Which **appetizer** would you like to have before dinner?

LIST WORDS

appendage	approval	asset	appendix
appreciation	appraise	appetizer	appropriate
apparel	appease	apprentice	appliance
appeal	assassin	applaud	assurance
assortment	assert	assault	apparatus

Scrambled Letters

Unscramble each set of letters to write a **list word**.

1. sasasisn **assassin**
2. palpea **appeal**
3. zaptripee **appetizer**
4. paxdenpi **appendix**
5. isparpea **appraise**
6. palerap **apparel**
7. morsetants **assortment**
8. lapduap **applaud**
9. slatusa **assault**
10. cianipeap **appliance**

Puzzle

This is a crossword puzzle without clues. Use the length and the spelling of each **list word** to complete the puzzle.

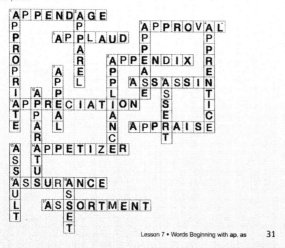

Proofreading

Use the proofreading marks to correct the mistakes in the article. Then, write the misspelled **list words** correctly on the lines.

Proofreading Marks
- ⟲ spelling mistake
- ⌄ add apostrophe
- ≡ capital letter
- ⊙ add end punctuation

Motion picture costume designers have difficult but rewarding jobs A designer usually begins by making sketches of the apparrel needed. Then, the designer gets the aproval of the actor who will wear the clothing. The films director must also appraize the costume sketches. If the film is set in the past, the garments must be apropriate for the time period. Once an idea has been approved, an asortment of fabrics to make the clothes must be ordered. It is up to the designer to make sure that the colors do not clash and that they photograph well. when everything is said and done, however, eye-catching costumes are an assett to any film

1. **apparel**
2. **approval**
3. **appraise**
4. **appropriate**
5. **assortment**
6. **asset**

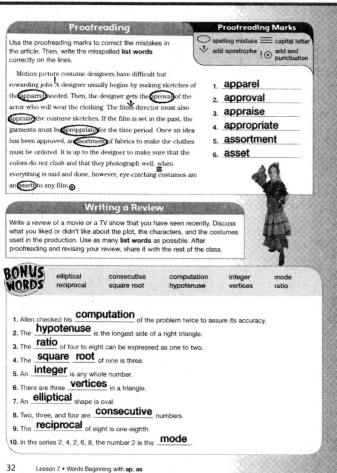

Writing a Review

Write a review of a movie or a TV show that you have seen recently. Discuss what you liked or didn't like about the plot, the characters, and the costumes used in the production. Use as many **list words** as possible. After proofreading and revising your review, share it with the rest of the class.

BONUS WORDS

elliptical	consecutive	computation	integer	mode
reciprocal	square root	hypotenuse	vertices	ratio

1. Allen checked his **computation** of the problem twice to assure its accuracy.
2. The **hypotenuse** is the longest side of a right triangle.
3. The **ratio** of four to eight can be expressed as one to two.
4. The **square root** of nine is three.
5. An **integer** is any whole number.
6. There are three **vertices** in a triangle.
7. An **elliptical** shape is oval.
8. Two, three, and four are **consecutive** numbers.
9. The **reciprocal** of eight is one-eighth.
10. In the series 2, 4, 2, 6, 8, the number 2 is the **mode**

Scrambled Letters
Before beginning the exercise, work with students to unscramble these letters to find a **list word**: *padgapeen*. (*appendage*)

Puzzle
Urge students to count the number of spaces in each answer blank to help them solve the puzzle.

Spelling and Writing   *Page 32*
Proofreading Have students provide examples demonstrating the proofreading marks, emphasizing the apostrophe and end punctuation marks.

Writing a Review Ask students how they determine if a movie or TV program is good or bad. Then, read aloud a current review of a popular movie or TV show. Discuss what aspects a writer might critique in a review, and encourage them to use these ideas while writing.

Bonus Words   *Page 32*
Math Terms Use math books, diagrams, and encyclopedias to define and discuss the **bonus words**. Relate them to students' knowledge of mathematical terms and functions.

Bonus Words Test
1. The **mode** is the number that occurs most often.
2. The base of a cone can form an **elliptical** shape.
3. One, two, and three are **consecutive** numbers.
4. Finish your **computation** and circle your answer.
5. The **square root** of sixteen is four.
6. Every whole number is an **integer**.
7. Mark the **vertices** of the angles with red dots.
8. The **ratio** of 3 to 9 is equal to 1 to 3.
9. We will calculate the **hypotenuse** of a triangle.
10. The **reciprocal** of three is one-third.

Final Test
1. Gloria designs sportswear **apparel**.
2. What a wonderful **assortment** of cheeses!
3. The manager will **appease** the unhappy workers.
4. Take a bow as the people **applaud** your speech.
5. The detective looked for a motive for the **assault**.
6. Cold shrimp is a delicious and elegant **appetizer**.
7. Her greatest **asset** is her brilliant mind.
8. Did the movie **appeal** to the critics?
9. A jeweler will **appraise** Aunt Helen's emerald pin.
10. Will you help assemble my exercise **apparatus**?
11. Was President McKinley killed by an **assassin**?
12. Write an **appropriate** thank-you note for the gift.
13. Franklin was an **apprentice** in a printer's shop.
14. I need his **assurance** that he'll clean his room.
15. An **appendix** is at the end of the resource book.
16. A dishwasher is an **appliance** that saves time.
17. I need their **approval** before I accept the job.
18. **Assert** yourself by speaking up at the meeting.
19. Blood flows to the tip of each **appendage**.
20. In **appreciation** for your help, I made you a gift.

Prefixes <u>ac</u>, <u>af</u>, <u>at</u>

Objective
To spell words with the prefixes *ac, af, at*

Pretest
1. Wow! Today's weather forecast was **accurate**.
2. Both parties finally reached an **accord**.
3. My mother is **accustomed** to taking a daily walk.
4. The wedding will be a small **affair** for family only.
5. The ambassador will send an **attaché** in his place.
6. My neighbor still speaks with a British **accent**.
7. Grandma Lopez will **accompany** us on our trip.
8. The bank will **acquire** two new branch offices.
9. Two agents had to **affirm** the truth of the report.
10. Certain music has no **attraction** for me.
11. Will the **accomplice** be punished for the crime?
12. This card gives you **access** to the library's books.
13. Will you **affix** mailing labels to the packages?
14. Be **attentive** and you will learn a great deal.
15. Jamal kept a positive **attitude** toward his work.
16. Can this car **accommodate** a large family?
17. Watch the ball **accelerate** down the steep slope.
18. I meant the note to be funny, not an **affront**.
19. My niece has a strong **attachment** to one toy.
20. Friends are **attune** to one another's needs.

Spelling Strategy   *Page 33*
After discussing the spelling rule, have students identify the prefix in each **list word** and note when it produces a doubled consonant. Ask students to identify the **list word** that does not contain a doubled letter. (*acquire*) Then, help students learn the meanings of the words, having them refer to dictionaries as needed.

Vocabulary Development Write "gain speed" on the board, and ask which **list word** the definition applies to. (*accelerate*) Have students give other definitions for **list words**.

Dictionary Skills Review the symbols for sound-spellings and discuss why they are useful. (*They teach a word's pronunciation.*) Point out the importance of applying the accent on the appropriate syllable.

Spelling Practice   *Pages 34–35*
Word Analysis Encourage students to try to complete this exercise without referring to the **list words** on page 35.

Analogies Review how analogies compare words. Then, work through the first item with students, discussing why *accurate* is the correct answer.

Word Application Point out that the answers students choose must make sense in each sentence. Urge them to use context clues to choose each answer.

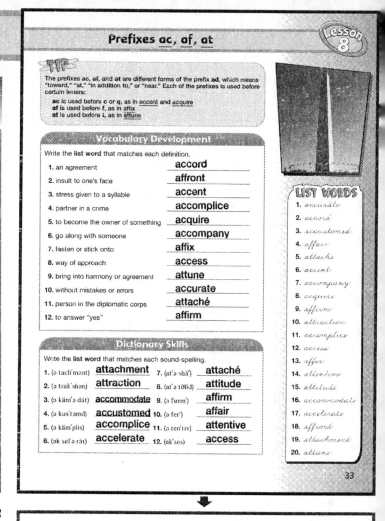

TIP
The prefixes **ac, af,** and **at** are different forms of the prefix **ad**, which means "toward," "at," "in addition to," or "near." Each of the prefixes is used before certain letters:
ac is used before c or q, as in <u>ac</u>cent and <u>ac</u>quire
af is used before f, as in <u>af</u>fix
at is used before t, as in <u>at</u>tune

Vocabulary Development
Write the list word that matches each definition.
1. an agreement — accord
2. insult to one's face — affront
3. stress given to a syllable — accent
4. partner in a crime — accomplice
5. to become the owner of something — acquire
6. go along with someone — accompany
7. fasten or stick onto — affix
8. way of approach — access
9. bring into harmony or agreement — attune
10. without mistakes or errors — accurate
11. person in the diplomatic corps — attaché
12. to answer "yes" — affirm

Dictionary Skills
Write the list word that matches each sound-spelling.
1. (ə tach′mənt) attachment
2. (ə trak′shən) attraction
3. (ə käm′ə dāt) accommodate
4. (ə kus′təmd) accustomed
5. (ə käm′pliss) accomplice
6. (ak sel′ə rāt) accelerate
7. (at′ə shā′) attaché
8. (at′ə tōōd) attitude
9. (ə furm′) affirm
10. (ə fer′) affair
11. (ə ten′tiv) attentive
12. (ak′ses) access

LIST WORDS
1. accurate
2. accord
3. accustomed
4. affair
5. attaché
6. accent
7. accompany
8. acquire
9. affirm
10. attraction
11. accomplice
12. access
13. affix
14. attentive
15. attitude
16. accommodate
17. accelerate
18. affront
19. attachment
20. attune

33

DID YOU KNOW?
The root of the word **accommodate** comes from the Latin *modus*, which means "measure." It later became a term that defined a manner of singing, particularly, "in tune." *Modus* later came to mean "a manner of doing anything." The prefixes **ad**, meaning "to," and **com**, meaning "together," joined with *modus* to become *accommodate*, meaning "coming together in tune." Today, *accommodate* is used to describe the manner of making things come together in a pleasant way.

Spelling Practice
Word Analysis
Write the list word formed by adding the appropriate prefix to each root or base word given.
1. fair — affair   6. fix — affix
2. cess — access   7. tache — attaché
3. traction — attraction 8. celerate — accelerate
4. customed — accustomed 9. front — affront
5. curate — accurate   10. company — accompany

Analogies
Write a list word to complete each analogy.
1. Inaccurate is to incorrect as accurate is to correct.
2. Treaty is to pact as accord is to agreement.
3. Hurt is to offend as insult is to affront.
4. Negate is to no as affirm is to yes.
5. Hate is to love as detachment is to attachment.
6. Slow is to decelerate as fast is to accelerate.
7. Staple is to join as glue is to affix.
8. Lead is to guide as escort is to accompany.

Word Application
Replace the underlined word in each sentence with a list word. Write the list word on the line.
1. My friend Javier speaks English with a Spanish <u>tone</u>. accent
2. The balcony of this theater can <u>handle</u> 500 people. accommodate
3. As a new employee, Jack had to <u>adjust</u> himself to new work habits. attune
4. Eileen wore a long gown to a formal <u>event</u> last weekend. affair
5. Mt. Rushmore is a popular tourist <u>site</u> in South Dakota. attraction
6. We plan to <u>obtain</u> the empty lot next to our house. acquire
7. The students were alert as the principal spoke to them. attentive
8. I asked Cassie to <u>attach</u> postage stamps to the mail. affix

34   Lesson 8 • Prefixes ac, af, at

accent	affront	accomplice	attentive
accord	access	accustomed	accelerate
affix	acquire	accompany	attitude
affair	affirm	accommodate	attraction
attaché	attune	attachment	accurate

Puzzle
Use the **list words** to complete the crossword puzzle.

ACROSS
2. paying attention
3. something added or joined
4. agree something is right
7. adjust or make fit
9. agreement
11. fasten; stick
12. member of ambassador's staff
14. go along with
15. become the owner of
16. something that attracts notice or admiration

DOWN
1. a person's opinion or mind set
2. bring into harmony
4. way of approach
5. insult to one's face
6. event or occurrence
8. increase in speed
9. in the habit of
10. criminal helper
11. extra stress given to some syllables of a word
13. without mistakes or errors

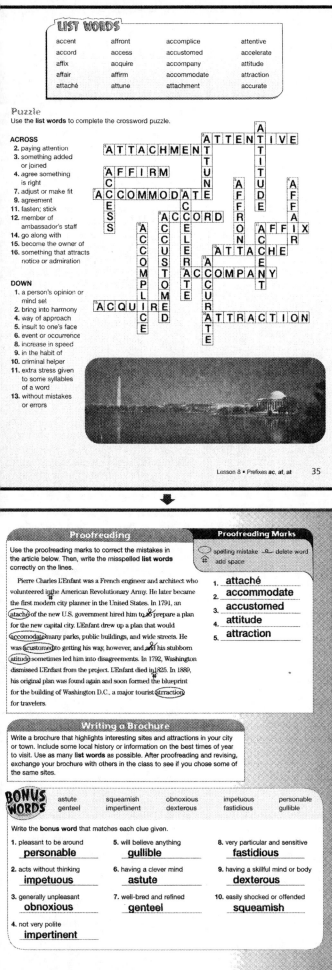

Proofreading

Use the proofreading marks to correct the mistakes in the article below. Then, write the misspelled **list words** correctly on the lines.

Proofreading Marks
⬭ spelling mistake   ⌇ delete word
add space

Pierre Charles L'Enfant was a French engineer and architect who volunteered in the American Revolutionary Army. He later became the first modern city planner in the United States. In 1791, an attaché of the new U.S. government hired him to prepare a plan for the new capital city. L'Enfant drew up a plan that would accommodate many parks, public buildings, and wide streets. He was accustomed to getting his way, however, and his stubborn attitude sometimes led him into disagreements. In 1792, Washington dismissed L'Enfant from the project. L'Enfant died in 1825. In 1889, his original plan was found again and soon formed the blueprint for the building of Washington D.C., a major tourist attraction for travelers.

1. attaché
2. accommodate
3. accustomed
4. attitude
5. attraction

Writing a Brochure
Write a brochure that highlights interesting sites and attractions in your city or town. Include some local history or information on the best times of year to visit. Use as many **list words** as possible. After proofreading and revising, exchange your brochure with others in the class to see if you chose some of the same sites.

BONUS WORDS

astute	squeamish	obnoxious	impetuous	personable
genteel	impertinent	dexterous	fastidious	gullible

Write the **bonus word** that matches each clue given.

1. pleasant to be around
   personable
2. acts without thinking
   impetuous
3. generally unpleasant
   obnoxious
4. not very polite
   impertinent
5. will believe anything
   gullible
6. having a clever mind
   astute
7. well-bred and refined
   genteel
8. very particular and sensitive
   fastidious
9. having a skillful mind or body
   dexterous
10. easily shocked or offended
   squeamish

Puzzle Remind students that they have two clues for each answer: its definition and the number of letters it contains.

Spelling and Writing   Page 36
Proofreading Use this sentence to demonstrate the proofreading marks in the lesson: *Hes nameis spelled wrong wrong.*

Writing a Brochure Explain that a tourist brochure functions as an advertisement, with a clear goal for a specific audience (in this case, to attract visitors). It uses a bold headline to lure readers, and breaks up information with headings and subheadings. Remind students to include *Who, What, Where, When, Why,* and *How* information in their brochures.

Bonus Words   Page 36
Personal Characteristics Explain that the **bonus words** name characteristics a person might have. Through discussion and dictionary use, help students understand the meaning of each word.

Bonus Words Test
1. An **impertinent** person often asks rude questions.
2. In grand society, people are **genteel**.
3. Everyone wanted the **personable** traveler to stay.
4. An **impetuous** person may later regret his action.
5. I refuse to spend time with **obnoxious** people.
6. A **gullible** person is easily fooled.
7. Few people can trick someone who is **astute**.
8. They are too **squeamish** to clean the fish.
9. That **fastidious** family does laundry daily.
10. For a **dexterous** person, juggling is simple.

Final Test
1. This room can **accommodate** a large crowd.
2. This car can **accelerate** quickly for passing.
3. That report is an **affront** to the mayor!
4. I have a strong **attachment** to my hometown.
5. Try to **attune** yourself to the clients' wishes.
6. The report said the driver was an **accomplice**.
7. Does this gate provide **access** to the field?
8. Will you please **affix** a name tag to each package?
9. Everyone was **attentive** to the announcer's words.
10. Our coach congratulated us on our good **attitude**.
11. People from Maine speak with a different **accent**.
12. A museum guide will **accompany** us on the tour.
13. My town was able to **acquire** the land it needed.
14. The court will **affirm** my claim to the money.
15. Those rose gardens are a great tourist **attraction**.
16. Are you sure the figures in this list are **accurate**?
17. Did the jury reach an **accord** on the verdict?
18. My dog is **accustomed** to sleeping under my bed.
19. The party was a huge **affair** with many guests.
20. Are you an **attaché** at the embassy?

Objective
To spell words that end with *ion* or *ation*

Pretest

1. I feel great **affection** for my childhood home.
2. His bright **expression** proves that he is pleased.
3. I have a firm **conviction** about justice.
4. The doctor prescribed a **lotion** for my poison ivy.
5. People once had the **notion** that the world is flat.
6. The stomach and liver aid **digestion**.
7. Mix an equal **proportion** of milk and water.
8. The doctor bandaged the **lesion** on Gina's arm.
9. Did the detective's **suspicion** prove to be correct?
10. Did Juan use red velvet to cover the sofa **cushion**?
11. My mother's **occupation** is sports writer.
12. You may sunburn if you have a light **complexion**.
13. Computers caused a **revolution** in office work.
14. Thank you for your **devotion** and hard work.
15. The long game created **tension** among the fans.
16. The Greek **civilization** inspired Western culture.
17. Is it your **intention** to become a doctor?
18. The staff's **cooperation** will simplify the work.
19. On this happy **occasion**, I'd like to thank my dad.
20. What an incredible **recitation** of the poem!

Spelling Strategy   Page 37

Discuss the spelling rule and examples. For more examples of words with the *ion* or *ation* suffixes, use *conversation, combination, radiation,* and *circulation*. For words ending in *ion* that come from early root words, use *potion, position, legion*. Then, discuss the structure, derivations, and meanings of the **list words**.

Vocabulary Development Have volunteers identify the **list words** that match these clues: "relationship in size or volume" (*proportion*); "facial look" (*expression*).

Dictionary Skills Before beginning the exercise, call on volunteers to define the function of guide words and point out examples in a dictionary.

Spelling Practice   Pages 38–39

Word Analysis Review that the suffixes *ion* and *ation* form nouns when added to verbs. Point out how the suffix *ation* and the verb *relax* form the noun *relaxation*.

Analogies To review analogies, write on the board: *Argument is to disagreement as _____ is to agreement.* Read this incomplete analogy aloud and have students select a **list word** to complete it. (*cooperation*)

Word Application Urge students to use context clues to determine the correct answers. To extend, have students create similar sentences for the exercise distractors.

34

Words Ending with <u>ion</u> or <u>ation</u>   Lesson 9

TIP

Often, the suffixes **ion** or **ation** are added to verbs to make nouns that mean "the act of."

Verb	Meaning	Plus Ending	New Meaning
recite	"to repeat from memory"	recitation	"the act of repeating something from memory"
digest	"to break down food"	digestion	"the act of breaking down food"

Many other nouns ending in **ion** have been derived from early root words. For example, the modern noun *cushion* comes from the Middle English word *cuisshin*, which in turn came from the Old French word *coissin*.

Vocabulary Development

Write the **list word** that matches each synonym or definition.

1. stress — tension
2. wound — lesion
3. job — occupation
4. sudden uprising — revolution
5. mistrust — suspicion
6. pillow — cushion
7. event — occasion
8. plan or goal — intention
9. joint effort — cooperation
10. cream — lotion

Dictionary Skills

Write the **list word** that comes between each pair of dictionary guide words.

1. dew/digit — digestion
2. rebel/rest — recitation
3. addition/again — affection
4. nose/noun — notion
5. proper/propose — proportion
6. common/control — complexion
7. especially/eye — expression
8. comply/cook — conviction
9. center/clue — civilization
10. desk/dice — devotion

LIST WORDS

1. affection
2. expression
3. conviction
4. lotion
5. notion
6. digestion
7. proportion
8. lesion
9. suspicion
10. cushion
11. occupation
12. complexion
13. revolution
14. devotion
15. tension
16. civilization
17. intention
18. cooperation
19. occasion
20. recitation

37

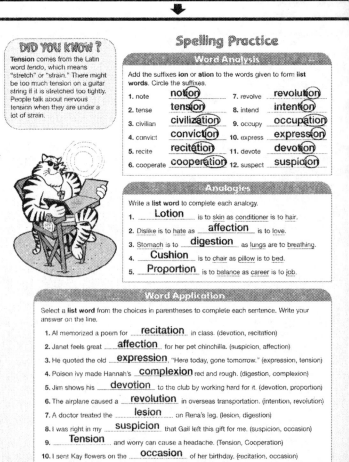

DID YOU KNOW?

Tension comes from the Latin word *tendo*, which means "stretch" or "strain." There might be too much tension on a guitar string if it is stretched too tightly. People talk about nervous tension when they are under a lot of strain.

Spelling Practice

Word Analysis

Add the suffixes **ion** or **ation** to the words given to form **list words**. Circle the suffixes.

1. note — not**ion**
2. tense — tens**ion**
3. civilian — civiliz**ation**
4. convict — convict**ion**
5. recite — recitat**ion**
6. cooperate — cooperat**ion**
7. revolve — revolut**ion**
8. intend — intent**ion**
9. occupy — occupat**ion**
10. express — express**ion**
11. devote — devot**ion**
12. suspect — suspic**ion**

Analogies

Write a **list word** to complete each analogy.

1. **Lotion** is to skin as conditioner is to hair.
2. Dislike is to hate as **affection** is to love.
3. Stomach is to **digestion** as lungs are to breathing.
4. **Cushion** is to chair as pillow is to bed.
5. **Proportion** is to balance as career is to job.

Word Application

Select a **list word** from the choices in parentheses to complete each sentence. Write your answer on the line.

1. Al memorized a poem for **recitation** in class. (devotion, recitation)
2. Janet feels great **affection** for her pet chinchilla. (suspicion, affection)
3. He quoted the old **expression**, "Here today, gone tomorrow." (expression, tension)
4. Poison ivy made Hannah's **complexion** red and rough. (digestion, complexion)
5. Jim shows his **devotion** to the club by working hard for it. (devotion, proportion)
6. The airplane caused a **revolution** in overseas transportation. (intention, revolution)
7. A doctor treated the **lesion** on Rena's leg. (lesion, digestion)
8. I was right in my **suspicion** that Gail left this gift for me. (suspicion, occasion)
9. **Tension** and worry can cause a headache. (Tension, Cooperation)
10. I sent Kay flowers on the **occasion** of her birthday. (recitation, occasion)

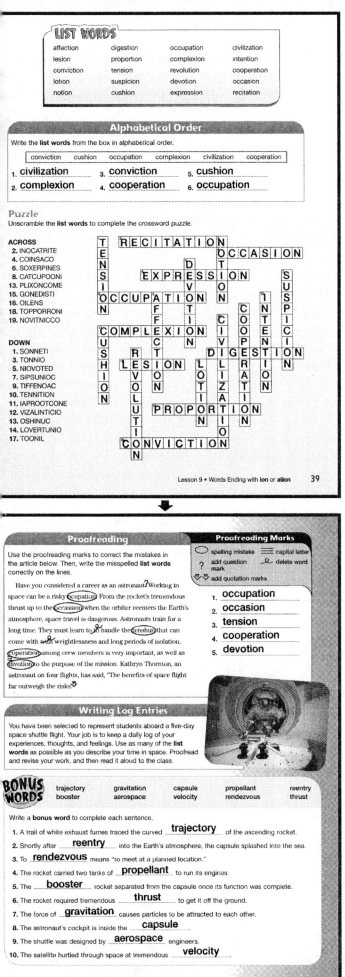

LIST WORDS

affection	digestion	occupation	civilization
lesion	proportion	complexion	intention
conviction	tension	revolution	cooperation
lotion	suspicion	devotion	occasion
notion	cushion	expression	recitation

Alphabetical Order

Write the **list words** from the box in alphabetical order.

conviction	cushion	occupation	complexion	civilization	cooperation

1. civilization
2. complexion
3. conviction
4. cooperation
5. cushion
6. occupation

Puzzle

Unscramble the **list words** to complete the crossword puzzle.

ACROSS
2. INOCATRITE
4. COINSACO
6. SOXERPINES
8. CATCUPOONI
13. PLIXONCOME
15. GONEDISTI
16. OILENS
18. TOPPORRONI
19. NOVITNICCO

DOWN
1. SONNETI
3. TONNIO
5. NIOVOTED
7. SIPSUNIOC
9. TIFFENOAC
10. TENNITION
11. IAPROOTCONE
12. VIZALINTICIO
13. OSHINUC
14. LOVERTUNIO
17. TOONIL

Crossword answers: RECITATION, OCCASION, EXPRESSION, OCCUPATION, COMPLEXION, SUSPICION, INTENTION, COOPERATION, CIVILIZATION, DIGESTION, LESION, REVOLUTION, LOTION, CUSHION, TENSION, NOTION, DEVOTION, AFFECTION, PROPORTION, CONVICTION

Lesson 9 • Words Ending with **ion** or **ation**   39

Proofreading

Use the proofreading marks to correct the mistakes in the article below. Then, write the misspelled **list words** correctly on the lines.

Have you considered a career as an astronaut? Working in space can be a risky occupation. From the rocket's tremendous thrust up to the occasion when the orbiter reenters the Earth's atmosphere, space travel is dangerous. Astronauts train for a long time. They must learn to handle the tension that can come with weightlessness and long periods of isolation. Cooperation among crew members is very important, as well as devotion to the purpose of the mission. Kathryn Thornton, an astronaut on four flights, has said, "The benefits of space flight far outweigh the risks."

1. occupation
2. occasion
3. tension
4. cooperation
5. devotion

Proofreading Marks
- ○ spelling mistake
- ≡ capital letter
- ? add question mark
- ℓ delete word
- ✓ add quotation marks

Writing Log Entries

You have been selected to represent students aboard a five-day space shuttle flight. Your job is to keep a daily log of your experiences, thoughts, and feelings. Use as many of the **list words** as possible as you describe your time in space. Proofread and revise your work, and then read it aloud to the class.

BONUS WORDS

| trajectory | gravitation | capsule | propellant | reentry |
| booster | aerospace | velocity | rendezvous | thrust |

Write a **bonus word** to complete each sentence.

1. A trail of white exhaust fumes traced the curved __trajectory__ of the ascending rocket.
2. Shortly after __reentry__ into the Earth's atmosphere, the capsule splashed into the sea.
3. To __rendezvous__ means "to meet at a planned location."
4. The rocket carried two tanks of __propellant__ to run its engines.
5. The __booster__ rocket separated from the capsule once its function was complete.
6. The rocket required tremendous __thrust__ to get it off the ground.
7. The force of __gravitation__ causes particles to be attracted to each other.
8. The astronaut's cockpit is inside the __capsule__.
9. The shuttle was designed by __aerospace__ engineers.
10. The satellite hurtled through space at tremendous __velocity__.

40   Lesson 9 • Words Ending with **ion** or **ation**

Alphabetical Order To extend, have students add to their list of alphabetized words: *conclusion, competition, coalition,* and *constitution.*

Puzzle Urge students to find clues in the scrambled letters and in the words as they are entered in the grid.

Spelling and Writing   Page 40

Proofreading Ask students for examples demonstrating the proofreading marks used in this lesson.

Writing Log Entries Read and discuss articles about space shuttle missions—including rendezvous and repair missions with satellites, photography sessions, and experiments. Have students suggest feelings they might have as assistants to the crews.

Bonus Words   Page 40

Space Travel Using dictionaries and diagrams or illustrations from an encyclopedia, define and discuss the **bonus words**. Relate them to the writing project and have students use the words in oral sentences.

Bonus Words Test
1. The space shuttle will **rendezvous** with a satellite.
2. Angelo hopes to become an **aerospace** engineer.
3. **Reentry** into the atmosphere will occur soon.
4. A chimpanzee piloted an early space **capsule**.
5. A technician tested the **booster** rocket.
6. Rocket engines create the **thrust** for take-off.
7. The **propellant** is measured periodically.
8. **Trajectory** is the curved path of a rocket.
9. **Velocity** is another term for "rate of speed."
10. **Gravitation** creates magnetism.

Final Test
1. A parade marked the **occasion** of the hero's birth.
2. Speak clearly during your **recitation** of the essay.
3. A balanced diet maintains a healthy **complexion**.
4. Your **cooperation** made the project simple.
5. My **intention** is to finish the report after dinner.
6. The pyramids are a legacy of an early **civilization**.
7. The **revolution** helped the colonists gain freedom.
8. Apply suntan **lotion** to protect your skin.
9. Do you enjoy your **occupation** as a journalist?
10. I have a **suspicion** that Alana planned a surprise.
11. The **digestion** of food creates energy.
12. What a silly **notion** that idea is!
13. My cat likes to take naps on that blue **cushion**.
14. Grandpa always greets me with **affection**.
15. Did you see the surprised **expression** on her face?
16. **Proportion** shows distance and dimension.
17. Cleanse the **lesion** with warm water.
18. Express your ideas with poise and **conviction**.
19. A writer with a deadline operates under **tension**.
20. She showed her **devotion** by working all night.

Lesson 10 — Words with French Derivations

Objective
To spell words with French derivations

Pretest
1. On what street is the **boutique** located?
2. The **boulevard** is lined with tall oak trees.
3. Mia works hard in her **pursuit** to be a musician.
4. What a moving speech the **chaplain** gave!
5. Mrs. Ishi will be a **chaperone** on the field trip.
6. My dad, who is a **gourmet**, writes a food column.
7. A **courteous** woman helped me to find the route.
8. Chameleons change color for **camouflage**.
9. Will a coat of **lacquer** protect the table's surface?
10. **Majestic** cliffs line the coast of West Wales.
11. Jorgé wore a mask to the **masquerade** party.
12. Should I carry a **passport** when traveling abroad?
13. The runners felt **fatigue** after the race.
14. I could see the tree's **silhouette** in the photo.
15. My family stayed in a **suite** at the Concord Hotel.
16. He recorded his **calorie** intake during his diet.
17. Through practice, Jill gained **expertise** as a skater.
18. My boss explained the daily **routine** of my job.
19. The **chauffeur** carefully parked the limousine.
20. Is a **lieutenant** required to salute a major?

Spelling Strategy
Page 41

Discuss the spelling rule, then work with students to find the following words in a college edition dictionary and discuss their etymologies: *restaurant, table, verb, vermin, plate, parasol, laissez faire, menu,* and *bouquet.* Use *laissez faire* and *bouquet* to stress the sounds that endings such as *ez* and *et* stand for in French, and that they are "borrowed" in the English language. Apply the discussion to the **list words** and work with students to define each word.

Vocabulary Development Before students begin the exercise, call on volunteers to identify the **list words** that match these definitions: "to disguise" (*camouflage*); "a masked ball" (*masquerade*).

Dictionary Skills Suggest students examine each etymology carefully to find clues as to the identity of the **list word**.

Spelling Practice
Pages 42–43

Word Analysis If needed, have students refer to the **list words** on page 43 to help them find each letter combination.

Word Application Before beginning the exercise, have students supply the **list word** to replace the underlined word in this sentence: *The lights along the street shine brightly at night illuminating the storefronts. (boulevard)*

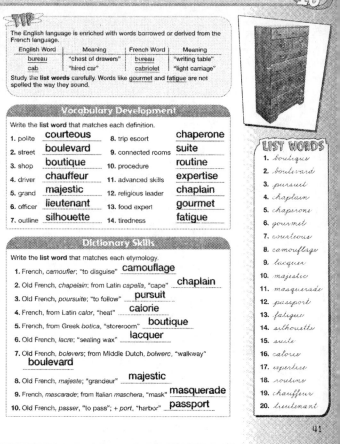

Words with French Derivations — Lesson 10

TIP The English language is enriched with words borrowed or derived from the French language.

English Word	Meaning	French Word	Meaning
bureau	"chest of drawers"	bureau	"writing table"
cab	"hired car"	cabriolet	"light carriage"

Study the **list words** carefully. Words like *gourmet* and *fatigue* are not spelled the way they sound.

Vocabulary Development
Write the **list word** that matches each definition.

1. polite — courteous
2. street — boulevard
3. shop — boutique
4. driver — chauffeur
5. grand — majestic
6. officer — lieutenant
7. outline — silhouette
8. trip escort — chaperone
9. connected rooms — suite
10. procedure — routine
11. advanced skills — expertise
12. religious leader — chaplain
13. food expert — gourmet
14. tiredness — fatigue

Dictionary Skills
Write the **list word** that matches each etymology.

1. French, *camoufler*; "to disguise" — camouflage
2. Old French, *chapelain*; from Latin *capella,* "cape" — chaplain
3. Old French, *poursuite*; "to follow" — pursuit
4. French, from Latin *calor,* "heat" — calorie
5. French, from Greek *botica,* "storeroom" — boutique
6. Old French, *lacre*; "sealing wax" — lacquer
7. Old French, *bolevers*; from Middle Dutch, *bolwerc,* "walkway" — boulevard
8. Old French, *majeste*; "grandeur" — majestic
9. French, *mascarade*; from Italian *maschera,* "mask" — masquerade
10. Old French, *passer,* "to pass"; + *port,* "harbor" — passport

LIST WORDS
1. boutique
2. boulevard
3. pursuit
4. chaplain
5. chaperone
6. gourmet
7. courteous
8. camouflage
9. lacquer
10. majestic
11. masquerade
12. passport
13. fatigue
14. silhouette
15. suite
16. calorie
17. expertise
18. routine
19. chauffeur
20. lieutenant

41

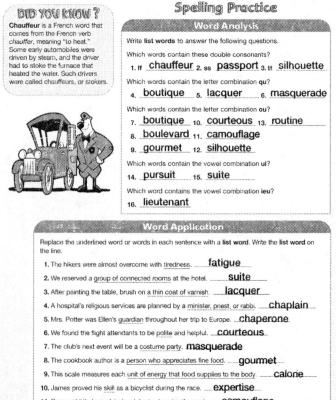

DID YOU KNOW?
Chauffeur is a French word that comes from the French verb *chauffer,* meaning "to heat." Some early automobiles were driven by steam, and the driver had to stoke the furnace that heated the water. Such drivers were called chauffeurs, or stokers.

Spelling Practice
Word Analysis
Write **list words** to answer the following questions.

Which words contain these double consonants?
1. ff — chauffeur 2. ss — passport 3. tt — silhouette

Which words contain the letter combination **qu**?
4. boutique 5. lacquer 6. masquerade

Which words contain the letter combination **ou**?
7. boutique 10. courteous 13. routine
8. boulevard 11. camouflage
9. gourmet 12. silhouette

Which words contain the vowel combination **ui**?
14. pursuit 15. suite

Which word contains the vowel combination **ieu**?
16. lieutenant

Word Application
Replace the underlined word or words in each sentence with a **list word**. Write the **list word** on the line.

1. The hikers were almost overcome with tiredness. — fatigue
2. We reserved a group of connected rooms at the hotel. — suite
3. After painting the table, brush on a thin coat of varnish. — lacquer
4. A hospital's religious services are planned by a minister, priest, or rabbi. — chaplain
5. Mrs. Potter was Ellen's guardian throughout her trip to Europe. — chaperone
6. We found the flight attendants to be polite and helpful. — courteous
7. The club's next event will be a costume party. — masquerade
8. The cookbook author is a person who appreciates fine food. — gourmet
9. This scale measures each unit of energy that food supplies to the body. — calorie
10. James proved his skill as a bicyclist during the race. — expertise
11. Some rabbits turn white in winter to disguise themselves. — camouflage
12. The investigators were in search of evidence and clues. — pursuit
13. His regular way of doing things is to start the day with breakfast. — routine

42   Lesson 10 • Words with French Derivations

36

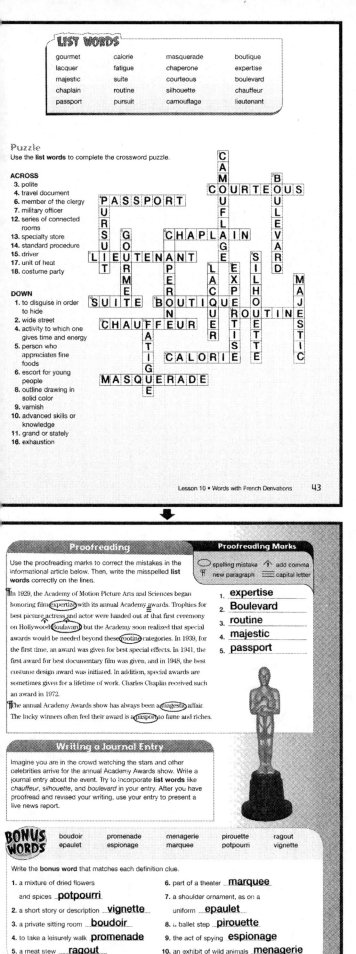

LIST WORDS

gourmet	calorie	masquerade	boutique
lacquer	fatigue	chaperone	expertise
majestic	suite	courteous	boulevard
chaplain	routine	silhouette	chauffeur
passport	pursuit	camouflage	lieutenant

Puzzle
Use the **list words** to complete the crossword puzzle.

ACROSS
3. polite
4. travel document
6. member of the clergy
7. military officer
12. series of connected rooms
13. specialty store
14. standard procedure
15. driver
17. unit of heat
18. costume party

DOWN
1. to disguise in order to hide
2. wide street
4. activity to which one gives time and energy
5. person who appreciates fine foods
6. escort for young people
8. outline drawing in solid color
9. varnish
10. advanced skills or knowledge
11. grand or stately
16. exhaustion

Lesson 10 • Words with French Derivations 43

Proofreading

Use the proofreading marks to correct the mistakes in the informational article below. Then, write the misspelled **list words** correctly on the lines.

Proofreading Marks
- ◯ spelling mistake
- ⁋ new paragraph
- ↑ add comma
- ≡ capital letter

In 1929, the Academy of Motion Picture Arts and Sciences began honoring film *expertize* with its annual Academy awards. Trophies for best picture, actress, and actor were handed out at that first ceremony on Hollywood *boulevard* but the Academy soon realized that special awards would be needed beyond these *rooting* categories. In 1939, for the first time, an award was given for best special effects. In 1941, the first award for best documentary film was given, and in 1948, the best costume design award was initiated. In addition, special awards are sometimes given for a lifetime of work. Charles Chaplin received such an award in 1972.

The annual Academy Awards show has always been a *magestic* affair. The lucky winners often feel their award is a *passort* to fame and riches.

1. expertise
2. Boulevard
3. routine
4. majestic
5. passport

Writing a Journal Entry

Imagine you are in the crowd watching the stars and other celebrities arrive for the annual Academy Awards show. Write a journal entry about the event. Try to incorporate **list words** like *chauffeur*, *silhouette*, and *boulevard* in your entry. After you have proofread and revised your writing, use your entry to present a live news report.

BONUS WORDS

| boudoir | promenade | menagerie | pirouette | ragout |
| epaulet | espionage | marquee | potpourri | vignette |

Write the **bonus word** that matches each definition clue.

1. a mixture of dried flowers and spices **potpourri**
2. a short story or description **vignette**
3. a private sitting room **boudoir**
4. to take a leisurely walk **promenade**
5. a meat stew **ragout**
6. part of a theater **marquee**
7. a shoulder ornament, as on a uniform **epaulet**
8. a ballet step **pirouette**
9. the act of spying **espionage**
10. an exhibit of wild animals **menagerie**

44 Lesson 10 • Words with French Derivations

Puzzle If needed, review the process for solving crossword puzzles, explaining the relationship between the clue numbers and those in the puzzle grid.

Spelling and Writing   Page 44
Proofreading Review the proofreading marks used in this lesson, and ask students to suggest examples illustrating each mark.

Writing a Journal Entry Discuss with students current movies that they have enjoyed. Have them name celebrities who might appear at the movies' premieres. Ask them how they'd feel if they were in the crowd clustered at the theater as the stars entered. Encourage them to take notes to use as they write.

Bonus Words   Page 44
French Words Have students find the **bonus words'** definitions and etymologies in dictionaries, and then use the words in oral sentences. Review what they have learned about the pronunciation of French words that have been "borrowed" by the English language.

Bonus Words Test
1. We saw a fierce Bengal tiger at the **menagerie**.
2. He wore a gold **epaulet** on each shoulder.
3. We selected new wallpaper for Joan's **boudoir**.
4. The **vignette** was written by Ernest Hemingway.
5. Please cut up two carrots for the **ragout**.
6. The attendant changed the theater **marquee**.
7. Partners **promenade** to begin the square dance.
8. The ballerina danced a graceful **pirouette**.
9. The movie describes the life of an **espionage** agent.
10. Fran used dried rose petals to make **potpourri**.

Final Test
1. After dinner, we strolled along the **boulevard**.
2. Does your **passport** include a current picture?
3. The **expertise** of the artist shows in her work.
4. Write a **courteous** note to acknowledge the gift.
5. A hot shower and a nap will cure your **fatigue**.
6. For **camouflage**, caterpillars blend in with leaves.
7. Val took a vacation to escape her daily **routine**.
8. Good luck in your **pursuit** of a career!
9. Did you know that my father is a **gourmet** cook?
10. The annual **masquerade** ball is on February 14.
11. Becky bought her new dress at a **boutique**.
12. Did you know that a **calorie** is a unit of heat?
13. Stir the **lacquer** thoroughly before using it.
14. My shadow made a **silhouette** on the wall.
15. Uncle Hank has a part-time job as a **chauffeur**.
16. The **chaplain** will conduct a service at noon.
17. A **suite** is more expensive than a single room.
18. Our **chaperone** will meet us at the airport.
19. What a **majestic** sight the Grand Canyon is!
20. My mother served as a **lieutenant** in the army.

37

Lesson 11 — Latin Roots

Objective
To spell words with Latin roots

Pretest

1. Therapy helped him overcome his **affliction**.
2. He orders people around like a **dictator**.
3. Because she was **persistent**, she got a refund.
4. The lawyer advised her client to sign the **contract**.
5. Tom and Ramón resolved their **conflict** peacefully.
6. Your actions must cease and **desist** now!
7. Does the village church have a new **minister**?
8. Human bones **consist** of hard and soft tissue.
9. Lizzie **fractured** her ankle playing baseball.
10. The actress used clear **diction** as she spoke.
11. As a result of the **impact**, both cars were dented.
12. When will **construction** of the new school begin?
13. Please don't try to **distract** me while I'm studying.
14. Some people are **resistant** to change.
15. Kendra read a **historical** account of the Civil War.
16. Joe's studio apartment was small and **compact**.
17. Dad pointed out the financial **district** of the city.
18. Will the leg cast **restrict** your movements?
19. This tight collar will **constrict** my breathing.
20. Lena was **tactful** when she told Al about his error.

Spelling Strategy
Page 45
Discuss the spelling rule, then help students find the Latin roots or Latin derivations of these words in a dictionary: *inflict, dictate, assist, attract, administer, fragment, compactor, structure, history, strictly,* and *tactile.* Discuss how the meaning of each word is related to the meaning of the Latin root or Latin word. Apply the discussion to the **list words** and help students to define each word.

Word Analysis To start, have students identify the **list word** containing the same root as *administration.* (*minister*) Encourage students to refer to the **list words**, if needed, to determine the words with the same roots.

Vocabulary Development Before students begin, have them identify the **list words** that are synonyms for *broken* (*fractured*), *tyrant* (*dictator*), and *stop* (*desist*).

Spelling Practice
Pages 46–47
Classification To review classification skills, ask students to select the **list word** that belongs in the following series: *limit, confine, _____.* (*restrict*) To extend the activity, have students create similar classification series using the remaining **list words** that classmates can solve.

Word Application Urge students to use context clues to find the **list words** that best complete the letter.

Latin Roots — Lesson 11

TIP

Many English words are formed with Latin roots.

Latin Root	Meaning	English Word	Meaning
dict, dic	"say"	diction	"manner of speaking"

Other English words are borrowed or derived from Latin words.

Latin Word	Meaning	English Word	Meaning
minister	"servant"	minister	"preacher"

All the **list words** are based on Latin roots or Latin words. Study these words carefully and practice spelling them.

Word Analysis

Write the **list words** that have the same Latin root as the word given.

predict	1. dictator		2. diction	
infraction	3. fractured			
consistency	4. persistent		5. consist	
	6. desist		7. resistant	
prehistoric	8. historical			
contact	9. tactful			
instruct	10. construction			
inflict	11. affliction		12. conflict	
traction	13. contract		14. distract	
stricter	15. district		16. restrict	
	17. constrict			

LIST WORDS
1. affliction
2. dictator
3. persistent
4. contract
5. conflict
6. desist
7. minister
8. consist
9. fractured
10. diction
11. impact
12. construction
13. distract
14. resistant
15. historical
16. compact
17. district
18. restrict
19. constrict
20. tactful

Vocabulary Development

Write the **list word** that matches each synonym.

1. agreement	contract	7. small	compact
2. sickness	affliction	8. region	district
3. squeeze	constrict	9. limit	restrict
4. struggle	conflict	10. crash	impact
5. preacher	minister	11. divert	distract
6. include	consist	12. discreet	tactful

45

DID YOU KNOW?
Contract is from the Latin *contractor.* It is formed from *con-,* meaning "together," and *tractus,* meaning "drawn." That is why we "draw up" a contract.

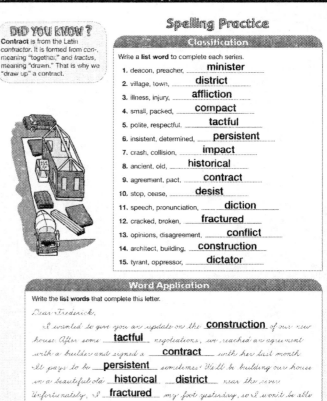

Spelling Practice
Classification

Write a **list word** to complete each series.

1. deacon, preacher, _____ minister
2. village, town, _____ district
3. illness, injury, _____ affliction
4. small, packed, _____ compact
5. polite, respectful, _____ tactful
6. insistent, determined, _____ persistent
7. crash, collision, _____ impact
8. ancient, old, _____ historical
9. agreement, pact, _____ contract
10. stop, cease, _____ desist
11. speech, pronunciation, _____ diction
12. cracked, broken, _____ fractured
13. opinions, disagreement, _____ conflict
14. architect, building, _____ construction
15. tyrant, oppressor, _____ dictator

Word Application

Write the **list words** that complete this letter.

Dear Frederick,

I wanted to give you an update on the **construction** of our new house. After some **tactful** negotiations, we reached an agreement with a builder and signed a **contract** with her last month. It pays to be **persistent** sometimes! We'll be building our house in a beautiful old **historical** **district** near the river. Unfortunately, I **fractured** my foot yesterday, so I won't be able to go to the groundbreaking tomorrow. I should be up and about soon. Hope all is well.

Regards,
Corinne

46   Lesson 11 • Latin Roots

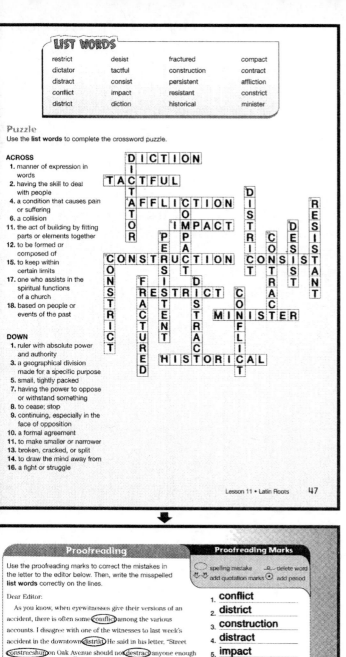

LIST WORDS

restrict	desist	fractured	compact
dictator	tactful	construction	contract
distract	consist	persistent	affliction
conflict	impact	resistant	constrict
district	diction	historical	minister

Puzzle
Use the **list words** to complete the crossword puzzle.

ACROSS
1. manner of expression in words
2. having the skill to deal with people
4. a condition that causes pain or suffering
6. a collision
11. the act of building by fitting parts or elements together
12. to be formed or composed of
15. to keep within certain limits
17. one who assists in the spiritual functions of a church
18. based on people or events of the past

DOWN
1. ruler with absolute power and authority
3. a geographical division made for a specific purpose
5. small, tightly packed
7. having the power to oppose or withstand something
8. to cease; stop
9. continuing, especially in the face of opposition
10. a formal agreement
11. to make smaller or narrower
13. broken, cracked, or split
14. to draw the mind away from
16. a fight or struggle

Crossword answers: DICTION, TACTFUL, AFFLICTION, DISTRICT, RESISTANT, IMPACT, DESIST, CONTRACT, CONSIST, CONSTRUCTION, CONSTRICT, FRACTURED, RESTRICT, DISTRACT, MINISTER, CONFLICT, PERSISTENT, HISTORICAL, DICTATOR

Lesson 11 • Latin Roots   47

Proofreading

Use the proofreading marks to correct the mistakes in the letter to the editor below. Then, write the misspelled **list words** correctly on the lines.

Dear Editor:

As you know, when eyewitnesses give their versions of an accident, there is often some **conflict** among the various accounts. I disagree with one of the witnesses to last week's accident in the downtown **district**. He said in his letter, "Street **construction** on Oak Avenue should not **distract** anyone enough to to cause an accident. I believe that the confusion and sudden detours caused by street repairs have a great **impact** on the flow of traffic. Motorists need enough warning to deal with these problems, or accidents will continue to occur.

Proofreading Marks
- spelling mistake
- delete word
- add quotation marks
- add period

1. conflict
2. district
3. construction
4. distract
5. impact

Writing a Report
Imagine that you have just witnessed a car accident. The police want you to write a report describing the accident. Include information about the direction and speed of the cars and the road conditions at the scene. Use as many **list words** as you can. Proofread and revise your report, and then share it with other students.

BONUS WORDS

waiver	assailant	probation	disposition	felony
larceny	accusation	jurisdiction	exonerate	statute

Write the **bonus word** that matches each definition clue.

1. a claim or charge of breaking the law **accusation**
2. an established rule; formal regulation **statute**
3. the territorial range of authority **jurisdiction**
4. to declare or prove blameless **exonerate**
5. the act of relinquishing voluntarily a right, claim, or privilege **waiver**
6. the power or authority to arrange, settle, or manage **disposition**
7. a major crime punishable by imprisonment **felony**
8. the suspension of a prison sentence **probation**
9. a person who attacks physically and violently **assailant**
10. the taking of personal property without consent; theft **larceny**

48   Lesson 11 • Latin Roots

Puzzle If needed for review, work with students to complete one item across and one item down.

Spelling and Writing   Page 48
Proofreading Write the following sentence on the board and have students help you correct it using the proofreading marks from the lesson: *The car was was going to fast, said Alex*

Writing a Report Discuss the kinds of details that might be important to the investigation of an accident. As students suggest ideas, write them on the board. Encourage students to use these ideas as they write. When finished, you may wish to have students share their eyewitness reports in small groups.

Bonus Words   Page 48
Legal Terms Have students work in pairs to find the meanings of the **bonus words** in dictionaries. For words with more than one meaning, have students identify the meaning of the word that is related to law.

Bonus Words Test
1. A **felony** is a serious crime, punishable by law.
2. My client will not sign a **waiver** of her rights.
3. This case is beyond the **jurisdiction** of the state.
4. The **disposition** of your case is in the jury's hands.
5. This **statute** allows stores to open on holidays.
6. The facts will **exonerate** my client of all guilt.
7. The **assailant** was quickly captured by the police.
8. He was released on **probation** for good behavior.
9. The defendant denied the **accusation**.
10. The police investigated a **larceny** at the store.

Final Test
1. The two teams had a **conflict** over the rules.
2. Speak with clear, precise **diction** to be understood.
3. This story is **historical** fiction set in the 1800s.
4. Kate was **tactful** when she spoke to her boss.
5. According to the **contract**, the job pays well.
6. The X-rays showed that the bone was **fractured**.
7. Is the carpet in the family room **resistant** to stains?
8. A tourniquet will help **constrict** the flow of blood.
9. He was **persistent** and would never stop trying.
10. How many members did the committee **consist** of?
11. The loud music may **distract** the bus driver.
12. The fence will **restrict** the puppy to the backyard.
13. The people feared the tyrannical **dictator**.
14. The **minister** spoke about the homeless.
15. Mr. Diaz will oversee **construction** of the house.
16. Three towns make up our school **district**.
17. Chicken pox is a common childhood **affliction**.
18. "**Desist** your noisy chatter now!" said the librarian.
19. Did the **impact** of the baseball crack the window?
20. The wood was piled in small, **compact** bundles.

Objective
To review spelling words with prefixes, suffixes, and French and Latin origins

Spelling Strategy   Page 49

Read and discuss the spelling rules. To reinforce, ask students to name other words that illustrate the information summarized in each of the five sections. You may wish to have students turn back to the opening pages of Lessons 7–11 to review each spelling rule and then apply it to its full selection of **list words**.

Spelling Practice   Pages 49–51

Lesson 7 Review the meanings of the prefixes *ap* and *as* by discussing the Latin prefixes and roots in *appeal, approval, assert,* and *assortment.* Remind students that *ap* precedes roots beginning with *p,* and *as* precedes roots beginning with *s.* Apply the discussion to the **list words,** and have students use them in oral sentences. Point out the additional write-on lines and encourage students to add two words from Lesson 7 that they found difficult, or assign words that seemed difficult for everyone. (Repeat this procedure for each lesson in the Review.) To extend the exercise, have students create context-clue sentences for the additional words.

Lesson 8 Review the meanings of the prefixes *ac, af,* and *at* by discussing the prefixes and roots in *accompany, affront,* and *attune.* Have students name the roots that follow each prefix. Then, review the **list words,** having students use them in oral sentences. Have students write brief definitions for their additional words as well.

Lesson 9 To review nouns with the suffixes *ion* or *ation,* discuss the words *transportation, exploration, digestion,* and *vacation.* Have students name the verb to which each suffix was added. Repeat, using the **list words.**

Lesson 10 To review "spelling tricks" in words of French origin, discuss: *masquerade, suite, fatigue,* and *croquet.* Then, review the rest of the **list words.**

Lesson 11 To review words with Latin roots, have students look up the etymologies of *constrict, diction, contract,* and *conflict.* To extend the activity, have students write sentences using their additional words, and then scramble the words in each sentence. Have partners exchange and solve the "coded messages."

Show What You Know   Page 52

Point out that this review will help students know if they have mastered the words in Lessons 7–11. Have a volunteer restate the directions and tell which word in the first item should be marked. *(appendadge)* When finished, have students correct their misspelled words.

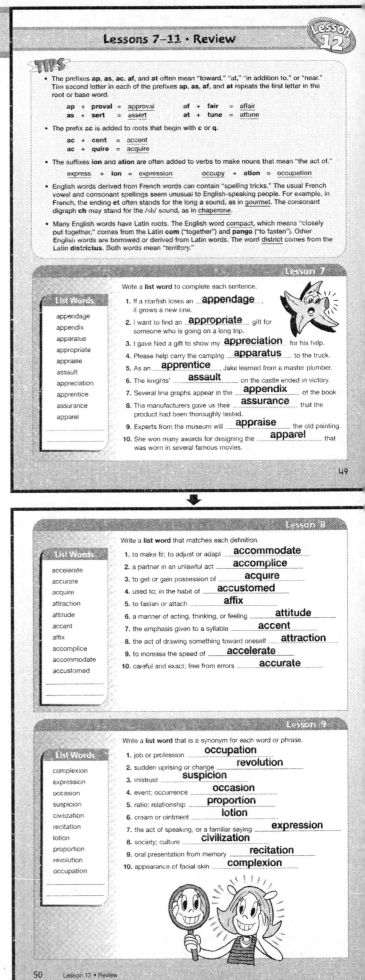

TIPS

- The prefixes **ap, as, ac, af,** and **at** often mean "toward," "at," "in addition to," or "near." The second letter in each of the prefixes **ap, as, af,** and **at** repeats the first letter in the root or base word.

  ap + proval = approval   af + fair = affair
  as + sert = assert   at + tune = attune

- The prefix **ac** is added to roots that begin with **c** or **q.**

  ac + cent = accent
  ac + quire = acquire

- The suffixes **ion** and **ation** are often added to verbs to make nouns that mean "the act of."

  express + ion = expression   occupy + ation = occupation

- English words derived from French words can contain "spelling tricks." The usual French vowel and consonant spellings seem unusual to English-speaking people. For example, in French, the ending **et** often stands for the long a sound, as in gourmet. The consonant digraph **ch** may stand for the /sh/ sound, as in chaperone.

- Many English words have Latin roots. The English word compact, which means "closely put together," comes from the Latin **com** ("together") and **pango** ("to fasten"). Other English words are borrowed or derived from Latin words. The word district comes from the Latin **districtus.** Both words mean "territory."

Lesson 7

Write a **list word** to complete each sentence.

List Words
appendage
appendix
apparatus
appropriate
appraise
assault
appreciation
apprentice
assurance
apparel

1. If a starfish loses an **appendage**, it grows a new one.
2. I want to find an **appropriate** gift for someone who is going on a long trip.
3. I gave Ned a gift to show my **appreciation** for his help.
4. Please help carry the camping **apparatus** to the truck.
5. As an **apprentice**, Jake learned from a master plumber.
6. The knights' **assault** on the castle ended in victory.
7. Several line graphs appear in the **appendix** of the book.
8. The manufacturers gave us their **assurance** that the product had been thoroughly tested.
9. Experts from the museum will **appraise** the old painting.
10. She won many awards for designing the **apparel** that was worn in several famous movies.

49

Lesson 8

Write a **list word** that matches each definition.

List Words
accelerate
accurate
acquire
attraction
attitude
accent
affix
accomplice
accommodate
accustomed

1. to make fit; to adjust or adapt **accommodate**
2. a partner in an unlawful act **accomplice**
3. to get or gain possession of **acquire**
4. used to; in the habit of **accustomed**
5. to fasten or attach **affix**
6. a manner of acting, thinking, or feeling **attitude**
7. the emphasis given to a syllable **accent**
8. the act of drawing something toward oneself **attraction**
9. to increase the speed of **accelerate**
10. careful and exact; free from errors **accurate**

Lesson 9

Write a **list word** that is a synonym for each word or phrase.

List Words
complexion
expression
occasion
suspicion
civilization
recitation
lotion
proportion
revolution
occupation

1. job or profession **occupation**
2. sudden uprising or change **revolution**
3. mistrust **suspicion**
4. event; occurrence **occasion**
5. ratio; relationship **proportion**
6. cream or ointment **lotion**
7. the act of speaking, or a familiar saying **expression**
8. society; culture **civilization**
9. oral presentation from memory **recitation**
10. appearance of facial skin **complexion**

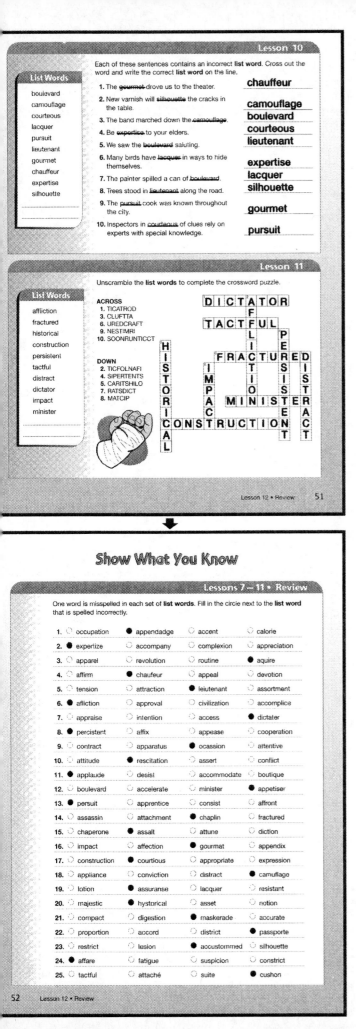

Final Test

1. A realtor will **appraise** the value of the house.
2. To show our **appreciation**, we cheered.
3. Use a hot iron to **affix** the nametag to your shirt.
4. Was the driver an **accomplice** to the crime?
5. A redhead usually has a very light **complexion**.
6. The law brought a **revolution** in health coverage.
7. Do you have a **suspicion** about who sent the note?
8. The cabinet showed great **expertise** in carpentry.
9. Did you use a clean brush to spread the **lacquer**?
10. The **lieutenant** was honored for his courage.
11. Glaucoma is an **affliction** affecting the eyes.
12. The **impact** of the rock smashed the windowpane.
13. She was polite and **tactful** during the discussion.
14. **Historical** fiction blends facts with imagination.
15. The dull feathers of the bird provide **camouflage**.
16. In the film, the **chauffeur** was the criminal.
17. I'll meet you on the **boulevard** at noon.
18. Jim's **recitation** of the poem was dramatic.
19. This **lotion** may ease the itchiness of poison ivy.
20. His **expression** showed that he was surprised.
21. That boat can really **accelerate**!
22. The waiter tried to **accommodate** our every need.
23. I've grown **accustomed** to the noise of the city.
24. Make sure a fact is **accurate** before you quote it.
25. A lobster has a claw at the tip of each **appendage**.
26. The tale told of a dragon's **assault** on the village.
27. They opened a shop that sells formal **apparel**.
28. Footnotes are in an **appendix** at the end of a book.
29. Is this suit **appropriate** for the wedding?
30. Will the museum **acquire** a Mary Cassatt painting?
31. Ana's cheerful **attitude** makes her a great friend.
32. The four sides of a square are in equal **proportion**.
33. We studied the **civilization** of ancient Greece.
34. His thank-you note was prompt and **courteous**.
35. Use black paper to make the **silhouette**.
36. Juan hopes to become a **minister**.
37. A government run by a **dictator** is oppressive.
38. I **fractured** one of my toes during the soccer game.
39. Will the loud music **distract** the workers?
40. We were delayed due to the highway **construction**.
41. What a terrible, **persistent** cough!
42. Julia Child is a famous **gourmet** cook.
43. The team was in **pursuit** of the state championship.
44. What a wonderful **occasion** to have a party!
45. I'd like to have an **occupation** as a travel agent.
46. The **accent** is on the first syllable in *kitten*.
47. Ted has an **attraction** to rural comforts.
48. She became an **apprentice** to a fine goldsmith.
49. Did the coach order new gymnastics **apparatus**?
50. Ken gave his **assurance** that he'd repay the loan.

Suffixes ial, ious

Objective
To spell words with the suffixes *ial* or *ious*

Pretest
1. The deceased sailor's **burial** was held at sea.
2. Please keep the information I told you **confidential**.
3. Cleanliness limits the spread of **infectious** diseases.
4. Zoe asked for all the **material** I had on Taiwan.
5. Do those windows make the room look **spacious**?
6. An **ambitious** person can go far in this company.
7. That 1938 hurricane was a **ferocious** storm!
8. Boris knows **influential** people in government.
9. These are **provincial** regions and those are urban.
10. He was a charming and **gracious** host.
11. Arthur is too **conscientious** to leave early.
12. Ms. Kearn understands **financial** matters.
13. Did you capitalize the **initial** letter of each word?
14. We could not pry off the **tenacious** barnacles.
15. Are the judge's **ceremonial** robes black?
16. Everyone was sorry to leave such a **glorious** beach.
17. Our voices created a **harmonious** melody.
18. The soldiers were stirred by the **martial** music.
19. When working, Jaina is **unconscious** of any noises.
20. An **impartial** person shows no favoritism.

Spelling Strategy
Page 53

After students have read the spelling rule, have them identify **list words** in which *i* takes the place of *y* and words in which it does not. Discuss the spelling patterns of the words and ways that students can remember them. Help students learn the meanings of the **list words**, referring them to dictionaries when necessary.

Vocabulary Development Write *plain* and *fancy* on the board, explaining that the words are antonyms. Have students give other examples of antonym pairs before completing the exercise independently.

Dictionary Skills Write *fair; just* on the board and ask students what **list word** matches the clue. *(impartial)* Point out that the clues in the exercise may be definitions or synonyms.

Spelling Practice
Pages 54–55

Word Analysis Write *the three red roses* on the board and use it to illustrate the difference between nouns and adjectives. Then, have students complete the exercise. When finished, ask volunteers which words had both *A* and *N* beside them. *(material, initial)*

Word Application Work through the first item with students, asking them to explain why *financial* is the correct answer. *(It has to do with money.)*

42

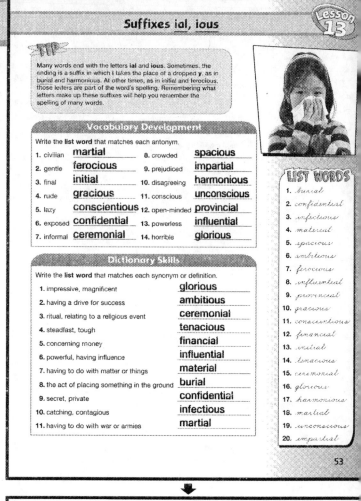

Suffixes ial, ious

TIP Many words end with the letters **ial** and **ious**. Sometimes, the ending is a suffix in which **i** takes the place of a dropped **y**, as in burial and harmonious. At other times, as in initial and ferocious, those letters are part of the word's spelling. Remembering what letters make up these suffixes will help you remember the spelling of many words.

Vocabulary Development

Write the **list word** that matches each antonym.

1. civilian	martial		8. crowded	spacious
2. gentle	ferocious		9. prejudiced	impartial
3. final	initial		10. disagreeing	harmonious
4. rude	gracious		11. conscious	unconscious
5. lazy	conscientious		12. open-minded	provincial
6. exposed	confidential		13. powerless	influential
7. informal	ceremonial		14. horrible	glorious

Dictionary Skills

Write the **list word** that matches each synonym or definition.

1. impressive, magnificent — glorious
2. having a drive for success — ambitious
3. ritual, relating to a religious event — ceremonial
4. steadfast, tough — tenacious
5. concerning money — financial
6. powerful, having influence — influential
7. having to do with matter or things — material
8. the act of placing something in the ground — burial
9. secret, private — confidential
10. catching, contagious — infectious
11. having to do with war or armies — martial

LIST WORDS
1. burial
2. confidential
3. infectious
4. material
5. spacious
6. ambitious
7. ferocious
8. influential
9. provincial
10. gracious
11. conscientious
12. financial
13. initial
14. tenacious
15. ceremonial
16. glorious
17. harmonious
18. martial
19. unconscious
20. impartial

53

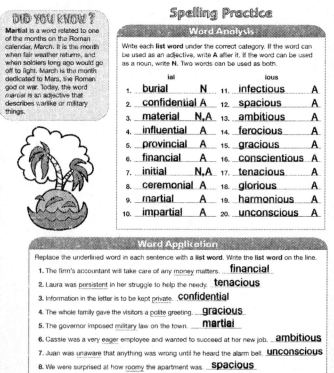

DID YOU KNOW? **Martial** is a word related to one of the months on the Roman calendar, *March*. It is the month when fair weather returns, and when soldiers long ago would go off to fight. March is the month dedicated to Mars, the Roman god of war. Today, the word *martial* is an adjective that describes warlike or military things.

Spelling Practice
Word Analysis

Write each **list word** under the correct category. If the word can be used as an adjective, write **A** after it. If the word can be used as a noun, write **N**. Two words can be used as both.

ial
1. burial — N
2. confidential — A
3. material — N,A
4. influential — A
5. provincial — A
6. financial — A
7. initial — N,A
8. ceremonial — A
9. martial — A
10. impartial — A

ious
11. infectious — A
12. spacious — A
13. ambitious — A
14. ferocious — A
15. gracious — A
16. conscientious — A
17. tenacious — A
18. glorious — A
19. harmonious — A
20. unconscious — A

Word Application

Replace the underlined word in each sentence with a **list word**. Write the **list word** on the line.

1. The firm's accountant will take care of any money matters. — financial
2. Laura was persistent in her struggle to help the needy. — tenacious
3. Information in the letter is to be kept private. — confidential
4. The whole family gave the visitors a polite greeting. — gracious
5. The governor imposed military law on the town. — martial
6. Cassie was a very eager employee and wanted to succeed at her new job. — ambitious
7. Juan was unaware that anything was wrong until he heard the alarm bell. — unconscious
8. We were surprised at how roomy the apartment was. — spacious
9. Only family members will be permitted to attend the funeral. — burial
10. Please leave the building supplies at the side of the garage. — material
11. The savage storm caused widespread damage to the island. — ferocious
12. Urban politicians need to know that country attitudes may differ. — provincial

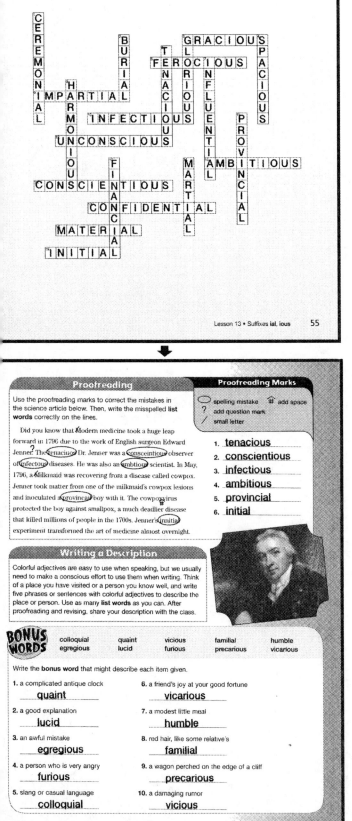

Puzzle

This is a crossword puzzle without clues. Use the length and the spelling of each **list word** to complete the puzzle.

Proofreading

Use the proofreading marks to correct the mistakes in the science article below. Then, write the misspelled **list words** correctly on the lines.

Did you know that Modern medicine took a huge leap forward in 1796 due to the work of English surgeon Edward Jenner? The tenacious Dr. Jenner was a consceintious observer of infectous diseases. He was also an ambtious scientist. In May, 1796, a milkmaid was recovering from a disease called cowpox. Jenner took matter from one of the milkmaid's cowpox lesions and inoculated a provincal boy with it. The cowpox virus protected the boy against smallpox, a much deadlier disease that killed millions of people in the 1700s. Jenner's innitial experiment transformed the art of medicine almost overnight.

Proofreading Marks

- ⭕ spelling mistake
- ? add question mark
- / small letter
- # add space

1. tenacious
2. conscientious
3. infectious
4. ambitious
5. provincial
6. initial

Writing a Description

Colorful adjectives are easy to use when speaking, but we usually need to make a conscious effort to use them when writing. Think of a place you have visited or a person you know well, and write five phrases or sentences with colorful adjectives to describe the place or person. Use as many **list words** as you can. After proofreading and revising, share your description with the class.

BONUS WORDS

colloquial	quaint	vicious	familial	humble
egregious	lucid	furious	precarious	vicarious

Write the **bonus word** that might describe each item given.

1. a complicated antique clock
   quaint
2. a good explanation
   lucid
3. an awful mistake
   egregious
4. a person who is very angry
   furious
5. slang or casual language
   colloquial
6. a friend's joy at your good fortune
   vicarious
7. a modest little meal
   humble
8. red hair, like some relative's
   familial
9. a wagon perched on the edge of a cliff
   precarious
10. a damaging rumor
    vicious

Puzzle Have students discuss strategies for solving crossword puzzles without clues. Then, let them complete the puzzle independently.

Spelling and Writing   *Page 56*

Proofreading Use the question *Wasn't that an exiting Book* to demonstrate the proofreading marks that students will be using in this lesson.

Writing a Description Have students suggest categories of adjectives, such as color, size, shape, number, and feeling. It may help if students first think of nouns, and then name adjectives that describe these. Encourage students to think of unique or vivid places or people to describe in their writing.

Bonus Words   *Page 56*

Adjectives Explain that the **bonus words** are adjectives. Discuss each word's meaning, having students consult dictionaries for any unfamiliar terms. Ask volunteers to identify a noun that each adjective could describe. Then, have students take turns using the words in oral sentences.

Bonus Words Test

1. The family lived in a **humble** little cottage.
2. Allan's dog is not **vicious** and would never hurt you.
3. I was embarrassed to make such an **egregious** error!
4. We got **vicarious** joy from their wedding pictures.
5. We heard a **colloquial** chat, not a formal report.
6. We understood Dr. Chan's **lucid** explanation.
7. Move the lamp away from such a **precarious** spot.
8. My uncle and I have a strong **familial** resemblance.
9. Tourists flocked to visit the **quaint** little village.
10. The **furious** battle raged for weeks.

Final Test

1. Is Wanda a **conscientious** student?
2. Read the **financial** pages for information on stocks.
3. My **initial** reaction changed after I met her.
4. The raccoon was **tenacious** and would not let go.
5. Special rules apply at **ceremonial** events.
6. Lee's project was the most **ambitious** in the class.
7. The animal looked **ferocious**, so I stayed far away.
8. The **influential** person supported the candidate.
9. Traveling will broaden your **provincial** attitude.
10. Max's **gracious** acceptance speech was charming.
11. We are moving to a more **spacious** apartment.
12. The ruler was surrounded by **material** comforts.
13. A yawn is **infectious** and makes others yawn.
14. Will you allow me to read the **confidential** report?
15. The news reported the **burial** of a time capsule.
16. Let an **impartial** jury determine who is right.
17. Do you find the colors **harmonious**?
18. Art was **unconscious** of the time until the bell rang.
19. The new leader declared **martial** law.
20. This is the most **glorious** sunset in weeks!

Lesson 14 — Suffixes <u>al</u>, <u>ally</u>, <u>ic</u>, <u>ically</u>, <u>ly</u>

Objective
To spell words with the suffixes *al, ally, ic, ically, ly*

Pretest

1. **Academically**, June is a leader in her class.
2. The club's **annual** meeting will be held in February.
3. Toads are **basically** very similar to frogs.
4. The sunset cast a **dramatic** glow on the ocean.
5. **Incidentally**, Jack will be late for the meeting.
6. The president met with her **economic** advisors.
7. Tony's response was an **emphatic** "No, thank you!"
8. Is the Model T a **classic** American automobile?
9. There has been a **gradual** decline in temperature.
10. The **substantial** fog made driving difficult.
11. The amoeba is a **microscopic** organism.
12. **Frantically**, I searched for my lost dog.
13. **Comically**, the clowns scurried into the small car.
14. You acted **heroically** when you rescued the cat.
15. Father packed the car in a **systematic** way.
16. Was the decision to go to the movies **mutual**?
17. Jane Austen was a **prolific** writer.
18. The drought **drastically** reduced the water supply.
19. **Ideally**, the new highway will be finished by May.
20. Did the **tragic** story touch your heart?

Spelling Strategy
Page 57

Discuss the spelling rule. Then, have students analyze each **list word** to find its root or base word, its meaning and part of speech, the suffix that was added, and the meaning and part of speech of the new word.

Vocabulary Development Before beginning the exercise, have volunteers identify the **list words** that match these clues: *very sad* (tragic); *bravely* (heroically).

Dictionary Skills To start, have students refer to dictionaries to find the sound-spellings of *dramatic, emphatic,* and *drastically,* and write them on the board.

Spelling Practice
Pages 58–59

Word Analysis Before students complete this two-part exercise, have volunteers add suffixes to these adjectives to make adverbs: *beautiful* (beautifully); *final* (finally); and *typical* (typically); and add suffixes to these nouns to make adjectives: *democrat* (democratic); *rent* (rental); and *history* (historic).

Word Application Have students tell which **list word** is a synonym for the word in parentheses in these phrases: *a _____ procedure* (methodical); *_____ searching* (desperately). (systematic; frantically)

Analogies Review analogies by reading this example aloud and having students select a word to complete it:
Leash is to dog as bridle is to _____. (horse)

Suffixes <u>al</u>, <u>ally</u>, <u>ic</u>, <u>ically</u>, <u>ly</u> — Lesson 14

TIP
The suffixes **al, ally, ic, ically,** and **ly** are often added to roots and base words to form new words and new parts of speech.

Root or Base Word	Meaning	Plus Suffix	New Meaning
annus (Latin root)	"year" (noun)	annual	"yearly" (adj.)
comic	"humorous" (adj.)	comically	"humorously" (adv.)
ideal	"perfect" (adj.)	ideally	"perfectly" (adv.)

Vocabulary Development

Write the **list word** that matches each definition or synonym.

1. harshly — **drastically**
2. having to do with education — **academically**
3. having great substance; solid or firm — **substantial**
4. invisible to the naked eye; tiny — **microscopic**
5. very productive, fruitful — **prolific**
6. shared in common by two or more people — **mutual**
7. acting in a worried or hurried way — **frantically**
8. filled with action, emotion, or excitement — **dramatic**
9. developing little by little, over time — **gradual**
10. expressed or done with emphasis; forceful — **emphatic**
11. having a formal style — **classic**
12. orderly; planned — **systematic**
13. dreadful — **tragic**

Dictionary Skills

Write the **list word** that matches each sound-spelling.

1. {klas'ik} — **classic**
2. {kàm'ik'lē} — **comically**
3. {bā'sik'lē} — **basically**
4. {ī dē'əl ē} — **ideally**
5. {traj'ik} — **tragic**
6. {hi rō'ik'lē} — **heroically**
7. {sis'tə mat'ik} — **systematic**
8. {an'yōō wəl} — **annual**
9. {in'si den't'l ē} — **incidentally**
10. {ē'kə näm'ik} — **economic**

LIST WORDS
1. academically
2. annual
3. basically
4. dramatic
5. incidentally
6. economic
7. emphatic
8. classic
9. gradual
10. substantial
11. microscopic
12. frantically
13. comically
14. heroically
15. systematic
16. mutual
17. prolific
18. drastically
19. ideally
20. tragic

DID YOU KNOW?
The adjective **microscopic** comes to our language from the Greek words *mikros,* meaning "small," and *skopein,* meaning "to watch or view." In our language, a microscope is an instrument which helps us to view tiny objects. *Microscopic* is used to describe objects which cannot be seen with the naked eye.

Spelling Practice

Word Analysis

Form **list words** by adding suffixes to these adjectives to make adverbs.

1. drastic — **drastically**
2. academic — **academically**
3. incidental — **incidentally**
4. ideal — **ideally**
5. frantic — **frantically**
6. basic — **basically**
7. comic — **comically**
8. heroic — **heroically**

Form **list words** by adding suffixes to these nouns to make adjectives. Some nouns change form before suffixes are added.

9. system — **systematic**
10. economy — **economic**
11. class — **classic**
12. microscope — **microscopic**
13. drama — **dramatic**
14. substance — **substantial**

Word Application

Write the **list word** that is a synonym for the word in parentheses.

1. the **annual** meeting (yearly)
2. a **classic** play (traditional)
3. by **mutual** consent (shared)
4. a **prolific** plant (fruitful)
5. a **tragic** story (extremely sad)
6. **basically** the same (simply)
7. the **gradual** changes (little by little)
8. his **emphatic** reply (forceful)

Analogies

Write a **list word** to complete each analogy.

1. Single is to one as **mutual** is to two or more together.
2. School is to **academically** as hospital is to medically.
3. Funny is to comedy as **tragic** is to tragedy.
4. Huge is to elephant as **microscopic** is to bacteria.
5. Up is to down as **heroically** is to cowardly.
6. Seriously is to lecture as **comically** is to joke.
7. Economy is to **economic** as scene is to scenic.
8. Slow is to calmly as fast is to **frantically**.
9. Soft-spoken is to a period as **emphatic** is to an exclamation point.

LIST WORDS

academically	economic	basically	mutual
drastically	emphatic	frantically	prolific
microscopic	classic	comically	annual
substantial	gradual	heroically	ideally
incidentally	dramatic	systematic	tragic

Puzzle
Unscramble the **list words** to complete the crossword puzzle.

ACROSS
4. SLACCIS
7. TISRADCLAYL
11. MONCICOE
12. AMTLUU
15. LEDAILY
16. CRIGTA
19. DURGALA
19. TICNINYELLAD
20. YECADIMACALL

DOWN
1. PRICSOMOCIC
2. CABYILLAS
3. COILFRIP
5. STEAMCITYS
6. CHOIRLAYEL
8. TINTBUSSALA
9. CHEAPMIT
10. DIRTACMA
13. CALFNAILRTY
14. MAILYCCOL
18. LUNANA

Crossword answers:
CLASSIC, DRASTICALLY, PROLIFIC, BASICALLY, MICROSCOPIC, SYSTEMATIC, HEROICALLY, DRAMATIC, ECONOMIC, EMPHATIC, SUBSTANTIAL, MUTUAL, FRANTICALLY, COMICALLY, IDEALLY, TRAGIC, GRADUAL, ANNUAL, INCIDENTALLY, ACADEMICALLY

Lesson 14 • Suffixes al, ally, ic, ically, ly   59

Proofreading

Use the proofreading marks to correct the mistakes in the paragraph. Write the misspelled **list words** correctly on the lines.

Proofreading Marks
- ⟋ spelling mistake
- ⚯ add apostrophe
- ⚬ delete word
- ≡ capital letter

The history of women inventors is substantial and every bit as dramatic as that of their male counterparts. Sybilla Masters is often called the first woman inventor in the American colonies. In 1715, she invented a method of making cornmeal that drastically cut the time needed for that task. After her husbands death, Martha Coston perfected their mutual idea for colored signal flares, which were used by the navy in the civil war. Margaret Knight, whose inventions had an economic effect on shopkeepers, got a patent in 1868 for a machine that made square-bottomed paper bags. Think of margaret the next time a clerk asks "paper or plastic?"

1. substantial
2. dramatic
3. drastically
4. mutual
5. economic

Writing Topic Sentences

A topic sentence tells what a paragraph is about. Write topic sentences that could begin these paragraphs. After proofreading and revising, compare your topic sentences with classmates'.

1. **The laser was one of the most useful inventions of the second half of the twentieth century.**
A laser is a device that produces a thin beam of light. It is used in many areas, such as communications, industry, and medicine. It can burn a hole in a diamond, repair delicate eye tissue, or even track the flight path of a plane.

2. **The development of writing was the most important invention of the early civilizations.**
The Sumerians, who lived in southern Mesopotamia, developed a system of writing around 3100 B.C. The Egyptians also developed a writing system about 3000 B.C. The invention of writing meant that people no longer had to remember all that they had learned. They could write down ideas and information, and then use them later.

BONUS WORDS

piston	generator	carburetor	radiator	speedometer
throttle	distributor	crankshaft	chassis	odometer

Write the **bonus word** that matches each clue given.

1. measures total mileage **odometer**
2. cools the engine **radiator**
3. mixes air with gasoline **carburetor**
4. moves within cylinder **piston**
5. valve inside carburetor **throttle**
6. engine, frame, and wheels **chassis**
7. measures rate of movement **speedometer**
8. takes spark to spark plugs **distributor**
9. creates electricity **generator**
10. connecting rod for pistons **crankshaft**

60   Lesson 14 • Suffixes al, ally, ic, ically, ly

Puzzle Urge students to find clues not only in the scrambled letters, but also in the number of spaces in each answer and the letter clues found once some of the words have been entered into the grid.

Spelling and Writing   Page 60

Proofreading Use the following sentence to review the proofreading marks in this lesson: *Pauls cat wanderd over to to kims house.*

Writing Topic Sentences To review students' knowledge of topic sentences, have them find examples in such content-area texts as social studies and science. When students have finished writing, provide time for discussion of their topic sentences, pointing out the clarity that each adds to the paragraph.

Bonus Words   Page 60

Mechanical Terms With dictionaries and diagrams or illustrations from an encyclopedia, define and discuss the **bonus words**. Urge students to share their knowledge of generators, engines, and automobile parts.

Bonus Words Test
1. The mechanic replaced the damaged **crankshaft**.
2. The **distributor** sends electricity to the spark plugs.
3. The **generator** creates a steady flow of electricity.
4. In the **carburetor**, gasoline is mixed with air.
5. Then the **throttle** sends fuel vapors onward.
6. Road salt and sand may cause the **chassis** to rust.
7. Check your speed on the **speedometer**.
8. Check the **odometer** to see how far you've driven.
9. Antifreeze will prevent your **radiator** from freezing.
10. Inside each cylinder is a moving **piston**.

Final Test
1. Did you notice a **gradual** decrease in temperature?
2. Are puffins **ideally** suited to cold environments?
3. **Heroically**, the man entered the burning store.
4. The principal made a **dramatic** announcement.
5. Solve math problems in a **systematic** way.
6. **Incidentally**, my sister met your cousin last night.
7. Shakespeare wrote a **tragic** play about Caesar.
8. An atlas is a **substantial** source of information.
9. Jamal was **emphatic** in his refusal to wear a hat.
10. We had a terrific harvest from our **prolific** garden.
11. Late for a test, I **frantically** ran to my class.
12. The company's **annual** report outlined its profits.
13. Several **microscopic** organisms exist in water.
14. Tina and I have a **mutual** friend named Linda.
15. The nation's **economic** state improved last year.
16. Our school is **academically** superior to theirs.
17. Is the Kentucky Derby a **classic** sporting event?
18. Critics gave the movie a **basically** positive review.
19. The actors behaved **comically** in that movie.
20. The oil embargo caused prices to rise **drastically**.

Latin Roots

Objective
To spell words with Latin roots

Pretest

1. Did **animosity** between the countries lead to war?
2. The **emission** of sparks from the wire caused a fire.
3. An **inanimate** object has no life.
4. His father worked long, hard days at **manual** labor.
5. His **submission** for the contest won first prize.
6. Tina received a **commission** on the stereo she sold.
7. Water is a clear **fluid**.
8. Use your **influence** to change Carly's mind.
9. The pilot will **manipulate** the helicopter controls.
10. The radio **transmission** was not clear.
11. **Animation** brings cartoon characters to life.
12. The water supply in our town contains **fluoride**.
13. **Influenza** is a horrible illness!
14. I got lost because of the **omission** of street signs.
15. The decision of the judges was **unanimous**.
16. Will the new laws **emancipate** the citizens?
17. The interest payments on the loan will **fluctuate**.
18. Refreshments were served during **intermission**.
19. The queen issued a harsh **mandate**.
20. Is Chan **fluent** in Chinese, Japanese, and English?

Spelling Strategy   Page 61

Discuss the spelling rule, then work with students to find the Latin roots of these words in a dictionary: *magnanimous*, *admission*, *affluent*, and *manufacture*. Discuss how the meaning of each word is related to the meaning of the Latin root. Then, help students identify the Latin root in each **list word** and define the word.

Vocabulary Development Encourage students to refer to the spelling rule to recall the meaning of each root and to determine which **list words** contain that root.

Dictionary Skills Remind students that knowing how to pronounce a word may help them remember how to spell the word.

Spelling Practice   Pages 62–63

Word Analysis Point out that some words may be used as more than one part of speech. As an example, have students look up *manual* in the dictionary and tell its different parts of speech. To extend the activity, have students use the words in sentences.

Synonyms and Antonyms Review what synonyms and antonyms are and have students give several examples of each.

Word Application Have students use a **list word** to replace the underlined word in *Peace talks were scheduled to relieve the hatred between the two countries.* (animosity)

46

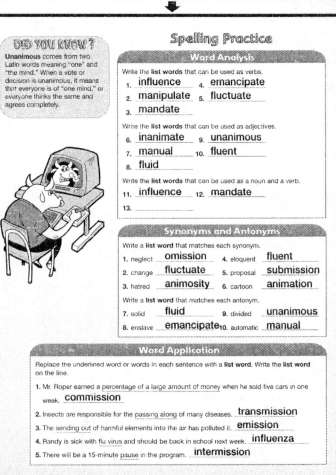

Latin Roots

TIP

Recognizing Latin roots in words can help you determine the meaning of unfamiliar words and remember how to spell them.

Latin Root	Meaning	English Word with Prefix	New Meaning
miss	"to send"	emission	"the act of sending out"
anim	"breath" or "soul"	inanimate	"not alive"
flu	"flow"	fluid	"able to flow"
man	"hand"	manipulate	"to operate by hand"

Vocabulary Development

Write the **list words** that have a Latin root that means "to send."

1. emission
2. submission
3. commission
4. transmission
5. omission
6. intermission

Write the **list words** that have a Latin root that means "breath" or "soul."

7. animosity
8. inanimate
9. animation
10. unanimous

Write the **list words** that have a Latin root that means "to flow."

11. fluid
12. influence
13. fluoride
14. influenza
15. fluctuate
16. fluent

Write the **list words** that have a Latin root that means "hand."

17. manual
18. manipulate
19. emancipate
20. mandate

Dictionary Skills

Write the **list word** that matches each sound-spelling.

1. {man′yoo wəl} manual
2. {mə nip′yə lāt} manipulate
3. {man′dāt} mandate
4. {in an′ə mit} inanimate
5. {floor′id} fluoride
6. {ō mish′ən} omission
7. {floo′id} fluid
8. {i mish′ən} emission

LIST WORDS
1. animosity
2. emission
3. inanimate
4. manual
5. submission
6. commission
7. fluid
8. influence
9. manipulate
10. transmission
11. animation
12. fluoride
13. influenza
14. omission
15. unanimous
16. emancipate
17. fluctuate
18. intermission
19. mandate
20. fluent

61

DID YOU KNOW?
Unanimous comes from two Latin words meaning "one" and "the mind." When a vote or decision is unanimous, it means that everyone is of "one mind," or everyone thinks the same and agrees completely.

Spelling Practice

Word Analysis

Write the **list words** that can be used as verbs.

1. influence
2. manipulate
3. mandate
4. emancipate
5. fluctuate

Write the **list words** that can be used as adjectives.

6. inanimate
7. manual
8. fluid
9. unanimous
10. fluent

Write the **list words** that can be used as a noun and a verb.

11. influence
12. mandate
13.

Synonyms and Antonyms

Write a **list word** that matches each synonym.

1. neglect — omission
2. change — fluctuate
3. hatred — animosity
4. eloquent — fluent
5. proposal — submission
6. cartoon — animation

Write a **list word** that matches each antonym.

7. solid — fluid
8. enslave — emancipate
9. divided — unanimous
10. automatic — manual

Word Application

Replace the underlined word or words in each sentence with a **list word**. Write the **list word** on the line.

1. Mr. Roper earned a percentage of a large amount of money when he sold five cars in one week. commission
2. Insects are responsible for the passing along of many diseases. transmission
3. The sending out of harmful elements into the air has polluted it. emission
4. Randy is sick with flu virus and should be back in school next week. influenza
5. There will be a 15-minute pause in the program. intermission

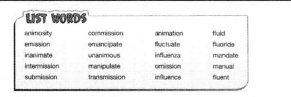

LIST WORDS

animosity	commission	animation	fluid
emission	emancipate	fluctuate	fluoride
inanimate	unanimous	influenza	mandate
intermission	manipulate	omission	manual
submission	transmission	influence	fluent

Puzzle
Use the **list words** to complete the crossword puzzle.

ACROSS
5. feeling of strong dislike or hatred
8. a chemical element
10. to work or operate with the hands
12. the act of sending out or giving forth
14. a cold-like illness
16. made or done with the hands
17. something that is left out
18. the art of making motion picture cartoons
19. showing complete agreement
20. rest or pause

DOWN
1. money paid to someone who makes a sale
2. the power to affect persons or things
3. rise and fall; keep changing
4. to set free
6. that which is submitted
7. the act of passing something along
9. any substance that flows
11. an order or command
13. without life
15. able to write and speak easily and clearly

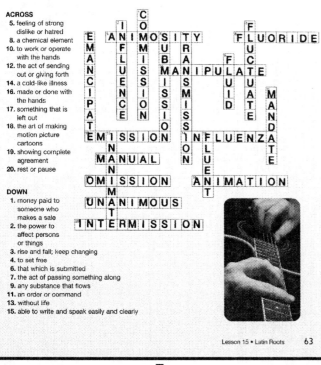

Lesson 15 • Latin Roots   63

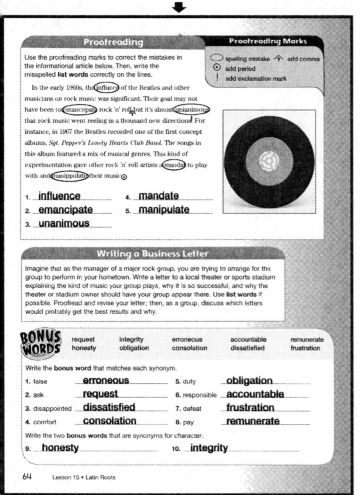

Proofreading
Use the proofreading marks to correct the mistakes in the informational article below. Then, write the misspelled **list words** correctly on the lines.

Proofreading Marks
- ◯ spelling mistake
- ⊙ add period
- ❗ add exclamation mark
- ⌃ add comma

In the early 1960s, the influence of the Beatles and other musicians on rock music was significant. Their goal may not have been to emancepate rock 'n' roll but it's almost unianimous that rock music went reeling in a thousand new directions. For instance, in 1967 the Beatles recorded one of the first concept albums, *Sgt. Pepper's Lonely Hearts Club Band*. The songs in this album featured a mix of musical genres. This kind of experimentation gave other rock 'n' roll artists a mandat to play with and manipulate their music.

1. influence   4. mandate
2. emancipate   5. manipulate
3. unanimous

Writing a Business Letter
Imagine that as the manager of a major rock group, you are trying to arrange for the group to perform in your hometown. Write a letter to a local theater or sports stadium explaining the kind of music your group plays, why it is so successful, and why the theater or stadium owner should have your group appear there. Use **list words** if possible. Proofread and revise your letter; then, as a group, discuss which letters would probably get the best results and why.

BONUS WORDS

request	integrity	erroneous	accountable	remunerate
honesty	obligation	consolation	dissatisfied	frustration

Write the **bonus word** that matches each synonym.

1. false — erroneous
2. ask — request
3. disappointed — dissatisfied
4. comfort — consolation
5. duty — obligation
6. responsible — accountable
7. defeat — frustration
8. pay — remunerate

Write the two **bonus words** that are synonyms for *character.*

9. honesty   10. integrity

64   Lesson 15 • Latin Roots

Puzzle Encourage students to think carefully about the meaning of each **list word** as they complete the crossword puzzle.

Spelling and Writing   Page 64
Proofreading Write this sentence on the board to review the proofreading marks used in this lesson: *He yelled "Help" when he saw the acident*

Writing a Business Letter Review with students how a business letter always includes a return address, an inside address, a salutation ending with a colon, and a closing with a signature block. Emphasize that students should use polite language, and be direct and clear in their writing.

Bonus Words   Page 64
Consumer Terms Have students look up the meanings of the **bonus words** in dictionaries. Discuss how the words apply to businesses and customers, then ask volunteers to use the words in oral sentences.

Bonus Words Test
1. The school must **remunerate** all its guest speakers.
2. As a **consolation**, the store refunded my money.
3. His **honesty** led him to return the extra change.
4. The store has an **obligation** to its valued customers.
5. In **frustration**, Jason demanded his money back.
6. Linda made a **request** to see the hat in the window.
7. The store is **accountable** for inferior merchandise.
8. The store owner was respected for his **integrity**.
9. A **dissatisfied** customer returned the shirt.
10. Al was overcharged due to an **erroneous** sales tag.

Final Test
1. The realtor earns a **commission** on every sale.
2. Research shows **fluoride** helps prevent cavities.
3. What terrible **animosity** between the two teams!
4. Everyone's story **submission** must be typewritten.
5. Is Patricia a **fluent** speaker on political issues?
6. The farmer hired **manual** laborers to pick apples.
7. Is that statue an **inanimate** object?
8. They detected the **emission** of radiation.
9. The committee's **mandate** angered many people.
10. Lincoln worked to **emancipate** the slaves.
11. An **omission** from the contract made it invalid.
12. Some new movies mix **animation** and real life.
13. The teacher has a great **influence** on his pupils.
14. Are fever and chills symptoms of **influenza**?
15. Computers quicken the **transmission** of ideas.
16. A greenish **fluid** leaked from the car's radiator.
17. The dancers changed costumes at **intermission**.
18. My report card shows how my grades **fluctuate**.
19. Ramón can **manipulate** complicated machines.
20. Julie was elected by a **unanimous** class vote.

Lesson 16

Suffixes able, ible

Objective
To spell words with the suffixes *able* or *ible*

Pretest
1. At home I am **responsible** for feeding the pets.
2. Our class donated money to a **charitable** group.
3. Today, diseases such as cancer are often **curable**.
4. What a nice, **livable** back yard this building has!
5. Sara carries a **portable** radio in her backpack.
6. The Delgados are **amiable** people to travel with.
7. Is my VCR **compatible** with your television?
8. The house needed work to make it **habitable**.
9. Many **notable** people were born in Texas.
10. A **disposable** flashlight is handy when you travel.
11. You can be successful if you set **attainable** goals.
12. Are colds very **communicable**?
13. Because of static, the words aren't **intelligible**.
14. Swimming is **permissible** in the roped-off area.
15. Many lines from that speech are **quotable**.
16. Is Paul **available** for work on Friday?
17. Pack the **consumable** items in a separate bag.
18. Is your name and address clearly **legible**?
19. The storm left the village in a **pitiable** state.
20. Anna is a **reliable** worker and seldom late.

Spelling Strategy   *Page 65*
After reading the spelling rule, have students tell which **list words** contain *s* or soft *g* followed by *ible*. Discuss ways students can remember each word's spelling. Then, encourage students to use dictionaries to find the words' meanings and to use them in oral sentences.

Vocabulary Development Students should be familiar with this type of exercise. Have them consult dictionaries if they encounter any difficulties.

Dictionary Skills Review the letters and symbols used in sound-spellings. When students have finished the exercise, encourage them to use a dictionary to check their answers.

Spelling Practice   *Pages 66–67*
Word Analysis Write this sentence on the board: *I live here.* Ask which word is a verb. (*live*) Point out that the **list word** *livable* is the adjectival form of the word. Then, have students read the directions. You may wish to work through the first item or two with students.

Analogies Remind students that analogies are used to show a relationship between words. Ask a volunteer to offer an example of an analogy.

Word Application To extend the activity, have students write similar sentences using the remaining **list words**, and then exchange them with classmates.

48

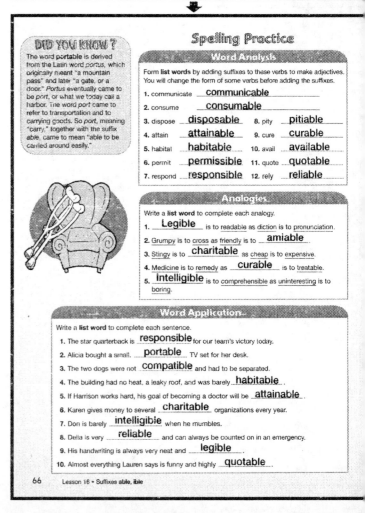

Suffixes able, ible
Lesson 16

TIP
The suffixes **able** and **ible** make adjectives from base words or roots. For instance, pity becomes pitiable. The more common suffix is **able**. The suffix **ible** is often used after s or soft g, as in responsible and legible. There are some words, such as compatible, which have to be remembered as exceptions.

Vocabulary Development
Write the **list word** that matches each definition.

1. able to be remedied or cured	curable
2. able to be carried around	portable
3. able to be thrown away	disposable
4. able to get along well together	compatible
5. worth noticing	notable
6. deserving scorn or contempt	pitiable
7. that which can be eaten or used up	consumable
8. that which can be understood easily	intelligible
9. able to be achieved by hard work	attainable
10. worth quoting	quotable

Dictionary Skills
Write the **list word** that matches each sound-spelling.

1. (liv′ə b'l)	livable
2. (ə vā′lə b'l)	available
3. (lej′ə b'l)	legible
4. (pər mis′ə b'l)	permissible
5. (ri li′ə b'l)	reliable
6. (kə myoo′ni kə b'l)	communicable
7. (char′ə tə b'l)	charitable
8. (ā′mē ə b'l)	amiable
9. (ri spän′sə b'l)	responsible
10. (hab′it ə b'l)	habitable

LIST WORDS
1. responsible
2. charitable
3. curable
4. livable
5. portable
6. amiable
7. compatible
8. habitable
9. notable
10. disposable
11. attainable
12. communicable
13. intelligible
14. permissible
15. quotable
16. available
17. consumable
18. legible
19. pitiable
20. reliable

65

DID YOU KNOW?
The word **portable** is derived from the Latin word *portus*, which originally meant "a mountain pass" and later "a gate, or a door." *Portus* eventually came to be *port*, or what we today call a harbor. The word *port* came to refer to transportation and to carrying goods. So *port*, meaning "carry," together with the suffix *able*, came to mean "able to be carried around easily."

Spelling Practice
Word Analysis
Form **list words** by adding suffixes to these verbs to make adjectives. You will change the form of some verbs before adding the suffixes.

1. communicate	communicable			
2. consume	consumable			
3. dispose	disposable	8. pity	pitiable
4. attain	attainable	9. cure	curable
5. habitat	habitable	10. avail	available
6. permit	permissible	11. quote	quotable
7. respond	responsible	12. rely	reliable

Analogies
Write a **list word** to complete each analogy.
1. **Legible** is to readable as diction is to pronunciation.
2. Grumpy is to cross as friendly is to **amiable**.
3. Stingy is to **charitable** as cheap is to expensive.
4. Medicine is to remedy as **curable** is to treatable.
5. **intelligible** is to comprehensible as uninteresting is to boring.

Word Application
Write a **list word** to complete each sentence.
1. The star quarterback is **responsible** for our team's victory today.
2. Alicia bought a small **portable** TV set for her desk.
3. The two dogs were not **compatible** and had to be separated.
4. The building had no heat, a leaky roof, and was barely **habitable**.
5. If Harrison works hard, his goal of becoming a doctor will be **attainable**.
6. Karen gives money to several **charitable** organizations every year.
7. Don is barely **intelligible** when he mumbles.
8. Della is very **reliable** and can always be counted on in an emergency.
9. His handwriting is always very neat and **legible**.
10. Almost everything Lauren says is funny and highly **quotable**.

66   Lesson 16 • Suffixes able, ible

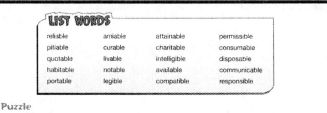

LIST WORDS

reliable	amiable	attainable	permissible
pitiable	curable	charitable	consumable
quotable	livable	intelligible	disposable
habitable	notable	available	communicable
portable	legible	compatible	responsible

Puzzle

Use the **list words** to complete the crossword puzzle.

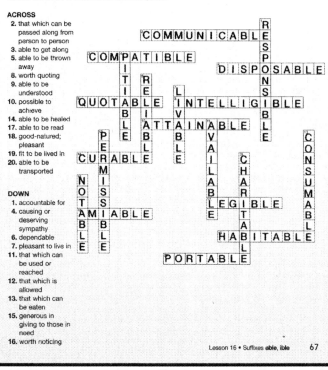

ACROSS

2. that which can be passed along from person to person
3. able to get along
5. able to be thrown away
8. worth quoting
9. able to be understood
10. possible to achieve
14. able to be healed
17. able to be read
18. good-natured; pleasant
19. fit to be lived in
20. able to be transported

DOWN

1. accountable for
4. causing or deserving sympathy
6. dependable
7. pleasant to live in
11. that which can be used or reached
12. that which is allowed
13. that which can be eaten
15. generous in giving to those in need
16. worth noticing

Lesson 16 • Suffixes **able**, **ible**   67

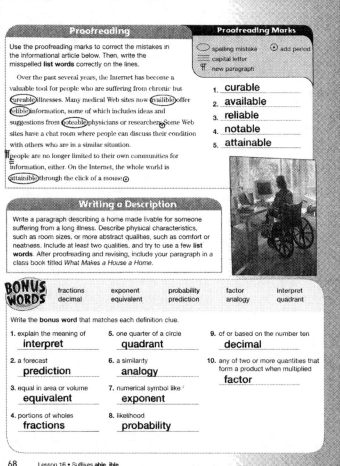

Proofreading

Use the proofreading marks to correct the mistakes in the informational article below. Then, write the misspelled **list words** correctly on the lines.

Over the past several years, the Internet has become a valuable tool for people who are suffering from chronic but cureable illnesses. Many medical Web sites now availible offer elible information, some of which includes ideas and suggestions from noteable physicians or researchers Some Web sites have a chat room where people can discuss their condition with others who are in a similar situation.

people are no longer limited to their own communities for information, either. On the Internet, the whole world is attainible through the click of a mouse

Proofreading Marks

○ spelling mistake   ⊙ add period
≡ capital letter
¶ new paragraph

1. curable
2. available
3. reliable
4. notable
5. attainable

Writing a Description

Write a paragraph describing a home made livable for someone suffering from a long illness. Describe physical characteristics, such as room sizes, or more abstract qualities, such as comfort or neatness. Include at least two qualities, and try to use a few **list words**. After proofreading and revising, include your paragraph in a class book titled *What Makes a House a Home*.

BONUS WORDS

fractions	exponent	probability	factor	interpret
decimal	equivalent	prediction	analogy	quadrant

Write the **bonus word** that matches each definition clue.

1. explain the meaning of
   interpret
2. a forecast
   prediction
3. equal in area or volume
   equivalent
4. portions of wholes
   fractions
5. one quarter of a circle
   quadrant
6. a similarity
   analogy
7. numerical symbol like ²
   exponent
8. likelihood
   probability
9. of or based on the number ten
   decimal
10. any of two or more quantities that form a product when multiplied
   factor

Puzzle Have students briefly review strategies for solving crossword puzzles. Remind them to use neatly printed uppercase letters.

Spelling and Writing   Page 68

Proofreading Review the proofreading marks used in the lesson, in particular, the mark that shows that a new paragraph should be indented.

Writing a Description Discuss the difference between *habitable*, or *fit to be lived in*, and *livable*, which implies *comfort*. Ask students what qualities contribute to livability. Have them brainstorm special changes or additions they might make to a home to help someone suffering from a long illness.

Bonus Words   Page 68

Math Explain that all the **bonus words** are related to mathematics. Through discussion and dictionary use, help students understand each word's meaning. Math books may provide examples of some terms.

Bonus Words Test

1. An **analogy** is a kind of comparison.
2. While not identical, the areas are **equivalent**.
3. Jan is very quick at multiplying **fractions**.
4. The number two is a **factor** in all even numbers.
5. One quarter of a circle is called a **quadrant**.
6. The **decimal** point separates dollars from cents.
7. If the **exponent** is two, the number is squared.
8. A **prediction** may or may not prove to be true.
9. A bar graph is easier to **interpret** than many lists.
10. The laws of **probability** explain what is likely.

Final Test

1. That candidate gave a highly **quotable** speech.
2. Is borrowing reference books **permissible**?
3. I heard sounds, but no **intelligible** speech.
4. **Communicable** diseases are easily spread.
5. Your goals seem realistic and **attainable**.
6. We have a fire extinguisher **available** at all times.
7. I shop frequently for **consumable** groceries.
8. That handwriting is barely **legible**!
9. The animal shelter had taken in a **pitiable** puppy.
10. The train is a **reliable** means of transportation.
11. Darla is certainly an **amiable** companion on a trip.
12. That color is not **compatible** with the red rug.
13. The hut wasn't fancy, but it was **habitable**.
14. Nothing **notable** happened all weekend.
15. Bring **disposable** utensils to the picnic.
16. Two people are **responsible** for today's victory.
17. Does Gregario donate time to **charitable** groups?
18. Luckily, you have an easily **curable** condition.
19. Your apartment has a nice **livable** feeling to it.
20. Did you bring along your **portable** radio?

Challenging Words

Objective
To spell difficult words with unusual spelling patterns

Pretest

1. Icebergs are common in **arctic** climates.
2. The actor will **endeavor** to learn his lines.
3. Your cat may feel **jealousy** if you get a new kitten.
4. When the **meteorite** landed, it created a crater.
5. The police **sergeant** spoke about highway safety.
6. The newspaper prints a **calendar** of local events.
7. Is vitamin C an **essential** daily nutrient?
8. Barb is the best player in the soccer **league**.
9. I'd hate to be an elephant with a **nasal** infection!
10. Angry is a **synonym** for furious.
11. He watched the wobbly tower of blocks **collapse**.
12. Tell the postal worker that this package is **fragile**.
13. Let's **maneuver** our way to the front of the crowd.
14. Instead of taking sides, I think I'll remain **neutral**.
15. May I help you carry your **valise** onto the train?
16. The **debtor** was given one year to repay the loan.
17. The temperature **gauge** reads 82 degrees.
18. Tomorrow's **matinee** will begin at two o'clock.
19. Halley's Comet is a rarely seen **phenomenon**.
20. Please put **mayonnaise** on my sandwich.

Spelling Strategy   *Page 69*

Discuss the spelling rule. Point out that students should memorize the spellings of challenging words to prevent mistakes. Have them analyze the **list words**, identifying the "trick" in each one, and then define the words. Encourage them to use the words in oral sentences.

Vocabulary Development Review with students that the clues in this exercise are either definitions or synonyms.

Dictionary Skills If needed, you may wish to use a dictionary to review guide words, pointing out examples and explaining their function.

Spelling Practice   *Pages 70–71*

Word Analysis Point out that this exercise will help students analyze the "tricks" in some of the **list words**. Urge them to check the **list words** on page 71 to find the various letter components.

Synonyms If needed, review synonyms by writing on the board: *To learn ballet, many people find that dance shoes are necessary.* Have students replace the underlined word with a **list word**. (*essential*)

Word Application Urge students to use context clues to find the missing **list words**. To extend, have students create similar sentences for other **list words** to give as challenges to classmates to solve.

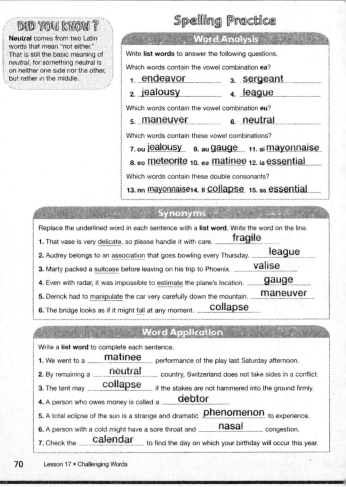

Challenging Words

TIP
Some words are hard to spell because they have silent letters or unusual vowel spellings or double consonants. Other challenging words contain the schwa sound /ə/ in unstressed syllables. Although it sounds like short e, the schwa sound may be spelled with any of the five vowels.

Word	"Trick"	Word	"Trick"
debtor	silent b	jealousy	ea = /ĕ/; ou = /ə/
matinee	ee = /ā/	mayonnaise	o = /ə/; double n
calendar	ar = /ər/	synonym	y = /ĭ/; o = /ə/

Vocabulary Development
Write the list word that matches each synonym or definition.

1. borrower — debtor
2. envy — jealousy
3. necessary — essential
4. breakable — fragile
5. suitcase — valise
6. attempt — endeavor
7. breakdown — collapse
8. measure — gauge
9. afternoon event — matinee
10. not taking sides — neutral
11. rare occurrence — phenomenon
12. a spread — mayonnaise
13. group of teams — league
14. schedule — calendar
15. of the nose — nasal
16. move; plot — maneuver

Dictionary Skills
Write the list word that comes between each pair of dictionary guide words.

1. senior/settle — sergeant
2. matrimony/maze — mayonnaise
3. game/get — gauge
4. empathy/escrow — endeavor
5. main/market — maneuver
6. endive/estate — essential
7. swim/system — synonym
8. merge/metric — meteorite
9. arbor/argue — arctic

JANUARY

LIST WORDS
1. arctic
2. endeavor
3. jealousy
4. meteorite
5. sergeant
6. calendar
7. essential
8. league
9. nasal
10. synonym
11. collapse
12. fragile
13. maneuver
14. neutral
15. valise
16. debtor
17. gauge
18. matinee
19. phenomenon
20. mayonnaise

69

DID YOU KNOW?
Neutral comes from two Latin words that mean "not either." That is still the basic meaning of *neutral*, for something neutral is on neither one side nor the other, but rather in the middle.

Spelling Practice
Word Analysis
Write list words to answer the following questions.

Which words contain the vowel combination ea?
1. endeavor   3. sergeant
2. jealousy   4. league

Which words contain the vowel combination eu?
5. maneuver   6. neutral

Which words contain these vowel combinations?
7. ou jealousy   9. au gauge   11. ai mayonnaise
8. eo meteorite 10. ee matinee 12. ia essential

Which words contain these double consonants?
13. nn mayonnaise 14. ll collapse 15. ss essential

Synonyms
Replace the underlined word in each sentence with a list word. Write the word on the line.

1. That vase is very delicate, so please handle it with care. — fragile
2. Audrey belongs to an association that goes bowling every Thursday. — league
3. Marty packed a suitcase before leaving on his trip to Phoenix. — valise
4. Even with radar, it was impossible to estimate the plane's location. — gauge
5. Derrick had to manipulate the car very carefully down the mountain. — maneuver
6. The bridge looks as if it might fall at any moment. — collapse

Word Application
Write a list word to complete each sentence.

1. We went to a ___ matinee ___ performance of the play last Saturday afternoon.
2. By remaining a ___ neutral ___ country, Switzerland does not take sides in a conflict.
3. The tent may ___ collapse ___ if the stakes are not hammered into the ground firmly.
4. A person who owes money is called a ___ debtor ___.
5. A total eclipse of the sun is a strange and dramatic ___ phenomenon ___ to experience.
6. A person with a cold might have a sore throat and ___ nasal ___ congestion.
7. Check the ___ calendar ___ to find the day on which your birthday will occur this year.

70   Lesson 17 • Challenging Words

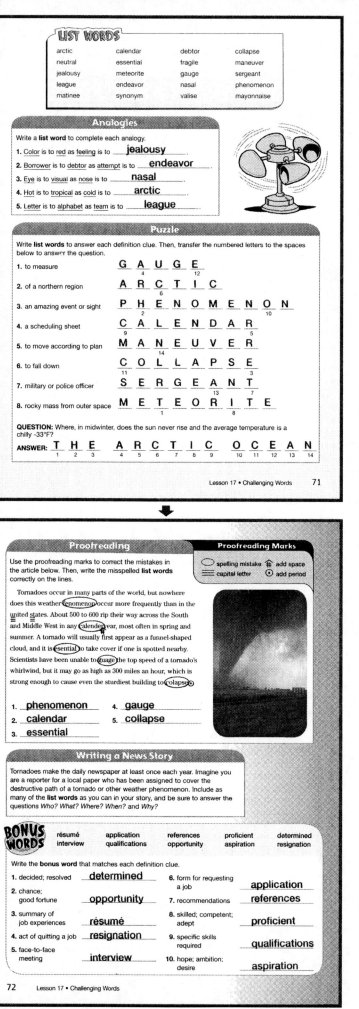

LIST WORDS

arctic	calendar	debtor	collapse
neutral	essential	fragile	maneuver
jealousy	meteorite	gauge	sergeant
league	endeavor	nasal	phenomenon
matinee	synonym	valise	mayonnaise

Analogies

Write a **list word** to complete each analogy.

1. Color is to red as feeling is to **jealousy**
2. Borrower is to debtor as attempt is to **endeavor**
3. Eye is to visual as nose is to **nasal**
4. Hot is to tropical as cold is to **arctic**
5. Letter is to alphabet as team is to **league**

Puzzle

Write **list words** to answer each definition clue. Then, transfer the numbered letters to the spaces below to answer the question.

1. to measure   G A U G E
2. of a northern region   A R C T I C
3. an amazing event or sight   P H E N O M E N O N
4. a scheduling sheet   C A L E N D A R
5. to move according to plan   M A N E U V E R
6. to fall down   C O L L A P S E
7. military or police officer   S E R G E A N T
8. rocky mass from outer space   M E T E O R I T E

QUESTION: Where, in midwinter, does the sun never rise and the average temperature is a chilly -33°F?

ANSWER: T H E   A R C T I C   O C E A N

Lesson 17 • Challenging Words   71

Proofreading

Use the proofreading marks to correct the mistakes in the article below. Then, write the misspelled **list words** correctly on the lines.

Proofreading Marks
- ◯ spelling mistake
- ≡ capital letter
- ⊕ add period
- ⫟ add space

Tornadoes occur in many parts of the world, but nowhere does this weather phenomenon occur more frequently than in the united states. About 500 to 600 rip their way across the South and Middle West in any calender year, most often in spring and summer. A tornado will usually first appear as a funnel-shaped cloud, and it is essential to take cover if one is spotted nearby. Scientists have been unable to gauge the top speed of a tornado's whirlwind, but it may go as high as 300 miles an hour, which is strong enough to cause even the sturdiest building to collapse.

1. phenomenon
2. calendar
3. essential
4. gauge
5. collapse

Writing a News Story

Tornadoes make the daily newspaper at least once each year. Imagine you are a reporter for a local paper who has been assigned to cover the destructive path of a tornado or other weather phenomenon. Include as many of the **list words** as you can in your story, and be sure to answer the questions Who? What? Where? When? and Why?

BONUS WORDS

résumé	application	references	proficient	determined
interview	qualifications	opportunity	aspiration	resignation

Write the **bonus word** that matches each definition clue.

1. decided; resolved **determined**
2. chance; good fortune **opportunity**
3. summary of job experiences **résumé**
4. act of quitting a job **resignation**
5. face-to-face meeting **interview**
6. form for requesting a job **application**
7. recommendations **references**
8. skilled; competent; adept **proficient**
9. specific skills required **qualifications**
10. hope; ambition; desire **aspiration**

Analogies To start, have students complete this analogy: *Lender is to debtor as antonym is to* _____ . (*synonym*)

Puzzle Remind students to write their answers carefully, one letter to each space.

Spelling and Writing   *Page 72*

Proofreading Use the sentence *My freinds are comingon tuesday* to demonstrate the proofreading marks.

Writing a News Story Discuss how a good lead or beginning paragraph in a news story should grab the reader's attention. Explain the inverted pyramid form of news writing, which prioritizes information by putting the most important details first. Encourage students to interview classmates who can pretend to be eyewitnesses to the weather phenomenon, and to incorporate classmates' quotes into their stories.

Bonus Words   *Page 72*

Job Applications Relate the **bonus words** to students' knowledge and experience. Discuss the features of a job application form and, if possible, display an example.

Bonus Words Test

1. My career **aspiration** is to be a doctor.
2. We accept your letter of **resignation** with sorrow.
3. Carlos is extremely **proficient** in math.
4. List all your job experiences on your **résumé**.
5. You've got the **qualifications** to be an able cook.
6. Peg listed two of her teachers as **references**.
7. Relax and stay calm during your job **interview**.
8. I am **determined** to become a chemical engineer.
9. Hal's job gives him an **opportunity** to travel.
10. The sales manager read Jane's **application** form.

Final Test

1. Each month, the **debtor** pays back part of the loan.
2. The **calendar** featured beautiful photographs.
3. Push this button to **collapse** the umbrella.
4. **Arctic** temperatures are rarely above freezing.
5. Joy will **maneuver** the boat through the channel.
6. Our basketball **league** competes in tournaments.
7. **Jealousy** can be a harmful emotion.
8. A **meteorite** usually looks like metallic rock.
9. The peace talks were held at a **neutral** site.
10. A falling star is a **phenomenon** many enjoy seeing.
11. Sinusitis can cause a **nasal** infection.
12. Is there a **matinee** on Wednesday at two o'clock?
13. The **sergeant** carried the flag during the parade.
14. Is *enormous* a **synonym** for *large*?
15. You can check your **valise** at the ticket counter.
16. Mario stirred **mayonnaise** into the chicken salad.
17. The pilot used radar to help **gauge** her position.
18. For a writer, a good dictionary is an **essential** tool.
19. How did the police **endeavor** to solve the crime?
20. Careful! Those dishes are **fragile**.

Lesson 18

Objective
To review spelling words with suffixes, Latin roots, and challenging words

Spelling Strategy
Page 73

This lesson will help students review the spelling patterns of words learned in Lessons 13–17. Read and discuss the spelling rules with students, having them identify root words and suffixes, where appropriate. Then, have students give other examples of challenging words, telling what makes each hard to spell.

Spelling Practice
Pages 73–75

Lesson 13 Use the words *luscious, glorious, special,* and *impartial* as examples of words in which *ial* and *ious* are suffixes or endings. Then, have students identify the **list words** that have suffixes. Point out the additional write-on lines and encourage students to add two words from Lesson 13 that they found especially difficult, or select and assign certain words that seemed difficult for everyone. (Repeat this procedure for each lesson in the Review.)

Lesson 14 Use these words to review the suffixes *al, ally, ic, ically,* and *ly: mutual, mutually, emphatic, emphatically,* and *simply.* Then, have students identify the suffix in each **list word**. Point out that in this exercise, students must provide the **list word** that fits each pair of words or phrases given.

Lesson 15 Write *manuscript, animated, fluency,* and *missile* on the board. Have students tell the meaning of each word. Then, use the words to review the Latin roots *miss, anim, flu,* and *man.* Have students identify which root helps form each **list word**.

Lesson 16 Review the suffixes *able* and *ible,* using these examples: *washable, admissible, edible,* and *eligible.* Discuss each word's meaning and ask which ending is more common. *(able)* Then, ask which two letters often come before the ending *ible. (s or soft g)* Have students note which letter precedes each ending in the **list words**.

Lesson 17 Write the words *endeavor, jealousy, nasal, collapse,* and *debtor* on the board. Use them to discuss how some words can be hard to spell. Have students suggest other words that are not spelled the way they sound, and then talk about different ways to remember the spelling of such words.

Show What You Know
Page 76

Point out to students that this review will help them know if they have mastered the words in Lessons 13–17. Have a volunteer restate the directions and tell which word in the first item should be marked. *(availible)* When finished, have students write their misspelled words correctly.

TIPS

- Some endings are suffixes, such as the **ial** and **ious** at the end of burial and gracious. Other words have endings that look like suffixes, but aren't, such as material and ferocious.
- Many suffixes change words to form other parts of speech. Notice the suffixes on the following words and how each changes the base word:

  substantial — substantially
  classic — classical, classically

- The suffixes **able** and **ible** both turn base words into adjectives. They sound alike, but **able** is the more common ending, as in notable. When the suffix is **ible**, it often follows s or soft g, as in intelligible and permissible.

- Knowing Latin roots can help you spell and understand many words. Read each word below and notice the meaning of its Latin root, which has been underlined.

Word with Latin Root	Meaning of Root
annual	"year"
emission	"to send"
animation	"breath" or "soul"
fluidity	"flow"
manage	"hand"

- A few words are tricky to spell because they have some unusual features, such as a silent letter, an odd vowel spelling, a double consonant, or the schwa sound spelled with a, i, o, or u. Notice what makes each word below hard to spell. Study carefully the spelling of such words.

  mayonnaise   arctic   matinee   debtor

Lesson 13

List Words
conscientious
confidential
harmonious
influential
unconscious
spacious
infectious
initial
financial
provincial

Replace the underlined word in each sentence with a **list word**. Write the **list word** on the line.

1. Carla consulted a money expert to help her make investment decisions. **financial**
2. What a pleasing sound those voices make! **harmonious**
3. This house has very roomy closets. **spacious**
4. Duane is a reliable student. **conscientious**
5. My cold is no longer catching. **infectious**
6. The family was unaware of the noise. **unconscious**
7. Please capitalize the first letter. **initial**
8. The doctor assured me that the information would be kept private. **confidential**
9. The most powerful advisors had the candidate's full attention. **influential**
10. Most of the countrified regions had narrow roads. **provincial**

73

Lesson 14

List Words
academically
drastically
economic
incidentally
systematic
mutual
annual
gradual
ideally
comically

Write the **list word** that goes with each pair of words.

1. scholarly, scholastically, **academically**
2. accidentally, by chance, **incidentally**
3. humorously, ridiculously, **comically**
4. financial, commercial, **economic**
5. methodical, orderly, **systematic**
6. radically, extremely, **drastically**
7. excellently, perfectly, **ideally**
8. slow, step-by-step, **gradual**
9. common, shared, **mutual**
10. weekly, monthly, **annual**

Lesson 15

List Words
commission
fluctuate
influence
intermission
omission
fluent
manual
manipulate
fluoride
inanimate

Write **list words** to answer the questions. Some words will be used more than once.

Which words contain the vowel combination **ue**?
1. **influence**   2. **fluent**

Which words contain the vowel combination **ua**?
3. **fluctuate**   4. **manual**

Which words contain the vowel combination **io or uo**?
5. **commission**   7. **omission**
6. **intermission**   8. **fluoride**

Which word completes each series?
9. power, authority, **influence**
10. handle, move, **manipulate**
11. still, unmoving, **inanimate**
12. teeth, dentist, **fluoride**
13. holiday, break, **intermission**
14. change, waver, **fluctuate**

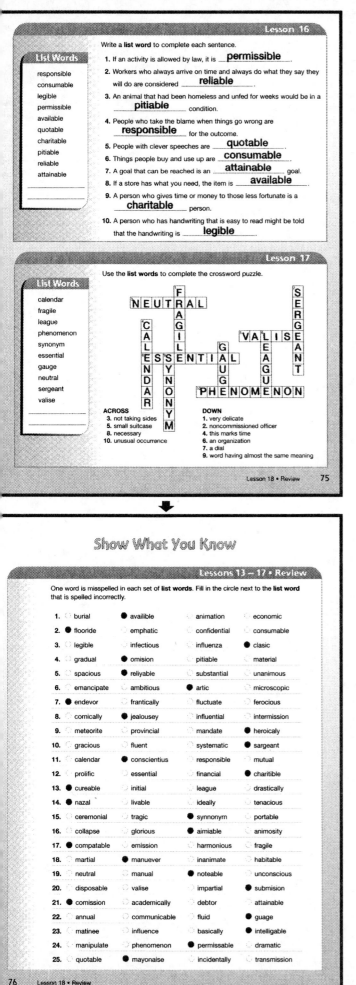

Lesson 16

List Words

responsible
consumable
legible
permissible
available
quotable
charitable
pitiable
reliable
attainable

Write a **list word** to complete each sentence.

1. If an activity is allowed by law, it is **permissible**
2. Workers who always arrive on time and always do what they say they will do are considered **reliable**
3. An animal that had been homeless and unfed for weeks would be in a **pitiable** condition.
4. People who take the blame when things go wrong are **responsible** for the outcome.
5. People with clever speeches are **quotable**
6. Things people buy and use up are **consumable**
7. A goal that can be reached is an **attainable** goal.
8. If a store has what you need, the item is **available**
9. A person who gives time or money to those less fortunate is a **charitable** person.
10. A person who has handwriting that is easy to read might be told that the handwriting is **legible**

Lesson 17

List Words

calendar
fragile
league
phenomenon
synonym
essential
gauge
neutral
sergeant
valise

Use the **list words** to complete the crossword puzzle.

```
      F
N E U T R A L              S
  C   A             V A L I S E
  A   G             E       R
'E S S E N T I A L  A       G
  N   L    G        G       E
  D   E    U        U       A
  A   S    G   P H E N O M E N O N
  R        O
           M
```

ACROSS
3. not taking sides
5. small suitcase
8. necessary
10. unusual occurrence

DOWN
1. very delicate
2. noncommissioned officer
4. this marks time
6. an organization
7. a dial
9. word having almost the same meaning

Lesson 18 • Review   75

Show What You Know

Lessons 13 – 17 • Review

One word is misspelled in each set of **list words**. Fill in the circle next to the **list word** that is spelled incorrectly.

1. burial	● availible	animation	economic
2. ● flooride	emphatic	confidential	consumable
3. legible	infectious	influenza	● clasic
4. gradual	● omision	pitiable	material
5. spacious	● reliyable	substantial	unanimous
6. emancipate	ambitious	● artic	microscopic
7. ● endevor	frantically	fluctuate	ferocious
8. comically	● jealousey	influential	intermission
9. meteorite	provincial	mandate	● heroicaly
10. gracious	fluent	systematic	● sargeant
11. calendar	● conscientius	responsible	mutual
12. prolific	essential	financial	● charitible
13. ● cureable	initial	league	drastically
14. ● nazal	livable	ideally	tenacious
15. ceremonial	tragic	● synnonym	portable
16. collapse	glorious	● aimiable	animosity
17. ● compatable	emission	harmonious	fragile
18. martial	● manuever	inanimate	habitable
19. neutral	manual	● noteable	unconscious
20. disposable	valise	impartial	● submision
21. ● comission	academically	debtor	attainable
22. annual	communicable	fluid	● guage
23. matinee	influence	basically	● intelligable
24. manipulate	phenomenon	● permissable	dramatic
25. quotable	● mayonaise	incidentally	transmission

Final Test

1. **Incidentally**, we both attended the same lecture.
2. Tien's family came from a **provincial** village.
3. At our **initial** meeting, we exchanged information.
4. That information is highly **confidential**!
5. The signature on this contract is barely **legible**.
6. After my **fluoride** treatment, I can't eat for an hour.
7. Our state budget has been cut **drastically** this year.
8. Is your rash very **infectious**?
9. What a beautiful, **spacious** apartment!
10. Make a **systematic** list of every drawer's contents.
11. My sister is **fluent** in three languages.
12. I have a **manual** typewriter, not an electric one.
13. You may have to **manipulate** the pieces into place.
14. We tried to solve our **economic** problems.
15. This artist paints **inanimate** objects, like rocks.
16. Will Kate be **responsible** for setting up the chairs?
17. Fruit is a **consumable** product.
18. Is this class for **academically** talented students?
19. I paid the agent a **commission** to sell my house.
20. A consultant will be **available** to help you decide.
21. Be careful with that **fragile** statue!
22. A mediator tries to stay **neutral** during arguments.
23. My brother has now achieved the rank of **sergeant**.
24. I think habit is a **synonym** for custom.
25. The moon has a direct **influence** on high tide.
26. Eric has always been a **conscientious** worker.
27. The bank questioned my **financial** history.
28. Those three colors make a **harmonious** pattern.
29. The president's secretary is very **influential**.
30. The boy was knocked **unconscious** by the ball.
31. A treaty is a **mutual** agreement between countries.
32. Mark the date of the party on your **calendar**.
33. Learning is a **gradual** process that never ends.
34. Is camping **permissible** in this park?
35. In one skit, the character was **comically** dressed.
36. Let me carry your **valise** to the train.
37. The prices of stocks and bonds **fluctuate** daily.
38. Lee told one particularly **quotable** story.
39. During **intermission**, we all bought popcorn.
40. The **omission** of your name can be corrected.
41. Mom's company has an **annual** picnic each July.
42. Several **charitable** groups asked for donations.
43. Many homeless people live in a **pitiable** state.
44. This clock is not **reliable**, so don't depend on it.
45. If I have help, this goal will be **attainable**.
46. **Ideally**, everyone will arrive at the same time.
47. The suitcase is full, so bring only **essential** items.
48. Keep the needle out of the red area on the **gauge**.
49. Scientists studied the **phenomenon** thoroughly.
50. Our baseball **league** is comprised of seven teams.

Words from Geography

Objective
To spell words from geography

Pretest
1. Danielle owns one **acre** of land near Lake Boone.
2. Southerners speak with a regional **dialect**.
3. A healthy plant should have thick, green **foliage**.
4. A narrow **isthmus** links the two larger islands.
5. We had a dry June, with no **precipitation**.
6. I took **aerial** photographs from a helicopter.
7. That massive oil spill was an **ecological** disaster!
8. The teacher drew **horizontal** lines across the map.
9. Are **meridian** lines used to measure longitude?
10. We must protect our nation's natural **resources**.
11. The earth rotates on an imaginary **axis**.
12. Columbus led an **expedition** to new lands.
13. The **hurricane** brought high winds and heavy rains.
14. We tasted a variety of **ethnic** foods at the festival.
15. Is the **reservoir** low because of the drought?
16. She paddled through the marshy **bayou** waters.
17. Mr. Lee planted vegetables in the rich, **fertile** soil.
18. The farmer learned new ways to **irrigate** crops.
19. The hikers set up camp on a wide **plateau**.
20. Here is a map of New York City and the **vicinity**.

Spelling Strategy
Page 77

Discuss the spelling rule. Encourage students to name other geography words they know. Then, have volunteers say and define the **list words**. For unfamiliar words, have students consult a dictionary or geography book. Point out that words from geography and other content areas are often more difficult to spell because they are not used regularly. Emphasize that they must study and practice these words.

Vocabulary Development Stress that students should think carefully about the meaning of each word as they complete the exercise.

Dictionary Skills To begin, you may wish to review diacritical marks and the sounds they stand for in **list words** such as *horizontal* and *hurricane*.

Spelling Practice
Pages 78–79

Word Analysis Remind students that many words are based on common roots or base words. As an example, discuss: *observe, reserve, preserve*. Have students look up the exercise words' definitions to learn how they differ from the **list words'** meanings.

Analogies Elicit that an analogy compares two pairs of things to show their relationship.

Word Application Remind students that each sentence has only one correct answer. Refer them to the dictionary if they forget the meanings of the **list words**.

54

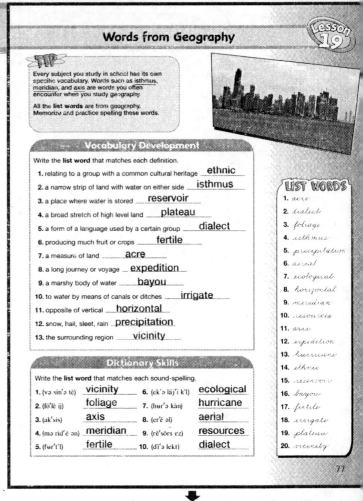

acre	precipitation	isthmus	dialect
axis	ecological	meridian	fertile
ethnic	horizontal	hurricane	foliage
aerial	expedition	plateau	irrigate
bayou	resources	reservoir	vicinity

Puzzle

Use the **list words** to complete the crossword puzzle.

ACROSS

2. high, level stretch of land
4. a form of language used by a certain group
7. a strong windstorm
8. a supply of things which fill a certain need
9. producing much fruit or crops
11. a marshy body of water
13. narrow strip of land with water on either side
14. a place to store rainfall
16. the surrounding region
19. rainfall or snowfall
20. straight line about which something turns

DOWN

1. a measure of land
3. of or in the air
5. to water by means of canals or ditches
6. a line across the surface of the Earth from one pole to the other
10. culturally similar
12. of the relationship between living things and the world
15. parallel to the horizon
17. a long journey
18. leaves, branches, flowers

```
          A  P L A T E A U
D I A L E C T              M
    R       R  HURRICANE   E
    R E S O U R C E S      R
    I       G              I
    G       F E R T I L E  D
  B A Y O U  E            I
    T        C    I S T H M U S
    R E S E R V O I R      N
    O        L             N
    L        O  V I C I N I T Y
  E X        G  O
  X P R E C I P I T A T I O N
  E D        A  I          O
  D I        L  Z          L
  I T           O          I
  T I           N          A
  I O           T          G
  O N           A  X I S   E
  N             L
```

Lesson 19 • Words from Geography   79

Puzzle Remind students to use capital letters and to print neatly as they complete the puzzle.

Spelling and Writing   Page 80

Proofreading You may wish to use this sentence to review the lesson's proofreading marks: *Maple avenue is Closed for Construktion.* Ask students for examples demonstrating the "new paragraph" mark.

Writing Questions and Answers To start, have students name a country they would like to visit and tell one thing they know about that country. After students have finished writing, provide time for volunteers to read their work aloud.

Bonus Words   Page 80

Countries Help students locate each country on a map. Make sure students notice on which continent each country is located. You may wish to have pairs of students consult an encyclopedia to find some significant facts about each country to report back to the class.

Bonus Words Test

1. Agriculture is the main industry of **Nicaragua**.
2. The capital of **Venezuela** is Caracas.
3. Many people of **Ethiopia** speak English or Arabic.
4. Patagonia is a dry plateau in southern **Argentina**.
5. **Thailand** was once known as Siam.
6. There are over twenty ethnic tribes in **Afghanistan**.
7. **Switzerland** was neutral during World War II.
8. **Libya** was once a part of the Roman Empire.
9. **Belgium** is a densely populated country in Europe.
10. More than 7,000 islands comprise the **Philippines**.

Final Test

1. The sheep grazed on the low mountain **plateau**.
2. The **hurricane** ripped trees out of the ground.
3. Some people in Quebec use a French **dialect**.
4. Is there an airport in the **vicinity** of the city?
5. The farmer planted corn on one **acre** of land.
6. Swimming is forbidden in the **reservoir**!
7. The gyroscope spun around on a steel **axis**.
8. Coal is one of our natural **resources**.
9. Scientists did **ecological** research on the island.
10. This map gives an **aerial** view of Cape Cod.
11. Are snow and rain forms of **precipitation**?
12. A path was cut through the thick jungle **foliage**.
13. The prime **meridian** passes through England.
14. **Horizontal** and vertical lines mark the chart.
15. The **isthmus** of Panama connects two continents.
16. Dad installed a pipeline to **irrigate** his crops.
17. Mae Jemison was a member of a space **expedition**.
18. Is the water in a **bayou** stagnant?
19. **Fertile** soil contains nutrients that help plants grow.
20. The musicians performed **ethnic** songs.

Proofreading

Proofreading Marks	
⬭ spelling mistake	/ small letter
¶ new paragraph	≡ capital letter

Use the proofreading marks to correct the mistakes in the article below. Then, write the misspelled **list words** correctly on the lines.

The Republic of Panama is the southernmost country in central America, situated on the isthmus which links North and south america. The country boasts tropical jungles, mountain ranges, furtile valleys and plains, and the Panama canal, which links the Atlantic and pacific oceans.

Temperatures are high year-round in Panama. The rainy season can last from May to September, and pricepitation is highest on the Caribbean coast. An aireal view of the country would reveal that most of the population lives around the Canal Area, in the capital—Panama City, and in the surrounding plateau.

1. isthmus   4. aerial
2. fertile   5. plateau
3. precipitation

Writing Questions and Answers

Imagine that you could visit any foreign country in the world. Think about why you would like to visit that country and what you would like to learn during your visit. Write five questions that you would like answered on your trip, using as many of the **list words** as you can. Then, use a geography book or encyclopedia to answer your questions. After proofreading and revising, share your questions and answers with a group.

BONUS WORDS

Venezuela	Libya	Nicaragua	Philippines	Belgium
Argentina	Ethiopia	Afghanistan	Switzerland	Thailand

Write the **bonus word** under the continent in which it is located.

Asia
1. Afghanistan
2. Thailand
3. Philippines

Europe
4. Switzerland
5. Belgium

Africa
8. Ethiopia
9. Libya

South America
6. Venezuela
7. Argentina

North America
10. Nicaragua

Lesson 20 — Words from Science

Objective
To spell words from science

Pretest

1. The chemist will **analyze** the compound.
2. I used a **compass** to find my way back to camp.
3. The **diagram** shows how to assemble the bicycle.
4. The **frequency** of rainfall is often unpredictable.
5. Every living creature has its own **specific** features.
6. We learn about past cultures through **archaeology**.
7. The shadow softened the **contour** of her face.
8. Health officials predict a flu **epidemic** this winter.
9. At what temperature will wax **liquefy**?
10. Dr. Won listened to my heart with a **stethoscope**.
11. Medical instruments are sterilized to kill **bacteria**.
12. It is **crucial** that they reach the hospital soon.
13. Will this class study the **evolution** of a frog?
14. My **sociology** report was on the homeless situation.
15. **Toxic** gases are harmful to people and animals.
16. Do botanists study the **characteristics** of plants?
17. The four seasons of the year complete a **cycle**.
18. The doctor showed us a **facsimile** of a heart.
19. The landscape artist used good **spatial** proportions.
20. That explosion caused a huge earth **tremor**!

Spelling Strategy — Page 81

Discuss the spelling rule with students. Encourage them to name and define other science words they know. Then, have volunteers define the **list words**, using a dictionary or science book for any unfamiliar words. Point out that because scientific words are often difficult to pronounce and spell, it is important to study and practice these words.

Vocabulary Development Have a volunteer explain the directions, then do the first item with students.

Dictionary Skills Remind students that knowing a word's sound-spelling can help them spell that word.

Spelling Practice — Pages 82–83

Word Analysis Urge students to refer to the **list words** on page 83 if needed to check each letter combination. To extend, have students identify **list words** containing the io vowel combination. *(evolution, sociology)*

Word Meaning Work through the first item with students so that they understand to replace the underlined word in each sentence with an underlined word from another sentence in the exercise.

Word Application Remind students to use context clues as a guide when choosing their answers. To extend the activity, have students create sentences using the distractors that classmates can solve.

Words from Science — Lesson 20

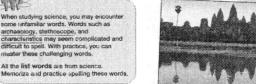

TIP When studying science, you may encounter some unfamiliar words. Words such as archaeology, stethoscope, and characteristics may seem complicated and difficult to spell. With practice, you can master these challenging words.

All the list words are from science. Memorize and practice spelling these words.

Vocabulary Development

Write the **list word** from column **B** that matches the synonym or definition in column **A**.

A		B
1. copy	facsimile	toxic
2. traits	characteristics	tremor
3. exact	specific	liquefy
4. examine	analyze	diagram
5. chart	diagram	facsimile
6. outline	contour	compass
7. melt	liquefy	specific
8. earthquake	tremor	crucial
9. poisonous	toxic	analyze
10. critical	crucial	characteristics
11. direction finder	compass	contour

LIST WORDS

1. analyze
2. compass
3. diagram
4. frequency
5. specific
6. archaeology
7. contour
8. epidemic
9. liquefy
10. stethoscope
11. bacteria
12. crucial
13. evolution
14. sociology
15. tone
16. characteristics
17. cycle
18. facsimile
19. spatial
20. tremor

Dictionary Skills

Write the **list word** that matches each sound-spelling.

1. (steth'ə skōp) stethoscope
2. (sō'sē.ăl'ə jē) sociology
3. (sī'k'l) cycle
4. (är'kē ăl'ə jē) archaeology
5. (ev'ə lōō'shən) evolution
6. (spā'shəl) spatial
7. (kum'pəs) compass
8. (bak tir'ē ə) bacteria
9. (ep'ə dem'ik) epidemic
10. (frē'kwən sē) frequency

81

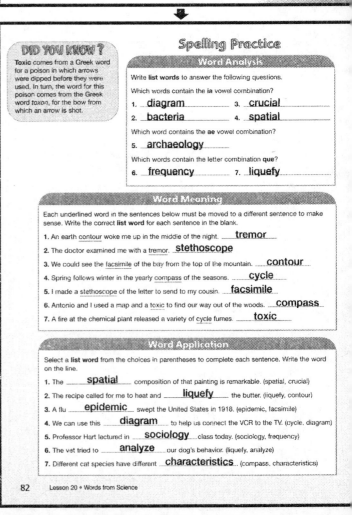

DID YOU KNOW?

Toxic comes from a Greek word for a poison in which arrows were dipped before they were used. In turn, the word for this poison comes from the Greek word *toxon*, for the bow from which an arrow is shot.

Spelling Practice

Word Analysis

Write **list words** to answer the following questions.

Which words contain the ia vowel combination?

1. diagram   3. crucial
2. bacteria   4. spatial

Which word contains the ae vowel combination?

5. archaeology

Which words contain the letter combination que?

6. frequency   7. liquefy

Word Meaning

Each underlined word in the sentences below must be moved to a different sentence to make sense. Write the correct **list word** for each sentence in the blank.

1. An earth contour woke me up in the middle of the night. **tremor**
2. The doctor examined me with a tremor. **stethoscope**
3. We could see the facsimile of the bay from the top of the mountain. **contour**
4. Spring follows winter in the yearly compass of the seasons. **cycle**
5. I made a stethoscope of the letter to send to my cousin. **facsimile**
6. Antonio and I used a map and a toxic to find our way out of the woods. **compass**
7. A fire at the chemical plant released a variety of cycle fumes. **toxic**

Word Application

Select a **list word** from the choices in parentheses to complete each sentence. Write the word on the line.

1. The **spatial** composition of that painting is remarkable. (spatial, crucial)
2. The recipe called for me to heat and **liquefy** the butter. (liquefy, contour)
3. A flu **epidemic** swept the United States in 1918. (epidemic, facsimile)
4. We can use this **diagram** to help us connect the VCR to the TV. (cycle, diagram)
5. Professor Hart lectured in **sociology** class today. (sociology, frequency)
6. The vet tried to **analyze** our dog's behavior. (liquefy, analyze)
7. Different cat species have different **characteristics**. (compass, characteristics)

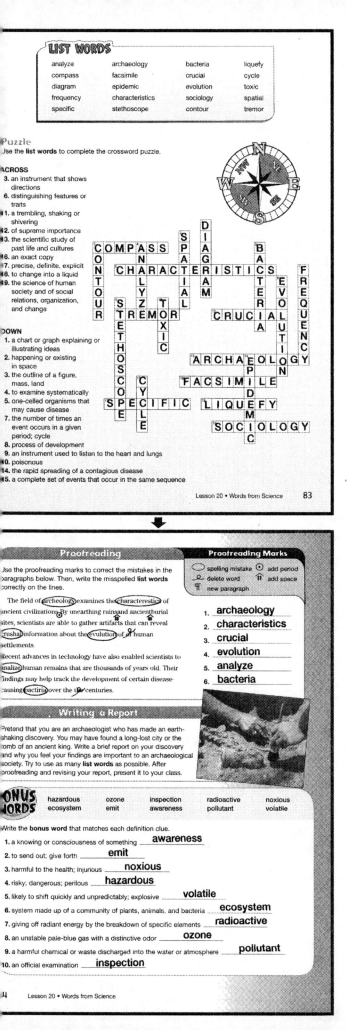

LIST WORDS

analyze	archaeology	bacteria	liquefy
compass	facsimile	crucial	cycle
diagram	epidemic	evolution	toxic
frequency	characteristics	sociology	spatial
specific	stethoscope	contour	tremor

Puzzle
Use the **list words** to complete the crossword puzzle.

ACROSS
3. an instrument that shows directions
6. distinguishing features or traits
11. a trembling, shaking or shivering
12. of supreme importance
13. the scientific study of past life and cultures
16. an exact copy
17. precise, definite, explicit
18. to change into a liquid
19. the science of human society and of social relations, organization, and change

DOWN
1. a chart or graph explaining or illustrating ideas
2. happening or existing in space
3. the outline of a figure, mass, land
4. to examine systematically
5. one-celled organisms that may cause disease
7. the number of times an event occurs in a given period; cycle
8. process of development
9. an instrument used to listen to the heart and lungs
10. poisonous
14. the rapid spreading of a contagious disease
15. a complete set of events that occur in the same sequence

Lesson 20 • Words from Science   83

Proofreading
Use the proofreading marks to correct the mistakes in the paragraphs below. Then, write the misspelled **list words** correctly on the lines.

The field of archeology examines the characterestics of ancient civilizations. By unearthing ruins and ancient burial sites, scientists are able to gather artifacts that can reveal crushal information about the evolutian of human settlements.

Recent advances in technology have also enabled scientists to analise human remains that are thousands of years old. Their findings may help track the development of certain disease-causing bactiria over the centuries.

Proofreading Marks
- ◯ spelling mistake
- ◉ add period
- ◵ delete word
- ⌗ add space
- ¶ new paragraph

1. archaeology
2. characteristics
3. crucial
4. evolution
5. analyze
6. bacteria

Writing a Report
Pretend that you are an archaeologist who has made an earth-shaking discovery. You may have found a long-lost city or the tomb of an ancient king. Write a brief report on your discovery and why you feel your findings are important to an archaeological society. Try to use as many **list words** as possible. After proofreading and revising your report, present it to your class.

BONUS WORDS

hazardous	ozone	inspection	radioactive	noxious
ecosystem	emit	awareness	pollutant	volatile

Write the **bonus word** that matches each definition clue.

1. a knowing or consciousness of something __awareness__
2. to send out; give forth __emit__
3. harmful to the health; injurious __noxious__
4. risky; dangerous; perilous __hazardous__
5. likely to shift quickly and unpredictably; explosive __volatile__
6. system made up of a community of plants, animals, and bacteria __ecosystem__
7. giving off radiant energy by the breakdown of specific elements __radioactive__
8. an unstable pale-blue gas with a distinctive odor __ozone__
9. a harmful chemical or waste discharged into the water or atmosphere __pollutant__
10. an official examination __inspection__

84   Lesson 20 • Words from Science

Puzzle Students will be familiar with the process for completing a crossword puzzle. Encourage them to print neatly and clearly as they write the letters in the boxes.

Spelling and Writing   Page 84

Proofreading Review the proofreading marks in the box, focusing on the "new paragraph" mark. Remind students that this mark is used to show where a new paragraph begins and should be indented. Have volunteers practice making the mark on the board.

Writing a Report Discuss the types of artifacts that could be found on an archaeological expedition. Ask students what those artifacts might reveal to researchers about that civilization. Encourage students to use these ideas when describing their discoveries.

Bonus Words   Page 84

Environmental Issues Have students look up the meanings of the **bonus words** in dictionaries. Discuss how the words apply to the environment and pollution. You may also wish to invite an environmental specialist to visit the class and discuss local ecological issues.

Bonus Words Test
1. Radon is a **radioactive** gas found in the earth.
2. Dispose of **hazardous** wastes carefully.
3. There is a delicate balance of life in the **ecosystem**.
4. A **pollutant** is a harmful waste.
5. **Noxious** gases can cause health problems.
6. After the rain, we could smell the **ozone**.
7. The chemical plant will **emit** pollutants into the air.
8. Nitroglycerine is **volatile** and will explode easily.
9. There is a great **awareness** of ecological issues.
10. After the **inspection**, the factory was shut down.

Final Test
1. Did you feel that earth **tremor** shake the house?
2. She had to make a **crucial** decision under stress.
3. The block of ice will **liquefy** into a puddle of water.
4. The chemical explosion produced **toxic** fumes.
5. Spring begins a new **cycle** of life in the garden.
6. A **compass** shows which direction you're traveling.
7. This **diagram** shows the human skeletal system.
8. What is the **frequency** of earthquakes in California?
9. The map showed the **contour** of the coastline.
10. Each experiment will produce **specific** results.
11. The **archaeology** professor visited the ancient ruins.
12. Each person has different physical **characteristics**.
13. The lawyer sent us a **facsimile** of the document.
14. Some **bacteria** are used to make medicines.
15. He has poor **spatial** vision.
16. A psychiatrist will **analyze** a person's behavior.
17. We discussed family life in **sociology** class.
18. Does **evolution** explain the development of life?
19. The doctor used a **stethoscope** to hear my heart.
20. That flu **epidemic** spread rapidly at school!

Words from Math

Objective
To spell words from mathematics

Pretest

1. Tell me the **absolute** truth!
2. Use this **equation** to find the area of a circle.
3. Don't waste! Use a **minimum** amount of paint.
4. A mistake will **skew** all the results.
5. I will show you how to prove this **theorem**.
6. Do these two triangles have **congruent** sides?
7. Draw an **equilateral** triangle and label the sides.
8. The angle will either be **obtuse**, right, or acute.
9. Is a ball one kind of **sphere**?
10. A **trapezoid** always has four sides.
11. The **denominator** of $\frac{3}{4}$ is four.
12. The diagram shows the **inequality** of the sides.
13. Use your **protractor** to draw an arc.
14. A **symmetrical** design is well-balanced.
15. The answers will be **variable**.
16. A **diagonal** line bisects the opposite angles.
17. Does an **isosceles** triangle have two equal sides?
18. All angles, except right angles, are **oblique**.
19. Draw the circle and the **tangent** described.
20. This **vertical** line is perpendicular to the base.

Spelling Strategy
Page 85

After students have read the spelling rule, have them discuss the meanings of the **list words** that they know. For unfamiliar words, have students consult dictionaries or math books. Show students how to find the mathematical meaning of words with multiple meanings by looking for the field labels *math*, *algebra*, or *geometry*. Then, discuss how students can best learn to spell the words.

Vocabulary Development Have students write the **list words** that can be easily matched to the given definitions first. For items that are more difficult, urge students to consult dictionaries.

Dictionary Skills Review as needed the letters and symbols used in sound-spellings. Point out the importance of placing accents in the correct positions.

Spelling Practice
Pages 86–87

Word Analysis Remind students that analyzing words makes it easier to remember how to spell them. If needed, review that the number of syllables in a word can be determined by the number of vowel sounds heard.

Word Application When students have finished the exercise, have them discuss the clues in the sentences that lead them to the correct answers.

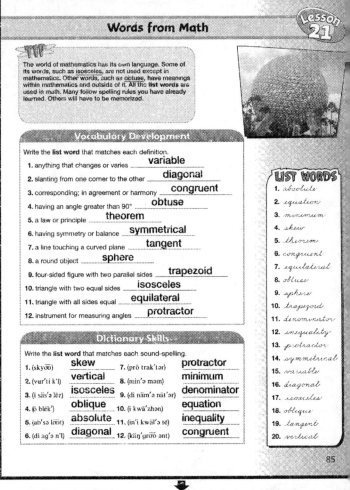

Words from Math

TIP
The world of mathematics has its own language. Some of its words, such as *isosceles*, are not used except in mathematics. Other words, such as *obtuse*, have meanings within mathematics and outside of it. All the **list words** are used in math. Many follow spelling rules you have already learned. Others will have to be memorized.

Vocabulary Development
Write the **list word** that matches each definition.

1. anything that changes or varies — **variable**
2. slanting from one corner to the other — **diagonal**
3. corresponding; in agreement or harmony — **congruent**
4. having an angle greater than 90° — **obtuse**
5. a law or principle — **theorem**
6. having symmetry or balance — **symmetrical**
7. a line touching a curved plane — **tangent**
8. a round object — **sphere**
9. four-sided figure with two parallel sides — **trapezoid**
10. triangle with two equal sides — **isosceles**
11. triangle with all sides equal — **equilateral**
12. instrument for measuring angles — **protractor**

LIST WORDS
1. absolute
2. equation
3. minimum
4. skew
5. theorem
6. congruent
7. equilateral
8. obtuse
9. sphere
10. trapezoid
11. denominator
12. inequality
13. protractor
14. symmetrical
15. variable
16. diagonal
17. isosceles
18. oblique
19. tangent
20. vertical

Dictionary Skills
Write the **list word** that matches each sound-spelling.

1. (skyo͞o) **skew**
2. (vur'ti k'l) **vertical**
3. (ī säs'ə lēz) **isosceles**
4. (ō blēk') **oblique**
5. (ab'sə lo͞ot) **absolute**
6. (dī ag'ə n'l) **diagonal**
7. (prō trak'tər) **protractor**
8. (min'ə məm) **minimum**
9. (di näm'ə nāt'ər) **denominator**
10. (i kwā'zhən) **equation**
11. (in'i kwäl'ə tē) **inequality**
12. (käŋ'gro͞o ənt) **congruent**

85

Spelling Practice

DID YOU KNOW?
When you have been absolved, you have been set free from something. If you have been set free from all ties, you are acting wholly on your own and are absolutely free. You have **absolute** power over yourself. The word *absolutely* comes from the Latin prefix *ab*, meaning "from," and *solvere*, meaning "to set free."

Word Analysis
Write **list words** to answer the following questions.

Which **list words** contain **equa** or **equi**?
1. **equation**
2. **equilateral**
3. **inequality**

Which **list words** end with the adjectival ending **al**?
4. **equilateral**
5. **symmetrical**
6. **diagonal**
7. **vertical**

Which **list words** contain five syllables?
8. **equilateral**
9. **denominator**
10. **inequality**

Word Application
Write a **list word** to complete each sentence.

1. Our teacher called for **absolute** silence during the test.
2. The patient must keep excitement down to a **minimum** during her recovery.
3. We will have to draw these triangles again if we **skew** the results.
4. This angle measures more than 90° so it must be **obtuse**.
5. We'd have to measure our basketball to determine whether it's a perfect **sphere**.
6. The weight of this object is **variable** depending on how much water it holds.
7. An **isosceles** triangle has two equal sides.
8. This **oblique** figure has a tilted axis.
9. The line is **tangent** to the circle, but it does not cut across its surface.
10. The two squares are the same size and have **congruent** sides.
11. Jeremy developed a **theorem** in math class and then attempted to prove it.

86   Lesson 21 • Words from Math

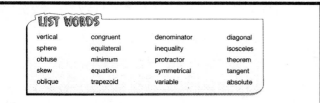

LIST WORDS

vertical	congruent	denominator	diagonal
sphere	equilateral	inequality	isosceles
obtuse	minimum	protractor	theorem
skew	equation	symmetrical	tangent
oblique	trapezoid	variable	absolute

Puzzle
Use the **list words** to complete the crossword puzzle.

ACROSS
3. a law or principle
5. straight up and down
8. smallest amount allowed
10. not equal in size or amount
11. whole; perfect; complete
14. line touching circle at only one point
15. triangle with two equal sides
17. instrument used for drawing and measuring
18. angle of more than 90°
19. to twist or slant

DOWN
1. number below the line in a fraction
2. something that changes
3. four-sided figure with two parallel sides
4. having a slanted position
6. triangle with equal sides
7. slanting from one corner to the opposite corner
9. having symmetry or balance
12. statement showing two quantities are equal
13. corresponding; in agreement or harmony
16. a round object

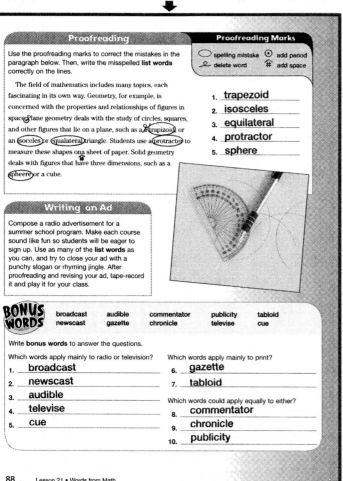

Lesson 21 • Words from Math   87

Proofreading
Use the proofreading marks to correct the mistakes in the paragraph below. Then, write the misspelled **list words** correctly on the lines.

Proofreading Marks
◯ spelling mistake   ⊙ add period
⌒ delete word   # add space

The field of mathematics includes many topics, each fascinating in its own way. Geometry, for example, is concerned with the properties and relationships of figures in space.Plane geometry deals with the study of circles, squares, and other figures that lie on a plane, such as a *trapezoid* or an *isoceles* or *equalateral* triangle. Students use a *protracter* to measure these shapes on a sheet of paper. Solid geometry deals with figures that have three dimensions, such as a *spheere* or a cube.

1. trapezoid
2. isosceles
3. equilateral
4. protractor
5. sphere

Writing an Ad
Compose a radio advertisement for a summer school program. Make each course sound like fun so students will be eager to sign up. Use as many of the **list words** as you can, and try to close your ad with a punchy slogan or rhyming jingle. After proofreading and revising your ad, tape-record it and play it for your class.

BONUS WORDS
broadcast   audible   commentator   publicity   tabloid
newscast   gazette   chronicle   televise   cue

Write **bonus words** to answer the questions.

Which words apply mainly to radio or television?
1. broadcast
2. newscast
3. audible
4. televise
5. cue

Which words apply mainly to print?
6. gazette
7. tabloid

Which words could apply equally to either?
8. commentator
9. chronicle
10. publicity

88   Lesson 21 • Words from Math

Puzzle By now, students should be able to complete the puzzle independently. Remind them to print neatly.

Spelling and Writing   *Page 88*
Proofreading Write this sentence on the board and ask volunteers to correct it using the proofreading marks from the lesson: *Pleaseopen the the vertikel blinds*

Writing an Ad Have small groups brainstorm fun elective courses a summer school program could offer, such as a fiction-writing workshop with a famous author, or a leadership-training ropes course. You may wish to point out that most radio ads are approximately 70 words long and fill a 30-second spot. Students may enjoy reading their ads as though on the radio.

Bonus Words   *Page 88*
Media Explain that all the **bonus words** are related to media, the forms of communication. Discuss familiar words and have students use dictionaries to find the meanings of unfamiliar terms. Point out if needed that *publicity*, *commentator*, and *chronicle* can apply to any media form.

Bonus Words Test
1. This story will be a **chronicle** of our trip.
2. The studio has a new **commentator**.
3. Our latest **broadcast** begins at midnight.
4. At the **cue**, Richard says his lines.
5. We bought an ad in a local weekly **tabloid**.
6. That story came in too late for the noon **newscast**.
7. The announcer spoke in a barely **audible** voice.
8. Channel 3 will **televise** the debates.
9. Look for our ad on page two of the local **gazette**.
10. Without **publicity**, the show would have failed.

Final Test
1. Is the **denominator** equal to the numerator?
2. Notice the **inequality** between the numbers.
3. A **protractor** will help you measure an angle.
4. The two halves of this figure are **symmetrical**.
5. The weight is **variable**, depending on the size.
6. Draw a **vertical** line down the side of the page.
7. The **tangent** touches the circle in one place only.
8. An **oblique** figure has a tilted axis.
9. Is this figure called an **isosceles** triangle?
10. The two **diagonal** lines cross in the center.
11. You can see that the two figures are **congruent**.
12. An **equilateral** figure has equal sides.
13. This angle is **obtuse** and that one is acute.
14. Our planet is not really a perfect **sphere**.
15. This **trapezoid** looks like a slanted box.
16. The **absolute** value of negative three is three.
17. Here is a simple **equation** that you will recognize.
18. Use a **minimum** amount of sugar in your food.
19. Be careful or you will **skew** those figures!
20. Can the **theorem** be proven to be true or false?

Lesson 22

Words from History

Objective
To spell words related to history

Pretest

1. The **aggressor** fought to conquer new territory.
2. The leaders held a **caucus** to select a candidate.
3. My aunt served in the state **legislature** of Ohio.
4. The campaign **propaganda** was false.
5. **Socialist** theory aims to equalize society.
6. The United States and Canada enjoy an **alliance**.
7. The government of China promotes **communism**.
8. Are atoms split to form **nuclear** energy?
9. The **rebellion** fought against the government.
10. We have a **strategic** plan to build our profits.
11. Support your opinions with an **arsenal** of facts.
12. Was Grandmother born in a European **ghetto**?
13. The **peasant** lives in a hut near the stream.
14. Did the **recession** cause interest rates to fall?
15. The admiral proved that he was not a **traitor**.
16. A **capitalist** believes in free enterprise.
17. They will **inaugurate** the president in January.
18. This restaurant has a **prohibition** on smoking.
19. Vote "No" on the **referendum** to lower taxes!
20. The nations' delegates signed the **armistice**.

Spelling Strategy   Page 89

After students have read the spelling rule, relate the history theme to a current social studies unit, having students name words that have significance to the events and issues being studied. Then, discuss the **list words**, using dictionaries and history texts for definitions, examples, and contextual references.

Vocabulary Development Before the exercise, have volunteers suggest short definitions for these history-related words: *democracy*, *migration*, and *monarchy*.

Dictionary Skills Before students begin, have a volunteer summarize the function of guide words and point out examples in a dictionary.

Spelling Practice   Pages 90–91

Word Analysis To extend the activity, you may wish to have students separate the words into syllables, using dictionaries to check their work.

Word Application Urge students to use context clues to find the **list word** that best completes each sentence. You may wish to have students create similar sentences for other **list words** to present as challenges to classmates.

Words from History   Lesson 22

TIP
The **list words** are related to government, politics, and social issues. Knowledge and use of such words as referendum, recession, and rebellion will help you in your study and in your discussion of historical events, as well as in your analysis of the causes and effects of those events.

Vocabulary Development

Write the **list word** that matches each definition.

1. an agreement to stop a conflict — armistice
2. a collection, usually of weapons — arsenal
3. a meeting to choose a leader or set policy — caucus
4. the person or group who starts a conflict — aggressor
5. one who betrays his or her country — traitor
6. a revolt or revolution — rebellion
7. to install an official or establish a policy — inaugurate
8. showing sound planning — strategic
9. a period of declining business activity — recession
10. persuasive language used to promote ideas — propaganda
11. a group of people who make laws — legislature
12. an order or law that forbids something — prohibition

LIST WORDS
1. aggressor
2. caucus
3. legislature
4. propaganda
5. socialist
6. alliance
7. communism
8. nuclear
9. rebellion
10. strategic
11. arsenal
12. ghetto
13. peasant
14. recession
15. traitor
16. capitalist
17. inaugurate
18. prohibition
19. referendum
20. armistice

Dictionary Skills

Write the **list word** that comes between each pair of dictionary guide words.

1. soap/soft — socialist
2. can/carry — capitalist
3. reef/regular — referendum
4. color/cope — communism
5. gem/give — ghetto
6. nuance/nugget — nuclear
7. patter/pepper — peasant
8. problem/project — prohibition
9. left/legitimate — legislature
10. ago/apartment — alliance

89

DID YOU KNOW?
In the late 1700s, a group of men who lived in Boston, Massachusetts, would hold regular meetings to discuss political issues. They called themselves the Caucus Club. Some believe that the name was taken from an Algonquin Indian word which means "advisor." Today, the word **caucus** is still a term reserved for political meetings.

Spelling Practice

Word Analysis

Write each **list word** under the correct category.

Words of Two Syllables
1. caucus   3. peasant
2. ghetto   4. traitor

Words of Three Syllables
5. aggressor   10. strategic
6. socialist   11. arsenal
7. alliance   12. recession
8. nuclear   13. armistice
9. rebellion

Words of Four Syllables
14. legislature   18. inaugurate
15. propaganda   19. prohibition
16. communism   20. referendum
17. capitalist

Word Application

Write a **list word** to complete each sentence.

1. Benedict Arnold is considered to be a ___traitor___ who betrayed the American patriots' cause.
2. The ___referendum___ on whether to build a new library will be decided by voters.
3. Advertisements often contain ___propaganda___ designed to persuade consumers to buy a product.
4. Under ___communism___, all property is owned by the community as a whole.
5. A ___capitalist___ believes in free enterprise, competitive business, and private ownership.
6. A ___socialist___ believes that all members of society should share work and profits equally.
7. Political leaders hold a ___caucus___ to select candidates and establish platforms.
8. A ___ghetto___ is an urban neighborhood in which many members of an ethnic group live because of poverty or prejudice.

90   Lesson 22 • Words from History

60

LIST WORDS

aggressor	recession	arsenal	capitalist
caucus	communism	ghetto	inaugurate
legislature	peasant	nuclear	prohibition
propaganda	rebellion	alliance	referendum
socialist	strategic	traitor	armistice

Word Analysis

Write the **list word** that contains the same root or base word as the word given.

1. recede **recession**
2. strategy **strategic**
3. society **socialist**
4. ally **alliance**
5. common **communism**
6. betray **traitor**
7. nucleus **nuclear**
8. legal **legislature**
9. rebel **rebellion**

Puzzle

This is a crossword puzzle without clues. Use the length and the spelling of each **list word** to complete the puzzle.

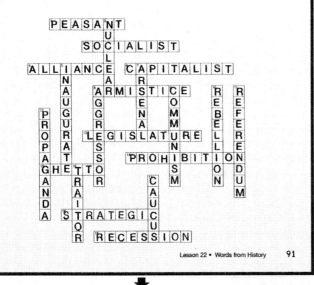

Lesson 22 • Words from History   91

Proofreading

Use the proofreading marks to correct the mistakes in the article below. Then, write the misspelled **list words** correctly on the lines.

Many legends have come from stories about real people. One such person was Davy Crockett. Davy Crockett was born in Tennessee in 1786. He served in the Tennessee legislachure and also in the U.S. House of Representatives. Crockett was often described as an agressor but every move he made was a strategik one. He is believed to have said, "Be always sure you are right, then go ahead." He died in 1836 at the Alamo in Texas while defending the arsenal during the rebelion against Mexico. Stories that have been told about him include his grinning down a raccoon, thawing out the frozen dawn, and saving the country from from a comet.

Proofreading Marks
- ⊙ spelling mistake
- ⊙ add period
- ᰠ add quotation marks
- ⌃ add comma
- ⌿ delete word

1. **legislature**
2. **aggressor**
3. **strategic**
4. **arsenal**
5. **rebellion**

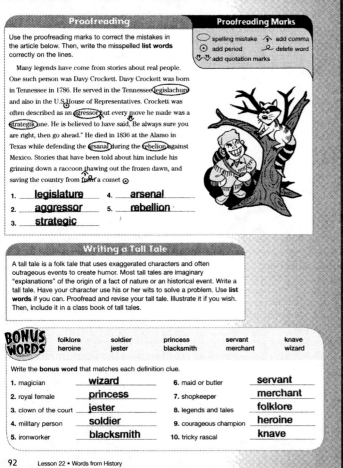

Writing a Tall Tale

A tall tale is a folk tale that uses exaggerated characters and often outrageous events to create humor. Most tall tales are imaginary "explanations" of the origin of a fact of nature or an historical event. Write a tall tale. Have your character use his or her wits to solve a problem. Use **list words** if you can. Proofread and revise your tall tale. Illustrate it if you wish. Then, include it in a class book of tall tales.

BONUS WORDS

folklore	soldier	princess	servant	knave
heroine	jester	blacksmith	merchant	wizard

Write the **bonus word** that matches each definition clue.

1. magician **wizard**
2. royal female **princess**
3. clown of the court **jester**
4. military person **soldier**
5. ironworker **blacksmith**
6. maid or butler **servant**
7. shopkeeper **merchant**
8. legends and tales **folklore**
9. courageous champion **heroine**
10. tricky rascal **knave**

92   Lesson 22 • Words from History

Word Analysis Point out that knowing the meanings of roots or base words will help students understand the technical words they encounter in history, science, and geography texts.

Puzzle Point out that each **list word** appears once.

Spelling and Writing   *Page 92*

Proofreading Review the proofreading marks with this sentence: *Omar said I've broght my my lunch*

Writing a Tall Tale Read and discuss the features of a popular tall tale, such as one about Pecos Bill or Paul Bunyan. Have students cite examples of exaggeration and outrageous events. Then, brainstorm story ideas with them. Urge students to take notes to help them organize their tales. When finished, invite students to share their work orally, and then combine their tales to create a bulletin board or a classroom anthology.

Bonus Words   *Page 92*

Literature Discuss the **bonus words**, relating them to familiar folk tales and to students' own knowledge of the words. Have students use the words in oral sentences.

Bonus Words Test

1. The **blacksmith** worked over an open forge.
2. In many folk tales, a **servant** becomes a great hero.
3. A **wizard** appears in the King Arthur legends.
4. In a famous tale, a **princess** falls in love with a frog.
5. The court **jester** was the castle's resident comedian.
6. The tin **soldier** is the hero of a well-known tale.
7. Germany is a country that is rich in **folklore**.
8. In one tale, a **knave** pretends that he's a king.
9. In another tale, a **merchant** is granted three wishes.
10. A young shepherdess is the **heroine** of this tale.

Final Test

1. The coach explained her **strategic** game plan.
2. All were jubilant when the **armistice** was signed.
3. The state **legislature** vetoed the bill.
4. Was the **traitor** exiled from the country?
5. Marx was a German philosopher and **socialist**.
6. Our company was hit hard by the **recession**.
7. There is a **referendum** question on the ballot.
8. The queen lowered taxes to prevent a **rebellion**.
9. Don't be swayed by **propaganda**!
10. At the **caucus**, Roberto presented his views.
11. The people in the **ghetto** were restless.
12. Russia turned to **communism** in 1922.
13. We will **inaugurate** our new class officers today.
14. The bordering nations formed a trade **alliance**.
15. Andrew Carnegie was a major American **capitalist**.
16. A knight's weapons **arsenal** included lances.
17. I ran from the **aggressor** to avoid a fight.
18. Is there a **nuclear** power plant near the city?
19. The **peasant** works in the field every day.
20. Many people support the **prohibition** of fireworks.

Lesson 23 — Words from Business

Objective
To spell words from business

Pretest
1. The **administration** of the business requires skill.
2. Mr. Inez added up the receipts on a **calculator**.
3. Ana's investments yield a monthly **dividend**.
4. He had to **justify** his expenses to his boss.
5. If you miss loan payments, they'll **repossess** the car.
6. Did the office supervisor **authorize** your raise?
7. Teachers must have proper **certification** to teach.
8. The company's **executive** offices are upstairs.
9. Trucks deliver **merchandise** to stores every day.
10. Leah's promotion meant an increase in **salary**.
11. That business tycoon is worth a **billion** dollars!
12. The bank requires **collateral** on the personal loan.
13. **Italics** are used to set off or emphasize an idea.
14. The **invoice** listed the item as a back order.
15. Is a **signature** required to cash a check?
16. The credit **bureau** checked Al's credit rating.
17. We exchanged U.S. dollars for German **currency**.
18. My statement shows the **interest** that I earned.
19. Lin sent a copy of the bill with her **remittance**.
20. **Statistics** show that the business is booming.

Spelling Strategy — Page 93
Introduce the lesson by discussing how to obtain a bank loan, why people seek loans, the use of collateral, how payments are made, and so on. Have volunteers define the **list words**, using dictionaries when needed.

Vocabulary Development To extend the activity, have students find synonyms for other **list words**, such as *calculator (adding machine)*, *dividend (profit)*, and *certification (verification)*.

Dictionary Skills Emphasize that students should be careful to not drop letters from any of the syllables as they write the words.

Spelling Practice — Pages 94–95
Word Analysis Students can refer to the **list words** on page 95 to find each letter combination. To extend, have students identify the words that contain the *st* letter combination. (*administration, justify, interest, statistics*)

Word Application To extend the activity, have students work in pairs to write ten sentences using **list words** not included in the exercise. Then, have student pairs share their sentences with the class.

Synonyms and Antonyms Ask students to tell which of these word pairs are synonyms, and which are antonyms, giving reasons for their answers: *profit, deficit (antonyms); merger, alliance (synonyms)*.

Words from Business — Lesson 23

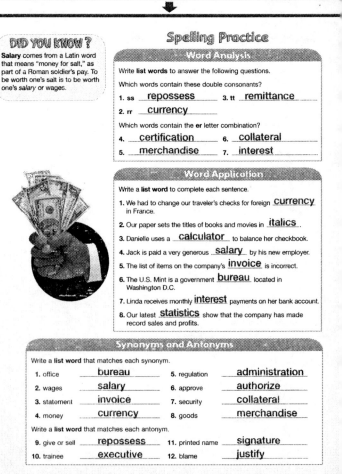

Vocabulary Development

Write the **list word** from column **B** that matches the synonym in column **A**.

	A		B
1.	autograph	signature	currency
2.	money	currency	administration
3.	bill	invoice	merchandise
4.	manager	executive	salary
5.	recover	repossess	statistics
6.	empower	authorize	executive
7.	figures	statistics	authorize
8.	pay	salary	signature
9.	goods	merchandise	repossess
10.	management	administration	invoice

LIST WORDS
1. administration
2. calculator
3. dividend
4. justify
5. repossess
6. authorize
7. certification
8. executive
9. merchandise
10. salary
11. billion
12. collateral
13. italics
14. invoice
15. signature
16. bureau
17. currency
18. interest
19. remittance
20. statistics

Dictionary Skills

Rewrite each of the following **list words** to show how they are divided into syllables.

1. remittance	re/mit/tance	6. italics	i/tal/ics
2. calculator	cal/cu/la/tor	7. bureau	bu/reau
3. dividend	div/i/dend	8. interest	in/ter/est
4. collateral	col/lat/er/al	9. billion	bil/lion
5. certification	cer/ti/fi/ca/tion	10. justify	jus/ti/fy

93

DID YOU KNOW?
Salary comes from a Latin word that means "money for salt," as part of a Roman soldier's pay. To be worth one's salt is to be worth one's *salary* or wages.

Spelling Practice

Word Analysis

Write **list words** to answer the following questions.

Which words contain these double consonants?
1. ss — repossess
2. rr — currency
3. tt — remittance

Which words contain the **er** letter combination?
4. certification
5. merchandise
6. collateral
7. interest

Word Application

Write a **list word** to complete each sentence.

1. We had to change our traveler's checks for foreign **currency** in France.
2. Our paper sets the titles of books and movies in **italics**.
3. Danielle uses a **calculator** to balance her checkbook.
4. Jack is paid a very generous **salary** by his new employer.
5. The list of items on the company's **invoice** is incorrect.
6. The U.S. Mint is a government **bureau** located in Washington D.C.
7. Linda receives monthly **interest** payments on her bank account.
8. Our latest **statistics** show that the company has made record sales and profits.

Synonyms and Antonyms

Write a **list word** that matches each synonym.

1. office	bureau	5. regulation	administration
2. wages	salary	6. approve	authorize
3. statement	invoice	7. security	collateral
4. money	currency	8. goods	merchandise

Write a **list word** that matches each antonym.

9. give or sell	repossess	11. printed name	signature
10. trainee	executive	12. blame	justify

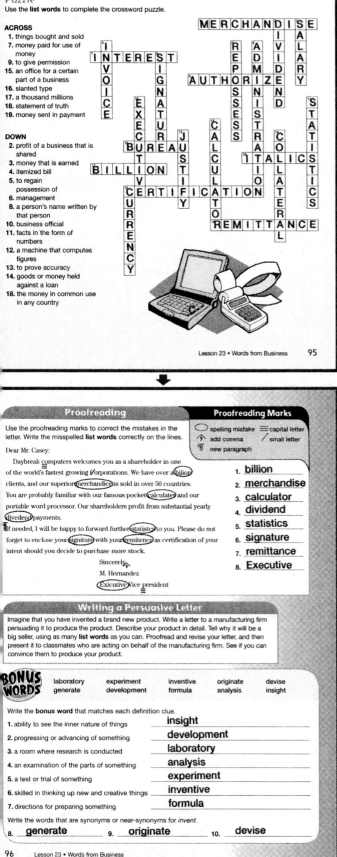

Puzzle
Use the **list words** to complete the crossword puzzle.

ACROSS
1. things bought and sold
7. money paid for use of money
9. to give permission
15. an office for a certain part of a business
16. slanted type
17. a thousand millions
18. statement of truth
19. money sent in payment

DOWN
2. profit of a business that is shared
3. money that is earned
4. itemized bill
5. to regain possession of
6. management
8. a person's name written by that person
10. business official
11. facts in the form of numbers
12. a machine that computes figures
13. to prove accuracy
14. goods or money held against a loan
18. the money in common use in any country

Crossword answers shown: MERCHANDISE, INTEREST, AUTHORIZE, BILLION, CERTIFICATION, ITALICS, REMITTANCE, BUREAU, INVOICE, EXECUTIVE, SIGNATURE, JUSTIFY, CURRENCY, CALCULATOR, ADMINISTRATION, REPOSSESS, DIVIDEND, SALARY, COLLATERAL, STATISTICS

Lesson 23 • Words from Business   95

Proofreading

Use the proofreading marks to correct the mistakes in the letter. Write the misspelled **list words** correctly on the lines.

Proofreading Marks
- ⟲ spelling mistake
- ⌃ add comma
- ¶ new paragraph
- ☰ capital letter
- / small letter

Dear Mr. Casey:

Daybreak computers welcomes you as a shareholder in one of the world's fastest growing Corporations. We have over a billion clients, and our superior merchandice is sold in over 50 countries. You are probably familiar with our famous pocket calculater and our portable word processor. Our shareholders profit from substantial yearly dividend payments. If needed, I will be happy to forward further statistcs to you. Please do not forget to enclose your signiture with your remitence as certification of your intent should you decide to purchase more stock.

Sincerely,
M. Hernandez
Exicutive Vice president

1. billion
2. merchandise
3. calculator
4. dividend
5. statistics
6. signature
7. remittance
8. Executive

Writing a Persuasive Letter
Imagine that you have invented a brand new product. Write a letter to a manufacturing firm persuading it to produce the product. Describe your product in detail. Tell why it will be a big seller, using as many **list words** as you can. Proofread and revise your letter, and then present it to classmates who are acting on behalf of the manufacturing firm. See if you can convince them to produce your product.

Write the **bonus word** that matches each definition clue.

1. ability to see the inner nature of things — insight
2. progressing or advancing of something — development
3. a room where research is conducted — laboratory
4. an examination of the parts of something — analysis
5. a test or trial of something — experiment
6. skilled in thinking up new and creative things — inventive
7. directions for preparing something — formula

Write the words that are synonyms or near-synonyms for *invent*.

8. generate   9. originate   10. devise

96   Lesson 23 • Words from Business

Puzzle Encourage students to think about the meanings of the **list words** as they complete the puzzle.

Spelling and Writing   Page 96
Proofreading Review the proofreading marks for this lesson using this sentence: *The ABC Companey, Located in ohio sells plants.* You may also wish to review the "new paragraph" mark and the use of commas in a letter.

Writing a Persuasive Letter Discuss ideas for inventions or new products. Ask students to describe their product, what made them think of inventing it, how it works or what it does, and why they think that it is important. To extend the activity, you may wish to have students create ads for their products to share in class.

Bonus Words   Page 96
Inventions Work with students to define the **bonus words**. Discuss how the words could apply to inventions. Encourage students to use the words in oral sentences. Point out that three of the words are synonyms: *generate, originate,* and *devise.*

Bonus Words Test
1. After careful **analysis**, I solved the problem.
2. As an **experiment**, she mixed the liquids together.
3. The **formula** for the new fuel was kept secret.
4. Jane is an **inventive** person with a creative mind.
5. Becky tried to **devise** a new way to package cereal.
6. Many new inventions **originate** out of necessity.
7. Paul worked in his **laboratory** on his new invention.
8. I aided the **development** of a new computer.
9. Inventors have **insight** into the needs of the future.
10. One invention may **generate** ideas for others.

Final Test
1. Mr. Hall must **justify** his annual tax deductions.
2. Did you receive a **dividend** on your stock?
3. Mrs. Vance is a top **executive** at the company.
4. If I pay now, the bank won't **repossess** my car.
5. The restaurant has served over a **billion** meals.
6. The contract's last paragraph was in **italics**.
7. The workers agreed to a temporary cut in **salary**.
8. Did you use a **calculator** to compute your taxes?
9. The bank will exchange foreign **currency** for a fee.
10. Businesses rely on **statistics** to chart their growth.
11. The new **administration** helped the company.
12. Ms. Wang's **signature** appears on our paychecks.
13. John used his car as **collateral** for a bank loan.
14. Did Leona check the figures listed on the **invoice**?
15. Full **remittance** on the bill is due in 30 days.
16. The state requires **certification** of all its plumbers.
17. The floor supervisor will **authorize** your refund.
18. The **interest** rate on our mortgage is 8.5 percent.
19. What a great sale on that **merchandise**!
20. Our Seattle **bureau** handles all our product sales.

Lessons 19–23 · Review

Objective
To review spelling words from fields of study

Spelling Strategy
Page 97

Tell students that in this lesson they will review the skills and spelling words they studied in Lessons 19–23. If needed, have students refer to previous spelling rules to review the information on words from geography, science, math, history, and business.

Spelling Practice
Pages 97–99

Lesson 19 Ask students to identify what the following words have in common: *meridian, bayou, axis, ecological,* and *precipitation. (They are all words related to the study of geography.)* Then, discuss the geographical meanings of the **list words**. Point out the additional write-on lines and encourage students to add two words from Lesson 19 that they found especially difficult, or assign certain words that seemed to be difficult for everyone. (Repeat this procedure for each lesson in the Review.) Emphasize that students should think of the meaning of each word as they complete the activity.

Lesson 20 Have students tell what subject they would be studying if they encountered these words: *molecular, fission, microbiology,* and *chemistry. (science)* Elicit that the **list words** are also from science, then discuss the words' meanings. Point out that each sentence contains clues to the answer.

Lesson 21 Write on the board: *theorem, equilateral, oblique,* and *tangent.* Elicit from students that these words are math terms. Have volunteers define the words. Point out that the **list words** are math terms and have students define them. Urge students to look closely at the spelling patterns of each word as they answer the questions.

Lesson 22 Ask students which of these words is not related to the study of history: *communism, socialist, therapy,* and *armistice. (therapy)* Elicit that the **list words** are from history, then discuss the words' meanings.

Lesson 23 Call on volunteers to tell how each of these words relates to business and finance: *dividend, invoice, interest,* and *merchandise.* Then, have students tell which of the following words would come between the guide words *itch* and *laugh* in a dictionary: *italics, itemize, interest, justify,* and *merchandise.*

Show What You Know
Page 100

Point out that this review will help students know if they have mastered the words in Lessons 19–23. Ask a volunteer to restate the directions and tell which word in the first item should be marked. *(capitolist)* When finished, have students write their misspelled words correctly.

64

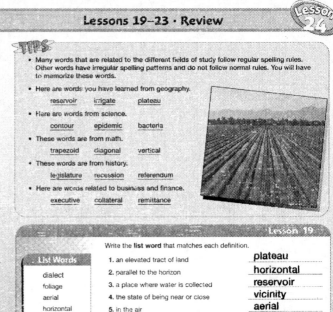

- Many words that are related to the different fields of study follow regular spelling rules. Other words have irregular spelling patterns and do not follow normal rules. You will have to memorize these words.
- Here are words you have learned from geography.
  reservoir   irrigate   plateau
- Here are words from science.
  contour   epidemic   bacteria
- These words are from math.
  trapezoid   diagonal   vertical
- These words are from history.
  legislature   recession   referendum
- Here are words related to business and finance.
  executive   collateral   remittance

Lesson 19

Write the list word that matches each definition.

List Words

dialect
foliage
aerial
horizontal
hurricane
reservoir
fertile
irrigate
plateau
vicinity

1. an elevated tract of land — plateau
2. parallel to the horizon — horizontal
3. a place where water is collected — reservoir
4. the state of being near or close — vicinity
5. in the air — aerial
6. a violent wind and rain storm — hurricane
7. leaves of a plant or a tree — foliage
8. language peculiar to a certain group of people — dialect
9. to supply land with water by means of ditches or artificial channels — irrigate
10. able to produce abundantly — fertile

97

Lesson 20

Write a list word to complete each sentence.

List Words

analyze
diagram
frequency
specific
contour
epidemic
bacteria
crucial
evolution
sociology

1. To discover how many times a wheel turns in an hour, determine the **frequency** of spins in one minute.
2. To assemble an object correctly, study a **diagram**.
3. A contagious disease may cause an **epidemic**.
4. If you examine something closely, you **analyze** it.
5. You may make many **crucial** decisions during a crisis.
6. Learn about the habits of people by studying **sociology**.
7. Dad practices **contour** farming in order to stop erosion.
8. If you have pneumonia, you may have **bacteria** in your lungs.
9. The process by which living things change is called **evolution**.
10. Choose a **specific** animal and study its characteristics.

Lesson 21

Write **list words** to answer the questions. Some words are used more than once.

List Words

symmetrical
minimum
trapezoid
denominator
protractor
equation
variable
diagonal
isosceles
vertical

Which words contain the ia vowel combination?
1. **variable**   2. **diagonal**

Which word contains the oi vowel combination?
3. **trapezoid**

Which word contains the io vowel combination?
4. **equation**

Which words contain three syllables?
5. **equation**   8. **protractor**
6. **minimum**   9. **vertical**
7. **trapezoid**

Which words contain four syllables?
10. **symmetrical**   12. **diagonal**
11. **variable**   13. **isosceles**

Which word contains five syllables?
14. **denominator**

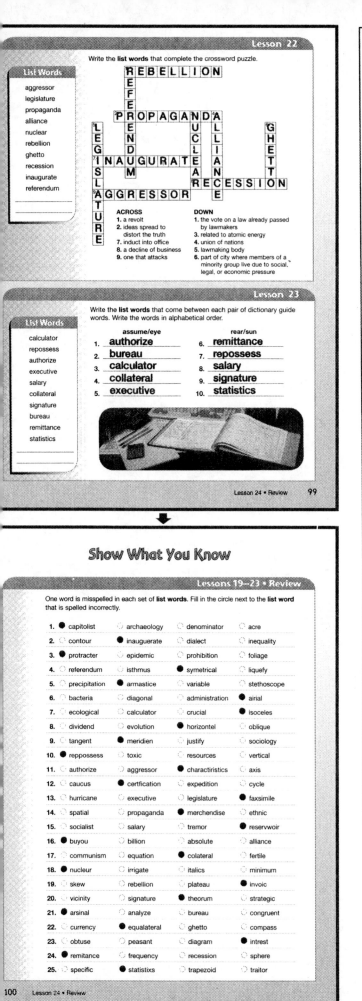

Lesson 22

Write the **list words** that complete the crossword puzzle.

List Words
- aggressor
- legislature
- propaganda
- alliance
- nuclear
- rebellion
- ghetto
- recession
- inaugurate
- referendum

ACROSS
1. a revolt
2. ideas spread to distort the truth
7. induct into office
8. a decline of business
9. one that attacks

DOWN
1. the vote on a law already passed by lawmakers
3. related to atomic energy
4. union of nations
5. lawmaking body
6. part of city where members of a minority group live due to social, legal, or economic pressure

Lesson 23

Write the **list words** that come between each pair of dictionary guide words. Write the words in alphabetical order.

List Words
- calculator
- repossess
- authorize
- executive
- salary
- collateral
- signature
- bureau
- remittance
- statistics

assume/eye
1. authorize
2. bureau
3. calculator
4. collateral
5. executive

rear/sun
6. remittance
7. repossess
8. salary
9. signature
10. statistics

Lesson 24 • Review   99

Show What You Know

Lessons 19–23 • Review

One word is misspelled in each set of **list words**. Fill in the circle next to the **list word** that is spelled incorrectly.

1. ● capitolist ○ archaeology ○ denominator ○ acre
2. ○ contour ● inauguerate ○ dialect ○ inequality
3. ● protracter ○ epidemic ○ prohibition ○ foliage
4. ○ referendum ○ isthmus ● symetrical ○ liquefy
5. ○ precipitation ● armastice ○ variable ○ stethoscope
6. ○ bacteria ○ diagonal ○ administration ● airial
7. ○ ecological ○ calculator ○ crucial ● isoceles
8. ○ dividend ○ evolution ● horizontel ○ oblique
9. ○ tangent ● meridien ○ justify ○ sociology
10. ● reppossess ○ toxic ○ resources ○ vertical
11. ○ authorize ○ aggressor ● charactiristics ○ axis
12. ○ caucus ● certfication ○ expedition ○ cycle
13. ○ hurricane ○ executive ○ legislature ● faxsimile
14. ○ spatial ○ propaganda ● merchendise ○ ethnic
15. ○ socialist ○ salary ○ tremor ● reservwoir
16. ● buyou ○ billion ○ absolute ○ alliance
17. ○ communism ○ equation ● colateral ○ fertile
18. ● nucleur ○ irrigate ○ italics ○ minimum
19. ○ skew ○ rebellion ○ plateau ● invoic
20. ○ vicinity ○ signature ● theorum ○ strategic
21. ● arsinal ○ analyze ○ bureau ○ congruent
22. ○ currency ● equalateral ○ ghetto ○ compass
23. ○ obtuse ○ peasant ○ diagram ● intrest
24. ● remitance ○ frequency ○ recession ○ sphere
25. ○ specific ● statistixs ○ trapezoid ○ traitor

100   Lesson 24 • Review

Final Test
1. Rosaria speaks the **dialect** of her native island.
2. Dr. Fermi will **analyze** the results of the blood test.
3. He wrote the mathematical **equation** on the board.
4. The **aggressor** nation was criticized by Congress.
5. Tim checked his addition with a **calculator**.
6. The tree's **foliage** turns bright orange in the fall.
7. The **diagram** shows all the bones of the hand.
8. The **minimum** payment is twenty dollars per month.
9. The state **legislature** enacts the laws of the state.
10. The store agreed not to **repossess** their furniture.
11. What a great **aerial** view from this tower!
12. They determined the **frequency** of rain in the area.
13. A **trapezoid** is a four-sided figure.
14. Is the newspaper spreading **propaganda**?
15. Mr. Juarez will have to **authorize** this loan.
16. A **horizontal** streak of red ran across the sky.
17. She researched the **specific** traits of mammals.
18. In the fraction $\frac{5}{6}$, six is the **denominator**.
19. The two nations formed a political **alliance**.
20. The company sent a top **executive** to the meeting.
21. A ferocious **hurricane** struck the Florida coast.
22. The scenic road follows the **contour** of the coast.
23. Should I use a **protractor** to measure the angle?
24. The treaty called for **nuclear** disarmament.
25. With an increase in **salary**, I can afford a new car.
26. Heavy rains increased the water in the **reservoir**.
27. Schools closed during the measles **epidemic**.
28. The **symmetrical** design is attractive.
29. The government worked to prevent a **rebellion**.
30. The Changs used their car as **collateral** for a loan.
31. The **fertile** land can support many species of plants.
32. Only a few **bacteria** lead to serious disease.
33. Weather in that region is quite **variable**.
34. Will the candidate campaign in the **ghetto**?
35. Ms. Town's **signature** appeared on the contract.
36. Dad will **irrigate** the corn fields.
37. That information is **crucial** for my report!
38. A **diagonal** line connects two corners of a square.
39. Many economists predict a long **recession**.
40. Sueann works at the federal **bureau** in the city.
41. The wind howled across the mountain **plateau**.
42. Fossils give proof to some theories of **evolution**.
43. An **isosceles** triangle has two or more equal sides.
44. When will we **inaugurate** our new president?
45. She sent her **remittance** in the form of a check.
46. Is there a restaurant in the **vicinity** of the hotel?
47. **Sociology** is the study of people and their behavior.
48. He drew a **vertical** line down the sidewalk.
49. The people voted on the seat belt **referendum**.
50. **Statistics** show when business is declining.

Words with ei and ie

Objective
To spell words with *ei* and *ie*

Pretest

1. Is that antique bowl a family **heirloom**?
2. The corner store has **convenient** weekend hours.
3. What a **fiend** that evil wizard is!
4. Macbeth committed a **heinous** act of murder.
5. This **receipt** shows that I paid for the sweater.
6. The curtains are made of **beige** and white fabric.
7. My new secretary is a very **efficient** person.
8. Speak to a **financier** about a savings program.
9. Will this chart show the company's **hierarchy**?
10. The storm gave us a brief **reprieve** from the heat.
11. Don't **besiege** Mrs. Delgado with questions.
12. Water freezes at thirty-two degrees **Fahrenheit**.
13. American settlers journeyed across the **frontier**.
14. The dentist spoke to us about good oral **hygiene**.
15. Let's walk out onto the **pier** and watch the boats.
16. Will too much **caffeine** make you nervous?
17. That sunset turned the sky a **fiery** red!
18. People do not always cry when they **grieve**.
19. The train is a little late, so please have **patience**.
20. The police used a **surveillance** camera.

Spelling Strategy
Page 101

After students have read the spelling rule, discuss which **list words** follow the rule and which do not. Make sure students know the meaning and pronunciation of the words, referring them to dictionaries when needed. Point out that *Fahrenheit* is capitalized because it comes from the name of a German scientist, Gabriel Daniel Fahrenheit, who developed the measurement scale.

Vocabulary Development You may wish to remind students to pay attention to the spelling of each **list word**, as well as its meaning.

Dictionary Skills If needed, briefly review the symbols used in sound-spellings. When students have completed the exercise, have them check any answers they are unsure of in a dictionary.

Spelling Practice
Pages 102–103

Word Analysis This exercise will help students remember the spelling of **list words** that both adhere to, and are exceptions to, this lesson's spelling rule.

Word Application Point out that each sentence has two underlined words to be replaced and that the answers students choose must make sense in the sentences and be spelled correctly.

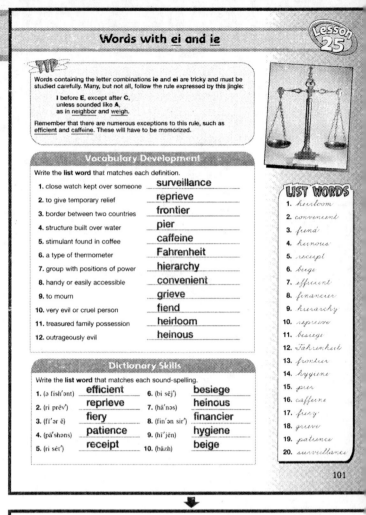

Words with ei and ie

TIP

Words containing the letter combinations ie and ei are tricky and must be studied carefully. Many, but not all, follow the rule expressed by this jingle:

I before E, except after C, unless sounded like A, as in neighbor and weigh.

Remember that there are numerous exceptions to this rule, such as efficient and caffeine. These will have to be memorized.

Vocabulary Development

Write the **list word** that matches each definition.

1. close watch kept over someone	surveillance
2. to give temporary relief	reprieve
3. border between two countries	frontier
4. structure built over water	pier
5. stimulant found in coffee	caffeine
6. a type of thermometer	Fahrenheit
7. group with positions of power	hierarchy
8. handy or easily accessible	convenient
9. to mourn	grieve
10. very evil or cruel person	fiend
11. treasured family possession	heirloom
12. outrageously evil	heinous

Dictionary Skills

Write the **list word** that matches each sound-spelling.

1. (ə fish'ənt) efficient 6. (bi sēj') besiege
2. (ri prēv') reprieve 7. (hā'nəs) heinous
3. (fī'ər ē) fiery 8. (fin'ən sir') financier
4. (pā'shəns) patience 9. (hī'jēn) hygiene
5. (ri sēt') receipt 10. (bāzh) beige

LIST WORDS

1. heirloom
2. convenient
3. fiend
4. heinous
5. receipt
6. beige
7. efficient
8. financier
9. hierarchy
10. reprieve
11. besiege
12. Fahrenheit
13. frontier
14. hygiene
15. pier
16. caffeine
17. fiery
18. grieve
19. patience
20. surveillance

101

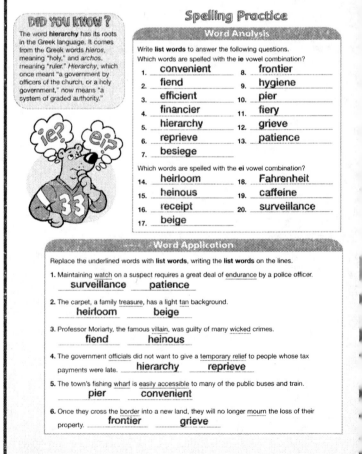

DID YOU KNOW?

The word **hierarchy** has its roots in the Greek language. It comes from the Greek words *hieros*, meaning "holy," and *archos*, meaning "ruler." *Hierarchy*, which once meant "a government by officers of the church, or a holy government," now means "a system of graded authority."

Spelling Practice

Word Analysis

Write **list words** to answer the following questions.
Which words are spelled with the **ie** vowel combination?

1. convenient 8. frontier
2. fiend 9. hygiene
3. efficient 10. pier
4. financier 11. fiery
5. hierarchy 12. grieve
6. reprieve 13. patience
7. besiege

Which words are spelled with the **ei** vowel combination?

14. heirloom 18. Fahrenheit
15. heinous 19. caffeine
16. receipt 20. surveillance
17. beige

Word Application

Replace the underlined words with **list words**, writing the **list words** on the lines.

1. Maintaining <u>watch</u> on a suspect requires a great deal of <u>endurance</u> by a police officer.
   surveillance patience

2. The carpet, a family <u>treasure</u>, has a light tan background.
   heirloom beige

3. Professor Moriarty, the famous <u>villain</u>, was guilty of many <u>wicked</u> crimes.
   fiend heinous

4. The government officials did not want to give a <u>temporary relief</u> to people whose tax payments were late. hierarchy reprieve

5. The town's fishing <u>wharf</u> is <u>easily accessible</u> to many of the public buses and train.
   pier convenient

6. Once they cross the <u>border</u> into a new land, they will no longer <u>mourn</u> the loss of their property. frontier grieve

102   Lesson 25 • Words with ei and ie

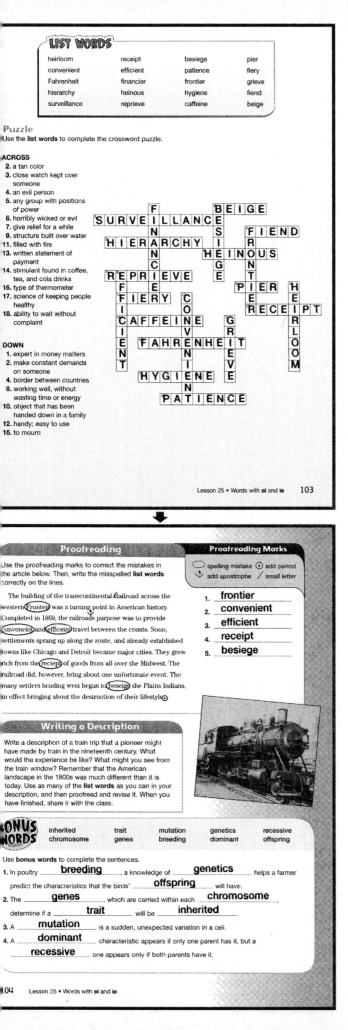

LIST WORDS

heirloom	receipt	besiege	pier
convenient	efficient	patience	fiery
Fahrenheit	financier	frontier	grieve
hierarchy	heinous	hygiene	fiend
surveillance	reprieve	caffeine	beige

Puzzle

Use the **list words** to complete the crossword puzzle.

ACROSS

2. a tan color
3. close watch kept over someone
4. an evil person
5. any group with positions of power
6. horribly wicked or evil
7. give relief for a while
9. structure built over water
11. filled with fire
13. written statement of payment
14. stimulant found in coffee, tea, and cola drinks
16. type of thermometer
17. science of keeping people healthy
18. ability to wait without complaint

DOWN

1. expert in money matters
2. make constant demands on someone
4. border between countries
8. working well, without wasting time or energy
10. object that has been handed down in a family
12. handy; easy to use
15. to mourn

Crossword solution:
BEIGE · SURVEILLANCE · FIEND · HIERARCHY · HEINOUS · REPRIEVE · PIER · FIERY · RECEIPT · CAFFEINE · FAHRENHEIT · HYGIENE · PATIENCE · FINANCIER · CONVENIENT · FRONTIER · GRIEVE · HEIRLOOM

Lesson 25 • Words with **ei** and **ie**   103

Proofreading

Use the proofreading marks to correct the mistakes in the article below. Then, write the misspelled **list words** correctly on the lines.

The building of the transcontinental railroad across the western Frontier was a turning point in American history. Completed in 1869, the railroads purpose was to provide Conveniet and efficeint travel between the coasts. Soon, settlements sprang up along the route, and already established towns like Chicago and Detroit became major cities. They grew rich from the reciept of goods from all over the Midwest. The railroad did, however, bring about one unfortunate event. The many settlers heading west began to beseige the Plains Indians, in effect bringing about the destruction of their lifestyle.

Proofreading Marks
- ⌒ spelling mistake
- ⊙ add period
- ⌄ add apostrophe
- / small letter

1. frontier
2. convenient
3. efficient
4. receipt
5. besiege

Writing a Description

Write a description of a train trip that a pioneer might have made by train in the nineteenth century. What would the experience be like? What might you see from the train window? Remember that the American landscape in the 1800s was much different than it is today. Use as many of the **list words** as you can in your description, and then proofread and revise it. When you have finished, share it with the class.

BONUS WORDS

| inherited | trait | mutation | genetics | recessive |
| chromosome | genes | breeding | dominant | offspring |

Use **bonus words** to complete the sentences.

1. In poultry __breeding__, a knowledge of __genetics__ helps a farmer predict the characteristics that the birds' __offspring__ will have.
2. The __genes__, which are carried within each __chromosome__, determine if a __trait__ will be __inherited__.
3. A __mutation__ is a sudden, unexpected variation in a cell.
4. A __dominant__ characteristic appears if only one parent has it, but a __recessive__ one appears only if both parents have it.

104   Lesson 25 • Words with **ei** and **ie**

Puzzle Remind students to use capital letters and to print neatly.

Spelling and Writing   Page 104

Proofreading Write *Ive lost my Blue jackit* on the board and use it to review the lesson's proofreading marks.

Writing a Description Discuss with students a long trip that they have taken. Have them contrast modern day traveling conditions with those of the nineteenth century. Point out that early passenger trains were much slower, had wooden benches, poor heat, and no air-conditioning. Urge students to consider these early traveling conditions when writing their descriptions.

Bonus Words   Page 104

Genetics Explain that the **bonus words** are related to genetics, the branch of biology that deals with heredity. Using dictionaries and biology books, help students learn the meanings of the words. Before students begin the exercise, have them use the **bonus words** in oral sentences to further their understanding of the words.

Bonus Words Test

1. Blue eyes are a **recessive** characteristic.
2. These cattle are being kept as **breeding** stock.
3. I **inherited** my left-handedness from my mother.
4. My father says artistic talent is in my **genes**.
5. Each **chromosome** carries genetic material.
6. One of the dog's **offspring** may have spots.
7. In some dogs, herding is a desirable **trait**.
8. That color is a normal variation, not a **mutation**.
9. Brown eyes are a **dominant** characteristic.
10. The average farmer today knows about **genetics**.

Final Test

1. Please don't **besiege** me with so much work!
2. Can you convert from **Fahrenheit** to Celsius?
3. Beyond the town is unexplored **frontier**.
4. Good **hygiene** helps prevent disease.
5. Is that your boat at the end of the **pier**?
6. This herbal tea has no **caffeine**.
7. The sun is actually a large **fiery** star.
8. I would prefer to **grieve** privately.
9. My **patience** resulted in a great photograph.
10. We kept the beehive under constant **surveillance**.
11. This pocket watch is an old family **heirloom**.
12. You look very attractive in that shade of **beige**.
13. Will the six o'clock train be the most **convenient**?
14. An **efficient** person can finish that task in an hour.
15. Dr. Jekyll became a **fiend** named Mr. Hyde.
16. A banker is only one kind of **financier**.
17. Such **heinous** crimes deserve long prison terms.
18. Anna worked her way up through the **hierarchy**.
19. I will need a **receipt** for that purchase.
20. Weekends are a **reprieve** from long work weeks.

Suffixes ance, ence, ce

Objective
To spell words with the suffixes ance, ence ce

Pretest
1. At what age does **adolescence** officially begin?
2. What a **coincidence** to meet you here!
3. A marathon runner needs to build up **endurance**.
4. The opening **performance** of the play is tonight.
5. I admire the **brilliance** of O'Keefe's paintings.
6. The **ambulance** arrived at the hospital.
7. Will the meeting **commence** promptly at noon?
8. The forest possessed the **essence** of tranquility.
9. Dr. Thompson has moved to a new **residence**.
10. Is it your **preference** to stay home?
11. **Arrogance** is not a positive personal quality.
12. I've kept all my **correspondence** from Uncle Ken.
13. The district attorney presented the **evidence**.
14. What is the **significance** of the stripes on the flag?
15. The ballerina moves with grace and **elegance**.
16. There is little **clearance** under that bridge.
17. A dog's **defiance** of commands is not good.
18. You should take your dog to **obedience** school.
19. Anger and **vengeance** can cause problems.
20. The thunder's sudden **occurrence** scared me.

Spelling Strategy
Page 105

Discuss the spelling rule with students. For more examples of verbs that take *ance* and *ence* to form nouns, use *allow*, *exist*, and *excel*. For adjectives ending in *ant* or *ent* that take *ce* to form nouns, use *silent*, *ignorant*, and *negligent*. Then, work with students to discuss and define each **list word**.

Vocabulary Development Before the exercise, have volunteers identify the **list words** that match the synonym *incident* (*occurrence*) and the definition "act of obeying; submission" (*obedience*).

Dictionary Skills Have students begin the exercise by writing the **list words** in alphabetical order. Next, have them separate the words into syllables. Finally, have students check their syllabication in dictionaries.

Spelling Practice
Pages 106–107

Word Analysis To show verbs that do or do not change when suffixes are added, use *disturb/disturbance*; *excel/excellence*; and *insure/insurance*. To show how adjectives change, use *silent/silence* and *ignorant/ignorance*.

Word Application Remind students to use context clues to decide which **list word** best completes each sentence. To extend, have students write sentences for the distractors that classmates can solve.

TIP
The suffixes **ance**, **ence**, and **ce** usually mean "the act of." The suffixes **ance** and **ence** are usually added to verbs to make nouns. The suffix **ce** is usually added to adjectives to make nouns.

Root Word	Meaning	Plus Suffix	New Meaning
occur (v.)	"to happen"	occurrence	"the act of occurring" (n)
endure (v.)	"to last"	endurance	"the act of lasting" (n)
arrogant (adj.)	"haughty"	arrogance	"the act of being haughty" (n)

Vocabulary Development
Write the **list word** that matches each synonym or definition.

1. revenge **vengeance**
2. begin **commence**
3. teen years **adolescence**
4. proof **evidence**
5. importance **significance**
6. medical vehicle **ambulance**
7. richness; grace **elegance**
8. letter writing **correspondence**
9. one's first choice **preference**
10. brightness **brilliance**

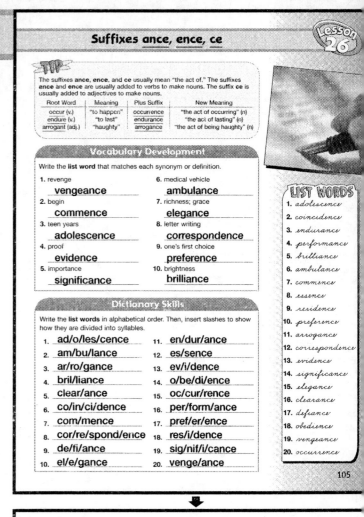

LIST WORDS
1. adolescence
2. coincidence
3. endurance
4. performance
5. brilliance
6. ambulance
7. commence
8. essence
9. residence
10. preference
11. arrogance
12. correspondence
13. evidence
14. significance
15. elegance
16. clearance
17. defiance
18. obedience
19. vengeance
20. occurrence

Dictionary Skills
Write the **list words** in alphabetical order. Then, insert slashes to show how they are divided into syllables.

1. ad/o/les/cence
2. am/bu/lance
3. ar/ro/gance
4. bril/liance
5. clear/ance
6. co/in/ci/dence
7. com/mence
8. cor/re/spond/ence
9. de/fi/ance
10. el/e/gance
11. en/dur/ance
12. es/sence
13. ev/i/dence
14. o/be/di/ence
15. oc/cur/rence
16. per/form/ance
17. pref/er/ence
18. res/i/dence
19. sig/nif/i/cance
20. venge/ance

105

DID YOU KNOW?
The word **commence** comes from the fourteenth century Middle English word *comencen* and the Middle French word *comencer*. Even earlier roots are in the Latin *com*, which means "with or together," and *initiare*, which means "to begin or initiate."

Spelling Practice
Word Analysis
Form **list words** by adding suffixes to these verbs to make nouns. You will need to change the form of some verbs before adding the suffix.

1. clear **clearance**
2. correspond **correspondence**
3. endure **endurance**
4. prefer **preference**
5. defy **defiance**
6. reside **residence**
7. perform **performance**
8. occur **occurrence**

Form **list words** by adding suffixes to these adjectives to make nouns. You will need to change the form of each adjective before adding the suffix.

9. brilliant **brilliance**
10. coincidental **coincidence**
11. significant **significance**
12. adolescent **adolescence**
13. arrogant **arrogance**
14. elegant **elegance**
15. obedient **obedience**
16. evident **evidence**

Word Application
Select a **list word** from the choices in parentheses to complete each sentence. Write your answer on the line.

1. Ken's **brilliance** is evident by his A+ average. (vengeance, brilliance)
2. Because it was going out of business, the store had a **clearance** sale. (coincidence, clearance)
3. I took my dog to **obedience** school because he was difficult to control. (obedience, vengeance)
4. By **coincidence**, Marcia and I wore the same outfit to school yesterday. (coincidence, commence)
5. Doug showed a great deal of **defiance** when he stood up to that bully. (obedience, defiance)
6. The tornado's sudden **occurrence** during the storm frightened people. (essence, occurrence)
7. The **ambulance** took Peter to the hospital. (ambulance, adolescence)
8. The Ackmans built a new **residence** on Oak Lane. (correspondence, residence)
9. His **arrogance** cost him several friends. (elegance, arrogance)
10. Della's **performance** in the play was super. (performance, preference)

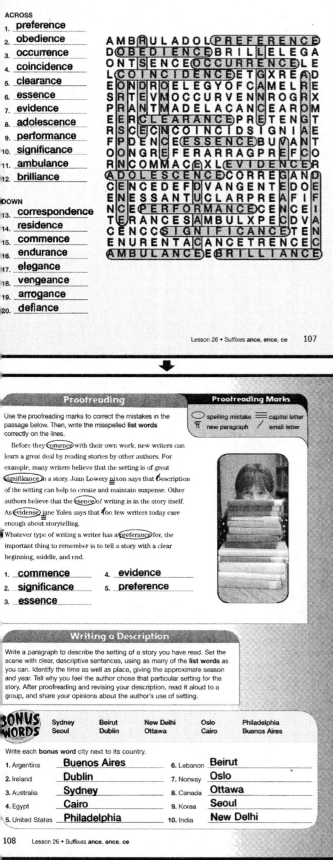

The left portion shows a reproduced student page:

LIST WORDS

adolescence	ambulance	essence	clearance
coincidence	commence	defiance	arrogance
endurance	significance	evidence	obedience
performance	residence	brilliance	vengeance
correspondence	preference	elegance	occurrence

Word Search Puzzle

The **list words** are hidden across and down in this puzzle. Circle the words in the puzzle and write them on the lines.

ACROSS
1. preference
2. obedience
3. occurrence
4. coincidence
5. clearance
6. essence
7. evidence
8. adolescence
9. performance
10. significance
11. ambulance
12. brilliance

DOWN
13. correspondence
14. residence
15. commence
16. endurance
17. elegance
18. vengeance
19. arrogance
20. defiance

Lesson 26 • Suffixes ance, ence, ce   107

Proofreading

Use the proofreading marks to correct the mistakes in the passage below. Then, write the misspelled **list words** correctly on the lines.

Proofreading Marks
◯ spelling mistake
¶ new paragraph
≡ capital letter
/ small letter

Before they comence with their own work, new writers can learn a great deal by reading stories by other authors. For example, many writers believe that the setting is of great significanse in a story. Joan Lowery nixon says that description of the setting can help to create and maintain suspense. Other authors believe that the esence of writing is in the story itself. As evidense jane Yolen says that too few writers today care enough about storytelling. Whatever type of writing a writer has a preferance for, the important thing to remember is to tell a story with a clear beginning, middle, and end.

1. commence
2. significance
3. essence
4. evidence
5. preference

Writing a Description

Write a paragraph to describe the setting of a story you have read. Set the scene with clear, descriptive sentences, using as many of the **list words** as you can. Identify the time as well as place, giving the approximate season and year. Tell why you feel the author chose that particular setting for the story. After proofreading and revising your description, read it aloud to a group, and share your opinions about the author's use of setting.

BONUS WORDS

| Sydney | Beirut | New Delhi | Oslo | Philadelphia |
| Seoul | Dublin | Ottawa | Cairo | Buenos Aires |

Write each **bonus word** city next to its country.

1. Argentina — Buenos Aires
2. Ireland — Dublin
3. Australia — Sydney
4. Egypt — Cairo
5. United States — Philadelphia
6. Lebanon — Beirut
7. Norway — Oslo
8. Canada — Ottawa
9. Korea — Seoul
10. India — New Delhi

108   Lesson 26 • Suffixes ance, ence, ce

Word Search Puzzle Make sure students understand that the words appear both horizontally and vertically, and that after they find and circle the words, they are to write them on the lines to the left of the puzzle.

Spelling and Writing   Page 108

Proofreading Review the proofreading marks for this lesson, including the "new paragraph" mark.

Writing a Description Remind students that a setting is a combination of time and place. Have students each select a favorite story, then call on volunteers to describe its setting. Urge students to draw prewriting webs to brainstorm more ideas about their settings. When finished, provide time for presentation and discussion.

Bonus Words   Page 108

Cities Help students to locate the **bonus word** cities on a globe or atlas. Point out the continent and country in which each city is located. Then, have students work in groups to research the cities and create brief paragraphs describing aspects of their settings, such as appearance, conditions, and climate.

Bonus Words Test
1. **Beirut** is the capital and chief port of Lebanon.
2. **Cairo**, the capital of Egypt, is on the Nile delta.
3. A museum of Viking ships exists in **Oslo**, Norway.
4. **Philadelphia** was founded in 1682.
5. **Ottawa**, Canada, is in the province of Ontario.
6. **Sydney** is Australia's oldest and largest city.
7. The summer Olympics were held in **Seoul**, Korea.
8. **Buenos Aires**, Argentina, was founded in 1536.
9. **Dublin**, Ireland, is located on the Liffey River.
10. **New Delhi** is the capital of India.

Final Test
1. My dentist maintains an office at her **residence**.
2. That grizzly bear fought with **vengeance**!
3. The Constitution is a document of **significance**.
4. The actors took a bow after their **performance**.
5. The **essence** of Thoreau's message is freedom.
6. **Obedience** and loyalty are attributes of dogs.
7. Did the witness present the letter as **evidence**?
8. Exercise will increase your physical **endurance**.
9. Boys' voices grow deeper during **adolescence**.
10. Her **arrogance** made her lose the election.
11. Dad drives an **ambulance** for the fire department.
12. The road crew is responsible for snow **clearance**.
13. I enjoy my **correspondence** with my pen pal.
14. The show will **commence** after these commercials.
15. By **coincidence**, Mr. Jones lives on Jones Street.
16. **Defiance** of the laws may lead to a person's arrest.
17. I admire the **brilliance** of the poet Maya Angelou.
18. The **elegance** of the palace is legendary.
19. Please cast your vote to indicate your **preference**.
20. Is the sighting of a comet a rare **occurrence**?

69

y as a Vowel

Objective
To spell words in which _y_ is a vowel

Pretest

1. Is _gleeful_ an **antonym** for _sorrowful?_
2. It was unkind of her to make that **cynical** remark.
3. Pan is a Greek **mythical** god of forests and fields.
4. The **python** is a very large, nonpoisonous snake.
5. Write a two-paragraph **synopsis** of the novel.
6. The **crystals** in her earrings reflected the sunlight.
7. Use an **encyclopedia** to verify facts in your report.
8. Is **oxygen** gas the main component of air?
9. The sauce will **solidify** if it isn't stirred.
10. Is nylon a **synthetic** fabric?
11. That **cyclone** is a violent windstorm!
12. **Hydrogen** gas explodes when it's near a flame.
13. A blizzard can **paralyze** a city.
14. A **sympathetic** friend cares about your problems.
15. Hot humid summers are **typical** in the South.
16. This juice can is an example of a **cylinder**.
17. A **pyramid** has triangular sides.
18. The **physician** examined Toby's sore throat.
19. We analyzed the **symbolic** elements in the art.
20. Erica played the **cymbals** in the school orchestra.

Spelling Strategy   **Page 109**

Discuss the spelling rule. Then, say the following words: _sinister, lyric, physical, disaster, dynamite, chimes,_ and _Wyoming._ Ask students if they can tell whether the long _i_ or short _i_ sounds in the words are spelled with _y._ Then, write the words on the board. Emphasize that the only way to know whether a word is spelled with a _y_ is to study and practice the word. Have students identify the sound for _y_ in the **list words**. Then, help students define the words and use them in oral sentences.

Vocabulary Development To extend, have students find antonyms for these words: _mythical_ (real), _sympathetic_ (uncaring), _solidify_ (melt), and _synthetic_ (natural).

Dictionary Skills If desired, have students find the sound-spellings for additional **list words** in dictionaries.

Spelling Practice   **Pages 110–111**
Word Analysis Refer students to their dictionaries if they are unsure of the pronunciation of _y_ in any **list words**.

Analogies Write on the board _Hawk is to bird as _____ is to snake._ Ask students which **list word** completes the analogy, and why. (_python; type of snake_)

Hidden Words. Write on the board, _The old horse loped along the trail._ Explain that some words "hide" in other words. Ask a volunteer to identify the **list word** containing the word _loped._ (_encyclopedia_)

y as a Vowel   Lesson 27

When the letter _y_ comes in the middle or at the end of a word, it is usually a vowel. The vowel _y_ can spell the long e sound, the long i sound, or the short i sound.

    everything   dry   python   mythical

In the **list words**, _y_ spells either the /ī/ sound or the /ĭ/ sound. There is no consistent rule to help you know when a word is spelled with an _i_ or with a _y_. You will have to memorize and practice spelling the words.

Vocabulary Development

Write the **list word** from column **B** that matches the definition or synonym in column **A**.

A		B
1. harden	solidify	paralyze
2. tornado	cyclone	mythical
3. doctor	physician	synthetic
4. outline	synopsis	cyclone
5. usual	typical	encyclopedia
6. mocking	cynical	cymbals
7. legendary	mythical	physician
8. artificial	synthetic	synopsis
9. caring	sympathetic	cynical
10. reference book	encyclopedia	sympathetic
11. instruments	cymbals	typical
12. immobilize	paralyze	solidify

Dictionary Skills

Write the **list word** that matches each sound-spelling.

1. (äk′si jən) oxygen
2. (an′tə nim) antonym
3. (kris′t'lz) crystals
4. (sim bäl′ik) symbolic
5. (hī′drə jən) hydrogen
6. (sil′ən dər) cylinder
7. (pir′ə mid) pyramid
8. (pī′thän) python

LIST WORDS
1. antonym
2. cynical
3. mythical
4. python
5. synopsis
6. crystals
7. encyclopedia
8. oxygen
9. solidify
10. synthetic
11. cyclone
12. hydrogen
13. paralyze
14. sympathetic
15. typical
16. cylinder
17. pyramid
18. physician
19. symbolic
20. cymbals

109

DID YOU KNOW ?
The Greek word from which we get **encyclopedia** is made up of three words, _en_ meaning "in," _kyklos_ meaning "a circle," and _paidea_ meaning "education." An _encyclopedia_ is, therefore, a work that deals with all subjects that lie within the circle of education.

Spelling Practice
Word Analysis

Write the **list words** in which _y_ spells the short i sound.

1. antonym
2. cynical
3. mythical
4. synopsis
5. crystals
6. oxygen
7. synthetic
8. sympathetic
9. typical
10. cylinder
11. pyramid
12. physician
13. symbolic
14. cymbals

Write the **list words** in which _y_ spells the long i sound.

15. python
16. encyclopedia
17. solidify
18. cyclone
19. hydrogen
20. paralyze

Analogies

Write a **list word** to complete each analogy.

1. Real is to factual as imaginary is to **mythical**.
2. **Oxygen** is to breathe as food is to eat.
3. Melt is to **solidify** as hot is to cold.
4. **Sympathetic** is to friend as uncaring is to enemy.
5. Square is to box as **cylinder** is to tin can.
6. Flute is to clarinet as **cymbals** are to drums.

Hidden Words

You will find part of a **list word** in italic type in each of the following clues. Write the **list word** on the line.

1. It towers _amid_ the stones. **pyramid**
2. The _symbol_ @ means "at" or "each." **symbolic**
3. An _ant_ is the opposite size of an elephant. **antonym**
4. No one would want to _clone_ a storm. **cyclone**
5. He gave his _sis_ a summary of the movie. **synopsis**
6. Put a _lid_ on the container or the liquid contents will harden. **solidify**

110   Lesson 27 • y as a Vowel

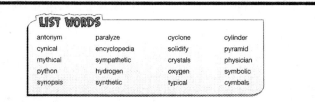

LIST WORDS

antonym	paralyze	cyclone	cylinder
cynical	encyclopedia	solidify	pyramid
mythical	sympathetic	crystals	physician
python	hydrogen	oxygen	symbolic
synopsis	synthetic	typical	cymbals

Puzzle
Use the **list words** to complete the crossword puzzle.

ACROSS
2. loss of the ability to move
4. book with information on all branches of knowledge
6. round brass plates used in percussion section of band
7. doubting others are sincere
10. round object with flat ends
11. a very large snake
12. a summary or short outline
15. a true example of its kind
16. showing feelings of kindness and understanding for another
17. a word opposite in meaning to another
18. a violent wind storm
19. a colorless, odorless gas; the lightest of all known substances

DOWN
1. huge triangular structure; royal tomb of the Egyptians
3. of or expressed by a sign or a mark that stands for something else
5. doctor
8. artificial; manufactured
9. clear transparent stones that look like glass
12. to harden; become solid
13. odorless, colorless gas that is essential to life
14. imaginary; not real

Crossword grid answers:
PARALYZE, PYRAMID, ENCYCLOPEDIA, SYMBOLIC, CYMBALS, PHYSICIAN, CYNICAL, CYLINDER, SYNTHETIC, CRYSTALS, PYTHON, SYNOPSIS, MYTHICAL, TYPICAL, SOLIDIFY, OXYGEN, SYMPATHETIC, ANTONYM, CYCLONE, HYDROGEN

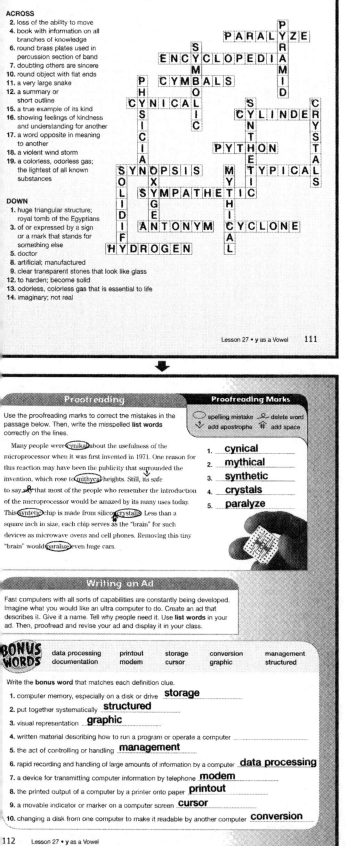

Proofreading

Use the proofreading marks to correct the mistakes in the passage below. Then, write the misspelled **list words** correctly on the lines.

Proofreading Marks
- ◯ spelling mistake
- ⚮ delete word
- ˅ add apostrophe
- # add space

Many people were cynikal about the usefulness of the microprocessor when it was first invented in 1971. One reason for this reaction may have been the publicity that surrounded the invention, which rose to mithycal heights. Still, its safe to say sy that most of the people who remember the introduction of the microprocessor would be amazed by its many uses today. This syntetic chip is made from silicon crystalls. Less than a square inch in size, each chip serves as the "brain" for such devices as microwave ovens and cell phones. Removing this tiny "brain" would paralize even huge cars.

1. cynical
2. mythical
3. synthetic
4. crystals
5. paralyze

Writing an Ad

Fast computers with all sorts of capabilities are constantly being developed. Imagine what you would like an ultra computer to do. Create an ad that describes it. Give it a name. Tell why people need it. Use **list words** in your ad. Then, proofread and revise your ad and display it in your class.

BONUS WORDS

data processing	printout	storage	conversion	management
documentation	modem	cursor	graphic	structured

Write the **bonus word** that matches each definition clue.

1. computer memory, especially on a disk or drive **storage**
2. put together systematically **structured**
3. visual representation **graphic**
4. written material describing how to run a program or operate a computer **documentation**
5. the act of controlling or handling **management**
6. rapid recording and handling of large amounts of information by a computer **data processing**
7. a device for transmitting computer information by telephone **modem**
8. the printed output of a computer by a printer onto paper **printout**
9. a movable indicator or marker on a computer screen **cursor**
10. changing a disk from one computer to make it readable by another computer **conversion**

Puzzle Remind students to use each puzzle clue and the number of letter boxes to determine an answer.

Spelling and Writing   Page 112

Proofreading Use this sentence to demonstrate the proofreading marks for the lesson: *Mias newcomputer isnt to wourking.*

Writing an Ad Discuss with students what they already know about computers. Then, invite students to suggest new functions that they would like computers to perform. Encourage students to be creative. Write their ideas on the board and have students refer to them as they complete the writing activity. You may wish to have students assemble their ads in a computer-type magazine.

Bonus Words   Page 112

Computers Work with students to define the **bonus words**. Discuss how these words apply to computers and information technology. If possible, illustrate some or all of the words with a computer demonstration.

Bonus Words Test
1. I converse with computer pals by using a **modem**.
2. A computer allows **management** of our records.
3. His computer came with much **documentation**.
4. This screen provides greater **graphic** capabilities.
5. Disk **conversion** makes computers compatible.
6. This program is **structured** for beginners.
7. This hard disk provides 40 megabytes of **storage**.
8. The store sent me a **printout** of my charges.
9. Our **data processing** department is upstairs.
10. Julio moved the **cursor** to the third line of the text.

Final Test
1. A heart is a **symbolic** expression of love.
2. He built a **pyramid** of cards on the kitchen table.
3. Horror movies **paralyze** me with fear.
4. Is a tornado an example of a **cyclone**?
5. Karen gave us a **synopsis** of the play she saw.
6. The Land of the Little People is a **mythical** place.
7. An **antonym** for *exciting* is *dull*.
8. What a loud crashing sound those **cymbals** make!
9. She was **sympathetic** to everyone's complaints.
10. **Hydrogen** is the lightest of all known substances.
11. **Crystals** were once used to build radios.
12. A **cynical** person mocks other people's ideas.
13. A **python** can coil around its victim and crush it.
14. Mercury does not **solidify** at room temperature.
15. I found that information in the **encyclopedia**.
16. Are red blood cells rich in **oxygen**?
17. **Synthetic** fibers are man-made substances.
18. A **typical** picnic includes chicken and watermelon.
19. The young **physician** will open a walk-in clinic.
20. Is a **cylinder** round with two flat ends?

Words from Music

Objective
To spell Words from music

Pretest

1. The singer sang an **aria** from my favorite opera.
2. Do the number of **decibels** represent the volume?
3. The **maestro** bowed as everyone applauded.
4. The conductor stood at the **podium**.
5. Six trumpets played the sharp **staccato** notes.
6. Our school **auditorium** has a large stage.
7. For an **encore**, the band played its theme song.
8. Listen to this **medley** of songs about summer.
9. I play violin for two groups, a trio and a **quartet**.
10. Our new car radio has **stereophonic** sound.
11. Is the **ballerina** in pink the lead dancer?
12. Last week, a local jazz **ensemble** gave a concert.
13. This is easy to sing, because it is so **melodic**.
14. My next selection will be a Russian **rhapsody**.
15. A **synthesizer** can sound like many instruments.
16. My brother wanted me to hear this **concerto**.
17. The melody in a **fugue** is heard in all the parts.
18. The **pianist** says that the piano needs tuning.
19. That music has great **rhythm**!
20. Each bar on a **xylophone** has a different pitch.

Spelling Strategy   *Page 113*

After students have read the spelling rule, discuss which **list words** are familiar to students and which are not. Through discussion and dictionary use, help students understand the meanings of the words. Discuss the spelling of each word and how students can best remember it.

Vocabulary Development Encourage students to check their answers against the entries in their dictionaries.

Dictionary Skills To check mastery of sound-spelling symbols and letters, encourage students to try to complete this exercise without any review. After students finish, discuss any problems they encountered.

Spelling Practice   *Pages 114–115*

Word Analysis To extend the activity, you may wish to have students find other words beginning with *deci, quar, syn, pod,* and *stereo*.

Word Application Point out that although more than one answer might possibly be correct, only one **list word** will make the most sense in each sentence. After students finish the exercise, discuss their answers and how they arrived at them.

72

Words from Music

TIP
The world of music has a language of its own. Many musical words, such as medley, are also used in other contexts. These **list words** are all related to music. Many of the words follow spelling rules that you know. Some will have to be learned by memory.

Vocabulary Development

Write the **list word** that matches each definition.

1. electronic sound reproducer	**synthesizer**
2. reproduction of sound with two speakers	**stereophonic**
3. form or pattern of movement in music	**rhythm**
4. one who plays the piano	**pianist**
5. selection of songs played as one piece	**medley**
6. room where an audience gathers	**auditorium**
7. female ballet dancer	**ballerina**
8. selection for solo instrument plus orchestra	**concerto**
9. master composer or conductor	**maestro**
10. variably-sized group of musicians	**ensemble**
11. a song in an opera or oratorio	**aria**

LIST WORDS
1. aria
2. decibels
3. maestro
4. podium
5. staccato
6. auditorium
7. encore
8. medley
9. quartet
10. stereophonic
11. ballerina
12. ensemble
13. melodic
14. rhapsody
15. synthesizer
16. concerto
17. fugue
18. pianist
19. rhythm
20. xylophone

Dictionary Skills

Write the **list word** that matches each sound-spelling.

1. (stə kät′ō) **staccato**
2. (kwôr tet′) **quartet**
3. (des′ə bəlz) **decibels**
4. (rap′sə dē) **rhapsody**
5. (zī′lə fōn) **xylophone**
6. (kən cher′tō) **concerto**
7. (mə läd′ik) **melodic**
8. (är′ē ə) **aria**
9. (fyōog) **fugue**
10. (än′kôr) **encore**
11. (pō′dē əm) **podium**
12. (mīs′trō) **maestro**

113

DID YOU KNOW?
A **rhapsody** in ancient Greece was a long epic poem that was recited without interruption. It came from a word meaning "one who strings songs together," from a Greek word meaning "to stitch." Probably, each *rhapsody* was so long as to seem like many songs "stitched together."

Spelling Practice

Word Analysis

Write the **list word** that contains the same prefix, root, or base word as the word given.

1. telephone	**xylophone**	5. decimal	**decibels**
2. quarter	**quartet**	6. melodious	**melodic**
3. stereogram	**stereophonic**	7. podiatry	**podium**
4. synthetic	**synthesizer**	8. audition	**auditorium**

Write the **list words** containing the elements given below.

ia		ue or ae	
9. **aria**		11. **maestro**	
10. **pianist**		12. **fugue**	

Write the **list words** containing one or two syllables.

13. **maestro**		16. **quartet**	
14. **encore**		17. **fugue**	
15. **medley**		18. **rhythm**	

Word Application

Write a **list word** to complete each sentence.

1. The **ballerina** strode to the center of the stage and began to dance.
2. The diva will sing an **aria** from the opera La Boheme.
3. A **synthesizer** can sound like any of a number of instruments.
4. Tina taught Matt how to play a scale on his toy **xylophone**.
5. Often, the **decibels** at a rock concert can be harmful to hearing.
6. The chorale's last selection was a **medley** of three popular songs.
7. A sharp **staccato** burst from the trumpet interrupted the violins.
8. Use the headset and you can listen in **stereophonic** sound.
9. At the end of the concert, the audience asked for an **encore**.
10. Nick stood at the **podium**, ready to conduct his first symphony.
11. An **ensemble** of voices rang joyously through the hall.
12. For the final concert, every seat in the **auditorium** was filled.

114   Lesson 28 • Words from Music

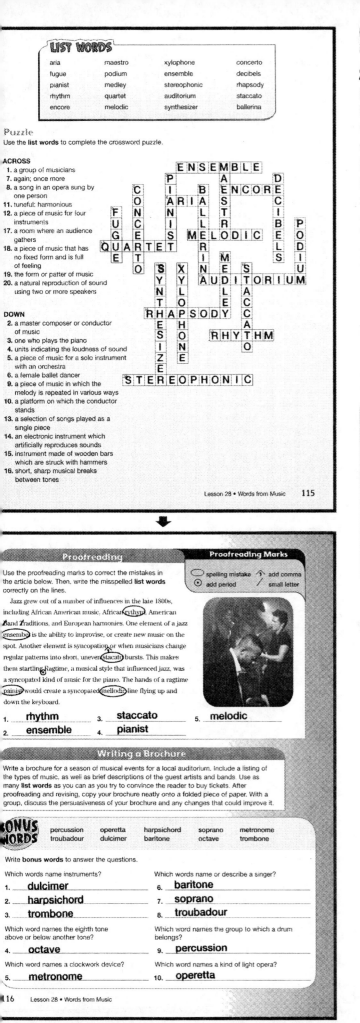

LIST WORDS

aria	maestro	xylophone	concerto
fugue	podium	ensemble	decibels
pianist	medley	stereophonic	rhapsody
rhythm	quartet	auditorium	staccato
encore	melodic	synthesizer	ballerina

Puzzle
Use the **list words** to complete the crossword puzzle.

ACROSS
1. a group of musicians
7. again; once more
8. a song in an opera sung by one person
11. tuneful; harmonious
12. a piece of music for four instruments
17. a room where an audience gathers
18. a piece of music that has no fixed form and is full of feeling
19. the form or patter of music
20. a natural reproduction of sound using two or more speakers

DOWN
2. a master composer or conductor of music
3. one who plays the piano
4. units indicating the loudness of sound
5. a piece of music for a solo instrument with an orchestra
6. a female ballet dancer
9. a piece of music in which the melody is repeated in various ways
10. a platform on which the conductor stands
13. a selection of songs played as a single piece
14. an electronic instrument which artificially reproduces sounds
15. instrument made of wooden bars which are struck with hammers
16. short, sharp musical breaks between tones

Lesson 28 • Words from Music   115

Proofreading
Use the proofreading marks to correct the mistakes in the article below. Then, write the misspelled **list words** correctly on the lines.

Jazz grew out of a number of influences in the late 1800s, including African American music, African rythm, American band traditions, and European harmonies. One element of a jazz ensemble is the ability to improvise, or create new music on the spot. Another element is syncopation, or when musicians change regular patterns into short, uneven staccato bursts. This makes them startling. Ragtime, a musical style that influenced jazz, was a syncopated kind of music for the piano. The hands of a ragtime painist would create a syncopated melodic line flying up and down the keyboard.

Proofreading Marks
- spelling mistake
- add period
- add comma
- small letter

1. rhythm
2. ensemble
3. staccato
4. pianist
5. melodic

Writing a Brochure
Write a brochure for a season of musical events for a local auditorium. Include a listing of the types of music, as well as brief descriptions of the guest artists and bands. Use as many **list words** as you can as you try to convince the reader to buy tickets. After proofreading and revising, copy your brochure neatly onto a folded piece of paper. With a group, discuss the persuasiveness of your brochure and any changes that could improve it.

BONUS WORDS

percussion	operetta	harpsichord	soprano	metronome
troubadour	dulcimer	baritone	octave	trombone

Write **bonus words** to answer the questions.

Which words name instruments?
1. dulcimer
2. harpsichord
3. trombone

Which word names the eighth tone above or below another tone?
4. octave

Which word names a clockwork device?
5. metronome

Which words name or describe a singer?
6. baritone
7. soprano
8. troubadour

Which word names the group to which a drum belongs?
9. percussion

Which word names a kind of light opera?
10. operetta

116   Lesson 28 • Words from Music

Puzzle Remind students that each answer has two clues: its definition and its number of letters.

Spelling and Writing   Page 116
Proofreading Write this sentence on the board and use it to demonstrate the proofreading marks: *Although the Concirt was sold out there were empty seats in the Hall*

Writing a Brochure Encourage students to think of the kinds of music they or their parents like to hear. Discuss local musical events that they have seen advertised. Tell students that for this activity, they can invent guest artists and bands, or name and describe real ones. When finished, you may wish to have students create a display of their brochures.

Bonus Words   Page 116
Music Explain that the **bonus words** are also related to music. If available, display a dictionary of musical terms. Otherwise, use any standard dictionary to research the meanings of unfamiliar words. Encourage students to talk about their own musical experiences and to use the **bonus words** in oral sentences.

Bonus Words Test
1. My mother is a **soprano** in our local chorus.
2. The singer accompanied himself on a **dulcimer**.
3. A drum is a **percussion** instrument.
4. The queen enjoyed the songs of the **troubadour**.
5. Each marcher in the first row played a **trombone**.
6. My brother has a beautiful **baritone** voice.
7. My fingers can span one **octave** on a piano.
8. An **operetta** combines music and dialogue.
9. A **harpsichord** sounds a little like a piano.
10. The beat of the **metronome** helps me keep time.

Final Test
1. Listen while they play the first **concerto**.
2. A **fugue** has repetitive parts for several voices.
3. That concert **pianist** practices six hours a day.
4. Tap out the **rhythm** on the bongo drums.
5. Is a **xylophone** played with mallets?
6. Can a **synthesizer** sound like an entire orchestra?
7. Is that piece called *Rhapsody in Blue*?
8. The musical had many upbeat **melodic** tunes.
9. Each member of the **ensemble** wore black.
10. A **ballerina** must be strong and graceful.
11. The opera has a beautiful tenor **aria**!
12. This gauge shows the number of **decibels**.
13. Quiet fell as the **maestro** raised his hands.
14. The conductor stood on the **podium** and bowed.
15. The music had a **staccato** sound, like a typewriter.
16. This **auditorium** holds about a thousand people.
17. For an **encore**, the singer sang an old favorite.
18. Here is a **medley** of popular Beatles' songs.
19. My neighbor plays the cello in a string **quartet**.
20. This television has **stereophonic** sound.

Words with Spanish Derivations

Objective
To spell words with Spanish derivations

Pretest
1. They built the wall with **adobe** bricks.
2. While in Mexico, June attended a **fiesta**.
3. The **palmetto** tree cast a shadow on the lawn.
4. The leaves on the **poinsettia** plant are often red.
5. John made me a delicious **tamale** for lunch.
6. I went into the **cabana** to change my clothes.
7. Let's find a shady spot for a brief **siesta**.
8. Did Roger name his **palomino** "Goldie"?
9. The **renegade** jumped onto his horse.
10. Marlene wrapped beans and lettuce in a **tortilla**.
11. A river flowed through the **canyon**.
12. Have you seen Joel's pet **iguana**?
13. Please call me back, **pronto**!
14. A **sombrero** is a type of hat.
15. The recipe called for two teaspoons of **vanilla**.
16. The **coyote** is a member of the dog family.
17. Does a **jaguar** resemble a leopard?
18. The **pimento** is a small red pepper.
19. Cattle often **stampede** if they are frightened.
20. Students work in the college **cafeteria**.

Spelling Strategy
Page 117

Read and discuss the spelling rule with students. For additional examples of words in the English language with Spanish roots, use *ranch, patio, mustang, pinto, barracuda, burro,* and *burrito.* Ask students to suggest others. Stress the pronunciation/spelling "tricks" that Spanish words can create for English-speaking people. Point out that many Spanish words end with the long *e* or long *o* sound. Also point out that *pimento* is the English spelling of the Spanish word *pimiento.* Then, relate the discussion to the **list words** and work with students to define each one.

Vocabulary Development Before the exercise, have volunteers suggest two **list words** that are members of the category *Mexican food. (tamale, tortilla)*

Dictionary Skills Ask a volunteer to summarize the function of dictionary guide words and show examples.

Spelling Practice
Pages 118–119

Word Analysis To extend this activity, you may wish to have students separate the **list words** into syllables, using dictionaries to check their work.

Classification To review, have students complete this series with a **list word:** *wolf, dog, _____. (coyote)*

Word Application Urge students to use context clues to find the **list word** that best fits in each blank.

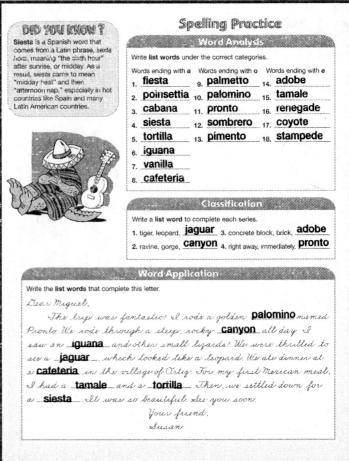

Words with Spanish Derivations Lesson 29

TIP

The English language has gained many words from the Spanish language. This is particularly true of American English due to the influence of early Spanish settlements in the Southwest, as well as the modern influx of language and culture brought by Spanish-speaking people from Mexico, Puerto Rico, and Cuba.

The **list words** are derived from Spanish words. Due to different vowel sounds, English-speaking people can find them tricky to spell. *Coyote* and *adobe* are examples of words with such "spelling tricks."

Vocabulary Development
Write the **list word** that names a member of each category.

1. sweet flavors — **vanilla**
2. celebrations — **fiesta**
3. building supplies — **adobe**
4. lizard — **iguana**
5. restaurants — **cafeteria**
6. horses — **palomino**
7. hats — **sombrero**
8. big cats — **jaguar**
9. flowers — **poinsettia**
10. trees — **palmetto**

LIST WORDS
1. adobe
2. fiesta
3. palmetto
4. poinsettia
5. tamale
6. cabana
7. siesta
8. palomino
9. renegade
10. tortilla
11. canyon
12. iguana
13. pronto
14. sombrero
15. vanilla
16. coyote
17. jaguar
18. pimento
19. stampede
20. cafeteria

Dictionary Skills
Write the **list word** that comes between each pair of dictionary guide words.

1. cab/cackle — **cabana**
2. pill/pine — **pimento**
3. tablet/top — **tamale**
4. pot/prune — **pronto**
5. clue/crayon — **coyote**
6. squash/steam — **stampede**
7. reach/repeat — **renegade**
8. set/sign — **siesta**
9. cake/coat — **canyon**
10. title/tune — **tortilla**

117

DID YOU KNOW?

Siesta is a Spanish word that comes from a Latin phrase, *sexta hora,* meaning "the sixth hour" after sunrise, or midday. As a result, *siesta* came to mean "midday heat" and then "afternoon nap," especially in hot countries like Spain and many Latin American countries.

Spelling Practice
Word Analysis
Write list words under the correct categories.

Words ending with a
1. **fiesta**
2. **poinsettia**
3. **cabana**
4. **siesta**
5. **tortilla**
6. **iguana**
7. **vanilla**
8. **cafeteria**

Words ending with o
9. **palmetto**
10. **palomino**
11. **pronto**
12. **sombrero**
13. **pimento**

Words ending with e
14. **adobe**
15. **tamale**
16. **renegade**
17. **coyote**
18. **stampede**

Classification
Write a **list word** to complete each series.

1. tiger, leopard, **jaguar**
2. ravine, gorge, **canyon**
3. concrete block, brick, **adobe**
4. right away, immediately, **pronto**

Word Application
Write the **list words** that complete this letter.

Dear Miguel,

The trip was fantastic! I rode a golden **palomino** named Pronto. We rode through a steep, rocky **canyon** all day. I saw an **iguana** and other small lizards! We were thrilled to see a **jaguar** which looked like a leopard. We ate dinner at a **cafeteria** in the village of Ortiz. For my first Mexican meal, I had a **tamale** and a **tortilla** Then, we settled down for a **siesta** It was so beautiful. See you soon.

Your friend,
Susan

118   Lesson 29 • Words with Spanish Derivations

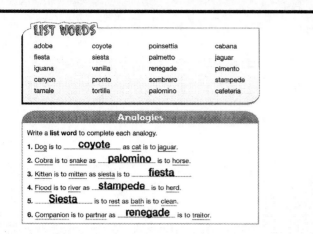

LIST WORDS

adobe	coyote	poinsettia	cabana
fiesta	siesta	palmetto	jaguar
iguana	vanilla	renegade	pimento
canyon	pronto	sombrero	stampede
tamale	tortilla	palomino	cafeteria

Analogies

Write a list word to complete each analogy.

1. Dog is to **coyote** as cat is to jaguar.
2. Cobra is to snake as **palomino** is to horse.
3. Kitten is to mitten as siesta is to **fiesta**.
4. Flood is to river as **stampede** is to herd.
5. **Siesta** is to rest as bath is to clean.
6. Companion is to partner as **renegade** is to traitor.

Puzzle

This is a crossword puzzle without clues. Use the length and the spelling of each **list word** to complete the puzzle.

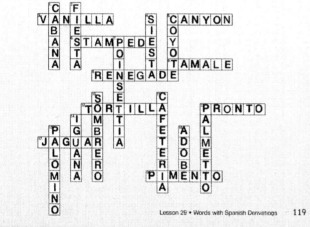

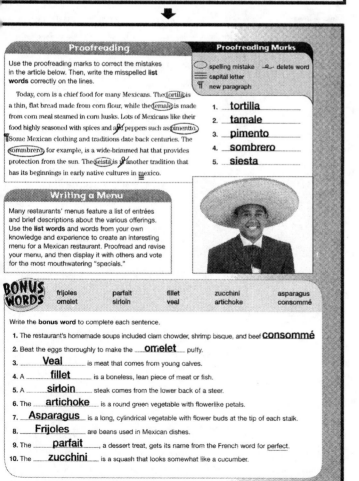

Proofreading

Use the proofreading marks to correct the mistakes in the article below. Then, write the misspelled **list words** correctly on the lines.

Today, corn is a chief food for many Mexicans. The tortilla is a thin, flat bread made from corn flour, while the tamale is made from corn meal steamed in corn husks. Lots of Mexicans like their food highly seasoned with spices and and peppers such as pimentto. Some Mexican clothing and traditions date back centuries. The sommbrero for example, is a wide-brimmed hat that provides protection from the sun. The siesta is another tradition that has its beginnings in early native cultures in mexico.

Proofreading Marks

- ⊙ spelling mistake
- ⟋ delete word
- ≡ capital letter
- ¶ new paragraph

1. tortilla
2. tamale
3. pimento
4. sombrero
5. siesta

Writing a Menu

Many restaurants' menus feature a list of entrées and brief descriptions about the various offerings. Use the **list words** and words from your own knowledge and experience to create an interesting menu for a Mexican restaurant. Proofread and revise your menu, and then display it with others and vote for the most mouthwatering "specials."

BONUS WORDS

frijoles	parfait	fillet	zucchini	asparagus
omelet	sirloin	veal	artichoke	consommé

Write the bonus word to complete each sentence.

1. The restaurant's homemade soups included clam chowder, shrimp bisque, and beef **consommé**
2. Beat the eggs thoroughly to make the **omelet** puffy.
3. **Veal** is meat that comes from young calves.
4. A **fillet** is a boneless, lean piece of meat or fish.
5. A **sirloin** steak comes from the lower back of a steer.
6. The **artichoke** is a round green vegetable with flowerlike petals.
7. **Asparagus** is a long, cylindrical vegetable with flower buds at the tip of each stalk.
8. **Frijoles** are beans used in Mexican dishes.
9. The **parfait**, a dessert treat, gets its name from the French word for perfect.
10. The **zucchini** is a squash that looks somewhat like a cucumber.

Analogies Have students complete this analogy: *English is to Great Britain as Spanish is to* _____. *(Cuba)*

Puzzle Urge students to count the number of spaces for each answer. Point out that each **list word** appears once.

Spelling and Writing   Page 120

Proofreading Review the use of the proofreading marks that students will be using in this lesson.

Writing a Menu If possible, display a menu that features descriptions or anecdotes about some of the dishes, then work with students to create a sample description or anecdote about a special cheeseburger. Students may enjoy creating complete menu layouts with illustrations of the food or pictures of the restaurant interior. Provide time for presentation and discussion.

Bonus Words   Page 120

Food Have students find the definitions of the **bonus words** in dictionaries. Ask volunteers to use the words in oral sentences. Provide time for students to discuss their eating and cooking experiences with each food.

Bonus Words Test

1. Jules filled the **omelet** with mushrooms and onions.
2. **Consommé** is served either hot or cold.
3. Roberto ordered a **sirloin** steak and a salad.
4. I steamed the **artichoke** for forty-five minutes.
5. She served the **veal** with a cheese sauce.
6. This **zucchini** is almost as big as a baseball bat!
7. George has a large **asparagus** patch in his garden.
8. Al filled the tacos with **frijoles** and lettuce.
9. For dessert, I'll have a strawberry **parfait**.
10. I'd like a **fillet** of halibut for dinner tonight.

Final Test

1. Maria felt refreshed after her midday **siesta**.
2. They made baskets out of **palmetto** leaves.
3. I've seen snakes and lizards in that **canyon**.
4. John, finish your homework, **pronto**!
5. The **palomino** has a glossy, golden coat.
6. Kate took a picture of a **jaguar**.
7. Add a teaspoon of **vanilla** to the cake batter.
8. The **cafeteria** on Elm Street serves delicious soup.
9. That **stampede** of horses caused a lot of dust!
10. **Adobe** bricks dry and harden in the sun.
11. Are the extra beach towels stored in the **cabana**?
12. The **poinsettia** was named after Joel R. Poinsett.
13. Use ground corn to make **tortilla** flour.
14. An **iguana** scurried across the big rock.
15. Is the **coyote** a protected animal?
16. Add two teaspoons of diced **pimento** to the sauce.
17. A **sombrero** has a broad brim to provide shade.
18. For the **fiesta**, we hung colored lights on the trees.
19. May I order a **tamale**, please?
20. The **renegade** horse ran away.

Objective

To review spelling words with *ie, ei; y* as vowels; suffixes *ance, ence,* and *ce;* and words from music and Spanish origins

Spelling Strategy   Page 121

Read and discuss the spelling rules. To reinforce, ask students to name other words that illustrate the information summarized in each of the five sections. You may wish to have students turn back to the opening pages of Lessons 25–29 to review each spelling rule separately and to apply it to its full selection of **list words**.

Spelling Practice   Pages 121–123

Lesson 25 Have students apply the rules of the "*i* before *e*" rhyme to each **list word**, telling which words follow the rule and which are exceptions. (*Exceptions include* heirloom, efficient, caffeine, *and* financier.) Point out the additional write-on lines to students and encourage them to add two words from Lesson 25 that they found especially difficult, or select and assign certain words that seemed to be difficult for everyone. (Repeat this procedure for each lesson in the Review.) To extend the exercise, have students create similar context-clue sentences for the additional words.

Lesson 26 Use the **list words** to stress the similar sounds of the suffixes *ance* and *ence,* urging students to memorize the spellings to avoid errors. Have students use the words in oral sentences to check their comprehension of the words' meanings.

Lesson 27 Before beginning the exercise, discuss these words to review the different sounds that *y* stands for: *antonym, solidify, energy, hydrogen,* and *cymbals.*

Lesson 28 If desired, have students turn back to review the complete selection of **list words** in Lesson 28. Discuss the definitions of each musical term and have students use the words in oral sentences. Point out the "spelling tricks" that occur.

Lesson 29 Urge students to use context clues to find the correct **list word** answers. To extend, have students challenge each other with similar "wrong word" sentences, using the **list words** they added to their lists.

Show What You Know   Page 124

Point out to students that this review will help them know if they have mastered the words in Lessons 25–29. Have a volunteer restate the directions and tell which word in the first item should be marked. (*adolesence*) When students have finished the exercise, have them write their misspelled words correctly.

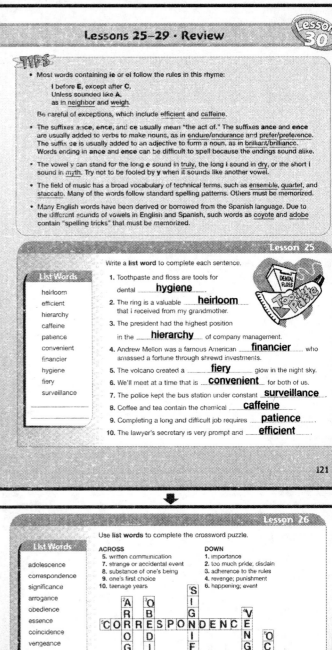

TIPS

- Most words containing ie or ei follow the rules in this rhyme:

  I before **E,** except after **C.**
  Unless sounded like **A,**
  as in n**ei**ghbor and w**ei**gh.

  Be careful of exceptions, which include ef**fi**cient and caf**fei**ne.

- The suffixes **ance, ence,** and **ce** usually mean "the act of." The suffixes **ance** and **ence** are usually added to verbs to make nouns, as in endure/endurance and prefer/preference. The suffix **ce** is usually added to an adjective to form a noun, as in brilliant/brilliance. Words ending in **ance** and **ence** can be difficult to spell because the endings sound alike.

- The vowel **y** can stand for the long **e** sound in truly, the long **i** sound in dry, or the short i sound in myth. Try not to be fooled by **y** when it sounds like another vowel.

- The field of music has a broad vocabulary of technical terms, such as ensemble, quartet, and staccato. Many of the words follow standard spelling patterns. Others must be memorized.

- Many English words have been derived or borrowed from the Spanish language. Due to the different sounds of vowels in English and Spanish, such words as coyote and adobe contain "spelling tricks" that must be memorized.

Lesson 25

Write a **list word** to complete each sentence.

List Words

heirloom
efficient
hierarchy
caffeine
patience
convenient
financier
hygiene
fiery
surveillance
_____
_____

1. Toothpaste and floss are tools for dental __hygiene__.
2. The ring is a valuable __heirloom__ that I received from my grandmother.
3. The president had the highest position in the __hierarchy__ of company management.
4. Andrew Mellon was a famous American __financier__ who amassed a fortune through shrewd investments.
5. The volcano created a __fiery__ glow in the night sky.
6. We'll meet at a time that is __convenient__ for both of us.
7. The police kept the bus station under constant __surveillance__.
8. Coffee and tea contain the chemical __caffeine__.
9. Completing a long and difficult job requires __patience__.
10. The lawyer's secretary is very prompt and __efficient__.

121

Lesson 26

Use **list words** to complete the crossword puzzle.

List Words

adolescence
correspondence
significance
arrogance
obedience
essence
coincidence
vengeance
occurrence
preference
_____
_____

ACROSS
5. written communication
7. strange or accidental event
8. substance of one's being
9. one's first choice
10. teenage years

DOWN
1. importance
2. too much pride; disdain
3. adherence to the rules
4. revenge; punishment
6. happening; event

[crossword puzzle grid with answers: ARROGANCE, OBEDIENCE, SIGNIFICANCE, CORRESPONDENCE, VENGEANCE, OCCURRENCE, COINCIDENCE, ESSENCE, PREFERENCE, ADOLESCENCE]

Lesson 27

Write **list words** to answer the questions. Some words are used more than once.

List Words

encyclopedia
sympathetic
physician
paralyze
synthetic
python
cylinder
cyclone
cynical
synopsis
_____
_____

In which words does the vowel y spell the short i sound?
1. __sympathetic__   4. __cylinder__
2. __physician__   5. __cynical__
3. __synthetic__   6. __synopsis__

In which words does the vowel y spell the long i sound?
7. __encyclopedia__   9. __python__
8. __paralyze__   10. __cyclone__

Which words contain the prefix **syn**?
11. __synthetic__   12. __synopsis__

Which words contain the root **cyclo**?
13. __encyclopedia__   14. __cyclone__

Which words contain only two syllables?
15. __python__   16. __cyclone__

List Words

aria
staccato
synthesizer
rhythm
podium
maestro
rhapsody
fugue
xylophone
pianist

Write a **list word** to answer each definition clue.

1. musician who plays a keyboard — **pianist**
2. with distinct breaks between tones — **staccato**
3. instrument consisting of a series of wooden bars — **xylophone**
4. piece of music in which the theme is repeated by different instruments — **fugue**
5. piece of music of irregular form, allowing improvisation — **rhapsody**
6. system of accented tones — **rhythm**
7. conductor's platform — **podium**
8. operatic melody — **aria**
9. great composer or conductor — **maestro**
10. electronic instrument that imitates many sounds — **synthesizer**

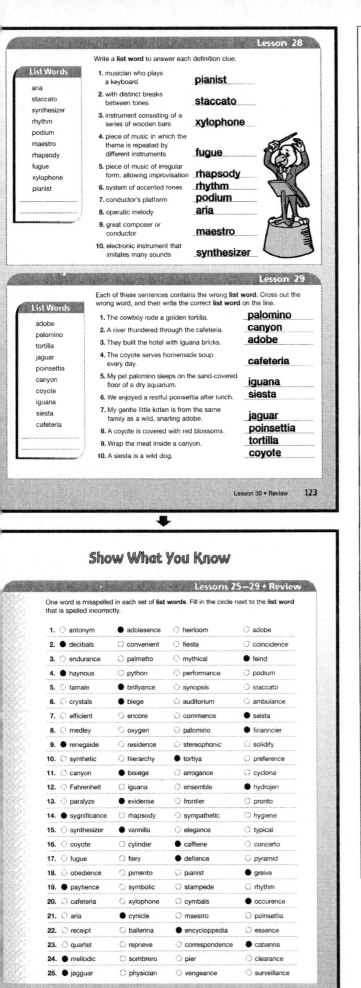

List Words

adobe
palomino
tortilla
jaguar
poinsettia
canyon
coyote
iguana
siesta
cafeteria

Each of these sentences contains the wrong list word. Cross out the wrong word, and then write the correct **list word** on the line.

1. The cowboy rode a golden tortilla. — **palomino**
2. A river thundered through the cafeteria. — **canyon**
3. They built the hotel with iguana bricks. — **adobe**
4. The coyote serves homemade soup every day. — **cafeteria**
5. My pet palomino sleeps on the sand-covered floor of a dry aquarium. — **iguana**
6. We enjoyed a restful poinsettia after lunch. — **siesta**
7. My gentle little kitten is from the same family as a wild, snarling adobe. — **jaguar**
8. A coyote is covered with red blossoms. — **poinsettia**
9. Wrap the meat inside a canyon. — **tortilla**
10. A siesta is a wild dog. — **coyote**

Lesson 30 • Review   123

Show What You Know

One word is misspelled in each set of **list words**. Fill in the circle next to the **list word** that is spelled incorrectly.

1. ○ antonym ● adolescence ○ heirloom ○ adobe
2. ● decibals ○ convenient ○ fiesta ○ coincidence
3. ○ endurance ○ palmetto ○ mythical ● feind
4. ● haynous ○ python ○ performance ○ podium
5. ○ tamale ● brillyance ○ synopsis ○ staccato
6. ○ crystals ● biege ○ auditorium ○ ambulance
7. ○ efficient ○ encore ○ commence ● seista
8. ○ medley ○ oxygen ○ palomino ● finanncier
9. ● renegaide ○ residence ○ stereophonic ○ solidify
10. ○ synthetic ○ hierarchy ● tortiya ○ preference
11. ○ canyon ● bisiege ○ arrogance ○ cyclone
12. ○ Fahrenheit ○ iguana ○ ensemble ● hydrojen
13. ○ paralyze ● evidense ○ frontier ○ pronto
14. ● significance ○ rhapsody ○ sympathetic ○ hygiene
15. ○ synthesizer ● vannilla ○ elegance ○ typical
16. ○ coyote ○ cylinder ● caffiene ○ concerto
17. ○ fugue ○ fiery ○ defiance ● pyramid
18. ○ obedience ○ pimento ○ pianist ● greive
19. ● paytience ○ symbolic ○ stampede ○ rhythm
20. ○ cafeteria ○ xylophone ○ cymbals ● occurence
21. ○ aria ● cynicle ○ maestro ○ poinsettia
22. ○ receipt ○ ballerina ● encycloppedia ○ essence
23. ○ quartet ○ reprieve ○ correspondence ● cabanna
24. ● mellodic ○ sombrero ○ pier ○ clearance
25. ● jagguar ○ physician ○ vengeance ○ surveillance

124   Lesson 30 • Review

Final Test

1. **Caffeine** can inhibit a person's ability to sleep.
2. The new shopping mall is at a **convenient** location.
3. The police put the house under **surveillance**.
4. A lawyer explains the **significance** of the evidence.
5. The family took their dog to **obedience** school.
6. **Adolescence** is a time of growth and discovery.
7. The **essence** of friendship is trust.
8. Did Fred check the facts in an **encyclopedia**?
9. Polio, an infectious disease, can **paralyze** a person.
10. Michelle was fascinated by a **python** at the zoo.
11. Weather forecasters warned of a **cyclone**.
12. Helen wrote a concise **synopsis** of the movie.
13. The soprano sang a beautiful **aria**!
14. Bill plays the drums and Kei plays the **synthesizer**.
15. Conductor Sarah Caldwell approached the **podium**.
16. Was the **fugue** written by Bach?
17. Jim ordered a **tortilla** at the Mexican restaurant.
18. Roy Rogers' **palomino** was named Trigger.
19. **Adobe** bricks harden in the sun.
20. Let's meet in the **cafeteria** around one o'clock.
21. Ms. Wan is fifth in the company **hierarchy**.
22. It takes **patience** and practice to learn how to ski.
23. The hostess wore a **fiery** red dress.
24. The friends shared a **correspondence** for years.
25. The play relates hope, **vengeance**, and despair.
26. What is your **preference** for dinner tonight?
27. Too much power led to the emperor's **arrogance**.
28. Are nylon and polyester **synthetic** materials?
29. The song is accented by a series of **staccato** notes.
30. As a young composer, Mozart was a **maestro**.
31. The **pianist** played an étude by Chopin.
32. A **jaguar** resembles a leopard.
33. The **iguana** dozed on a rock in the sun.
34. It is so relaxing to take a **siesta** after lunch!
35. This painting is a valuable family **heirloom**.
36. A **financier** spoke to us about the stock market.
37. By **coincidence**, the two friends met on the train.
38. Alicia's friend was **sympathetic** about her mistake.
39. Does a tin can have the shape of a **cylinder**?
40. A **cynical** person is ruled by doubt and suspicion.
41. Are snare drums and cymbals **rhythm** instruments?
42. One of Gershwin's famous songs is a **rhapsody**.
43. A **poinsettia** may be white, pink, or red.
44. We heard a **coyote** howling high up in the hills.
45. I took these photographs in the **canyon**.
46. The **occurrence** of snow is very rare in Florida.
47. Becky proved herself to be an **efficient** sales clerk.
48. The child's favorite toy is a miniature **xylophone**.
49. A veterinarian is a **physician** who treats animals.
50. Daphne wants a career in dental **hygiene**.

Latin Roots

Objective
To spell words with Latin roots

Pretest
1. Do **carnivorous** animals eat meat?
2. A mirage is just an **illusion**.
3. The clown's antics in the arena were **ludicrous**.
4. The lawyer began to **suspect** that Mr. Wu was lying.
5. A **versatile** musician can play many instruments.
6. A rabbit can **elude** a fox.
7. She clung to an **illusive** hope of winning.
8. In **retrospect**, Elena understood why she failed.
9. In the midst of the **tempest**, the boat keeled over.
10. Both my grandparents exude youthful **vitality**.
11. I used **extemporaneous** remarks in my speech.
12. Tom is an **introvert** and prefers to be alone.
13. Was the lifeguard able to **revive** the swimmer?
14. All life on earth is **temporal** and will eventually end.
15. Most milk is enriched with **vitamin** D.
16. An **extrovert** is an outgoing person.
17. The **inverse** of upside-down is right-side-up.
18. The fireworks display was **spectacular**!
19. We stayed in a **temporary** shelter after the fire.
20. The sunset was a **vivid** orange-red color.

Spelling Strategy   Page 125
Discuss the spelling rule, then work with students to identify the Latin roots in the following words: *voracious, diversion, spectator, contemporary, vivacious,* and *delude.* Discuss how the meaning of each word is related to the meaning of the Latin root. Then, apply the discussion to the **list words**. Be sure students notice the spelling patterns in *retrospect, introvert,* and *extrovert*—words that are often pronounced as if they were spelled with *a* instead of *o.*

Word Analysis Encourage students to refer to the **list words** to determine the words with the same roots.

Vocabulary Development To begin, have students identify the **list word** synonyms for these examples: *meat-eater (carnivorous), opposite (inverse),* and *bright (vivid).*

Spelling Practice   Pages 126–127
Word Application You may wish to have students review the meanings of the Latin roots in the spelling rule before completing this activity.

Word Meaning Encourage students to use context clues to find the correct **list word** to replace the underlined word in each sentence. To extend, have students challenge each other by writing similar word replacement sentences to exchange with classmates.

Latin Roots — Lesson 31

TIP
By recognizing Latin roots in the **list words**, you can make an intelligent guess at the meaning of the words.

Latin Root	Meaning	English Word	Meaning
vor	"devour; eat"	carnivorous	"meat eater"
lud, lus	"play"	ludicrous	"ridiculous"
vit, viv	"life," "live"	vitality	"full of life"
spect	"see"	spectacular	"showy"
ver	"turn"	extrovert	"outgoing"
temp	"time"	temporary	"for a short time"

Word Analysis
Write the **list words** that have the same Latin root as the word given.

inspector
1. suspect   3. spectacular
2. retrospect

vital
4. vitality   6. vitamin
5. revive   7. vivid

devour
8. carnivorous

convert
9. versatile   11. extrovert
10. introvert   12. inverse

Vocabulary Development
Write the **list word** that matches each synonym.
1. deceiving   illusive   5. storm   tempest
2. laughable   ludicrous   6. escape   elude
3. earthly   temporal   7. short-term   temporary
4. mirage   illusion   8. unrehearsed extemporaneous

LIST WORDS
1. carnivorous
2. illusion
3. ludicrous
4. suspect
5. versatile
6. elude
7. illusive
8. retrospect
9. tempest
10. vitality
11. extemporaneous
12. introvert
13. revive
14. temporal
15. vitamin
16. extrovert
17. inverse
18. spectacular
19. temporary
20. vivid

125

DID YOU KNOW?
The Latin word *vivere* means "to be alive or to live." The Romans used a form of the word, *viva,* as a salute, meaning "long live someone or something." *Viva* has lent its meaning to many of the words in our language. **Vivid** means "to be alive with color." **Revive** means "bring back to life." **Vivacious** means "full of life and energy."

Spelling Practice
Word Application
Write **list words** to answer the following questions.

Which words contain the Latin root that means "to turn"?
1. versatile   3. extrovert
2. introvert   4. inverse

Which words contain the Latin root that means "time"?
5. tempest   7. temporal
6. extemporaneous   8. temporary

Which words contain the Latin root that means "to see"?
9. suspect   11. spectacular
10. retrospect

Which words contain the Latin root that means "to play"?
12. illusion   14. elude
13. ludicrous   15. illusive

Which words contain the Latin root that means "to live"?
16. vitality   18. vitamin
17. revive   19. vivid

Which word contains the Latin root that means "to eat"?
20. carnivorous

Word Meaning
Each underlined word in the sentences below must be moved to a different sentence to make sense. Write the correct **list word** for each sentence in the blank.
1. Hannah, a ludicrous athlete, likes to play five different sports. ___versatile___
2. The spectacular operation of multiplication is division. ___inverse___
3. Milk is usually fortified with vitality D. ___vitamin___
4. Wearing casual sandals with a tuxedo would be carnivorous. ___ludicrous___
5. After jogging, inverse yourself with a glass of water. ___revive___
6. Some plants, like the Venus' flytrap, are vitamin and eat insects. ___carnivorous___
7. Exercise and a balanced diet help to promote revive. ___vitality___
8. The night sky was lit up by a versatile display of fireworks. ___spectacular___

126   Lesson 31 • Latin Roots

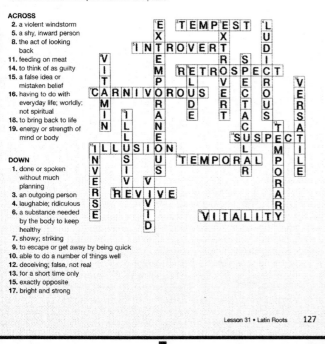

LIST WORDS

extrovert	elude	tempest	carnivorous
illusion	revive	introvert	retrospect
ludicrous	vivid	illusive	spectacular
suspect	inverse	temporal	temporary
versatile	vitality	vitamin	extemporaneous

Puzzle
Use the **list words** to complete the crossword puzzle.

ACROSS
2. a violent windstorm
5. a shy, inward person
8. the act of looking back
11. feeding on meat
14. to think of as guilty
15. a false idea or mistaken belief
16. having to do with everyday life; worldly; not spiritual
18. to bring back to life
19. energy or strength of mind or body

DOWN
1. done or spoken without much planning
3. an outgoing person
4. laughable; ridiculous
6. a substance needed by the body to keep healthy
7. showy; striking
9. to escape or get away by being quick
10. able to do a number of things well
12. deceiving; false, not real
13. for a short time only
15. exactly opposite
17. bright and strong

Lesson 31 • Latin Roots   127

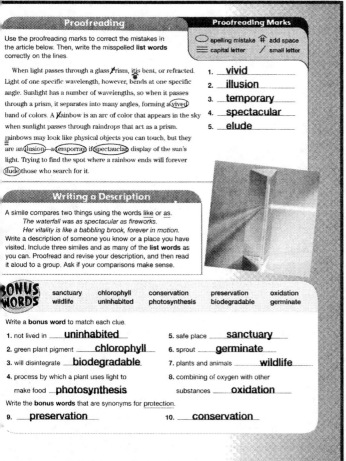

Proofreading
Use the proofreading marks to correct the mistakes in the article below. Then, write the misspelled **list words** correctly on the lines.

Proofreading Marks
◯ spelling mistake   ⊓ add space
☰ capital letter   / small letter

When light passes through a glass prism, it is bent, or refracted. Light of one specific wavelength, however, bends at one specific angle. Sunlight has a number of wavelengths, so when it passes through a prism, it separates into many angles, forming a vivid band of colors. A rainbow is an arc of color that appears in the sky when sunlight passes through raindrops that act as a prism. rainbows may look like physical objects you can touch, but they are an illusion—a temporary if spectacular display of the sun's light. Trying to find the spot where a rainbow ends will forever elude those who search for it.

1. __vivid__
2. __illusion__
3. __temporary__
4. __spectacular__
5. __elude__

Writing a Description
A simile compares two things using the words *like* or *as*.
  The waterfall was as spectacular as fireworks.
  Her vitality is like a babbling brook, forever in motion.
Write a description of someone you know or a place you have visited. Include three similes and as many of the **list words** as you can. Proofread and revise your description, and then read it aloud to a group. Ask if your comparisons make sense.

BONUS WORDS

sanctuary	chlorophyll	conservation	preservation	oxidation
wildlife	uninhabited	photosynthesis	biodegradable	germinate

Write a **bonus word** to match each clue.
1. not lived in __uninhabited__
2. green plant pigment __chlorophyll__
3. will disintegrate __biodegradable__
4. process by which a plant uses light to make food __photosynthesis__
5. safe place __sanctuary__
6. sprout __germinate__
7. plants and animals __wildlife__
8. combining of oxygen with other substances __oxidation__

Write the **bonus words** that are synonyms for protection.
9. __preservation__
10. __conservation__

128   Lesson 31 • Latin Roots

Puzzle Encourage students to think about the meaning of the **list words** as they complete the puzzle.

Spelling and Writing   Page 128
Proofreading Write this sentence on the board to demonstrate the lesson's proofreading marks: *From the empire State Building thecars looked like tinee Ants.*

Writing a Description Have students identify the two things being compared in each of the similes. (*waterfall, fireworks; vitality, babbling brook*) Then, have students orally repeat each simile replacing *fireworks* and *babbling brook* with ideas of their own. After students have finished their descriptions, encourage them to share their writing with the class.

Bonus Words   Page 128
Ecology Conduct a brief discussion on contemporary ecology issues, national and local, applying the **bonus words** to the discussion. Help students define each of the words, pointing out that *preservation* and *conservation* have similar meanings. ("keeping safe")

Bonus Words Test
1. My parents work for the **preservation** of whales.
2. The state created a **sanctuary** for animals.
3. In **photosynthesis**, a plant uses light to make food.
4. **Oxidation** of metal causes rust.
5. The animals in the **wildlife** refuge are protected.
6. **Chlorophyll** is the green pigment in plants.
7. The seeds will **germinate** in several days.
8. Solar heating is a method of energy **conservation**.
9. **Biodegradable** products won't harm nature.
10. We studied plants on the **uninhabited** islands.

Final Test
1. Her fame was **temporal** and faded quickly.
2. I have **vivid** memories of my vacation at the beach.
3. Exercise restored his **vitality** after the accident.
4. In **retrospect**, Franco admitted he was wrong.
5. An **extemporaneous** speech is unprepared.
6. What a silly, **ludicrous** statement he made!
7. **Carnivorous** animals eat meat.
8. Small details of past events **elude** my memory.
9. Winning the lottery is an **illusive** dream to people.
10. As an **introvert**, she keeps her feelings to herself.
11. A magician presents the **illusion** of magic.
12. I **suspect** that Cora has planned a surprise for me.
13. Joyful music will **revive** your low spirits.
14. Beneath her calm was a **tempest** ready to erupt.
15. This **versatile** gadget does many different things.
16. Is your job **temporary** or permanent?
17. The **inverse** of multiplication is division.
18. Fran is an **extrovert** and loves crowded parties.
19. The critics said his singing was **spectacular**.
20. Are citrus fruits a good source of **vitamin** C?

Lesson 32

Words from Sports

Objective
To spell words from sports

Pretest

1. The gymnasts performed their **acrobatics** routine.
2. A **toboggan** is a long sled with a curved front end.
3. I carried my bow and arrows to the **archery** range.
4. The **Olympics** are exciting to watch!
5. The **sportscaster** reported the results of the game.
6. Is **aerobics** an exercise that benefits the heart?
7. Jim registered as a **contestant** in the race.
8. Sue was the top **goalkeeper** in the soccer league.
9. The **referee** blew the whistle at half time.
10. A **sprinter** runs short distances at top speed.
11. Do you need an **agile** body to be a gymnast?
12. Does the **decathlon** consist of ten athletic events?
13. MayLin won a gold ribbon in **gymnastics**.
14. The **skiing** conditions were great last winter.
15. The **umpire** called a strike.
16. Reggie broke his **ankle** playing football.
17. The teams will **scrimmage** at the end of practice.
18. A **kayak** is a canoe for one person.
19. Is **soccer** a popular sport all over the world?
20. Field **hockey** is played with sticks and a small ball.

Spelling Strategy   *Page 129*

Discuss the spelling rule, then ask students to name sports or other physical activities in which they participate. Have them name words associated with those activities. For example, football words might include *quarterback*, *penalty*, *Super Bowl*, and so on. Discuss the definitions of the **list words**. Emphasize the spelling patterns of the more difficult words, such as *aerobics*, *decathlon*, *gymnastics*, and *kayak*. Point out that people often confuse the spelling of *empire* and *umpire*.

Vocabulary Development Tell students to think carefully about the meanings of the **list words** as they complete the activity.

Dictionary Skills Urge students to say each word slowly to themselves as they divide the words into syllables.

Spelling Practice   *Pages 130–131*

Word Analysis Urge students to study the spelling patterns of the **list words** before they begin this activity.

Analogies To review, have students identify the **list word** that completes this analogy: *Bicycle is to road as _____ is to river.* (kayak)

Word Application When students have completed the exercise, have volunteers read the sentences aloud, substituting their answers for the incorrect words.

80

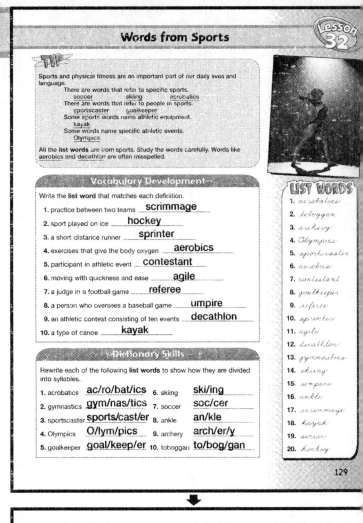

Words from Sports   Lesson 32

TIP

Sports and physical fitness are an important part of our daily lives and language.
There are words that refer to specific sports.
  soccer   skiing   acrobatics
There are words that refer to people in sports.
  sportscaster   goalkeeper
Some sports words name athletic equipment.
  kayak
Some words name specific athletic events.
  Olympics
All the list words are from sports. Study the words carefully. Words like aerobics and decathlon are often misspelled.

Vocabulary Development

Write the **list word** that matches each definition.

1. practice between two teams ___scrimmage___
2. sport played on ice ___hockey___
3. a short-distance runner ___sprinter___
4. exercises that give the body oxygen ___aerobics___
5. participant in athletic event ___contestant___
6. moving with quickness and ease ___agile___
7. a judge in a football game ___referee___
8. a person who oversees a baseball game ___umpire___
9. an athletic contest consisting of ten events ___decathlon___
10. a type of canoe ___kayak___

Dictionary Skills

Rewrite each of the following **list words** to show how they are divided into syllables.

1. acrobatics **ac/ro/bat/ics**   6. skiing **ski/ing**
2. gymnastics **gym/nas/tics**   7. soccer **soc/cer**
3. sportscaster **sports/cast/er**   8. ankle **an/kle**
4. Olympics **O/lym/pics**   9. archery **arch/er/y**
5. goalkeeper **goal/keep/er**   10. toboggan **to/bog/gan**

LIST WORDS
1. acrobatics
2. toboggan
3. archery
4. Olympics
5. sportscaster
6. aerobics
7. contestant
8. goalkeeper
9. referee
10. sprinter
11. agile
12. decathlon
13. gymnastics
14. skiing
15. umpire
16. ankle
17. scrimmage
18. kayak
19. soccer
20. hockey

129

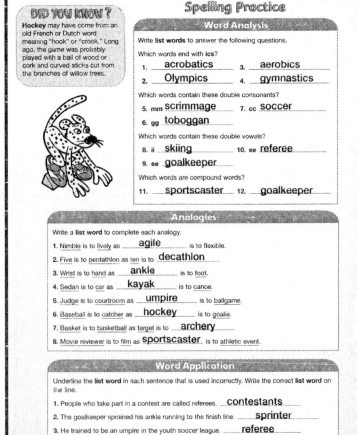

Spelling Practice

DID YOU KNOW?
Hockey may have come from an old French or Dutch word meaning "hook" or "crook." Long ago, the game was probably played with a ball of wood or cork and curved sticks cut from the branches of willow trees.

Word Analysis

Write **list words** to answer the following questions.

Which words end with **ics**?
1. ___acrobatics___   3. ___aerobics___
2. ___Olympics___   4. ___gymnastics___

Which words contain these double consonants?
5. mm ___scrimmage___   7. cc ___soccer___
6. gg ___toboggan___

Which words contain these double vowels?
8. ii ___skiing___   10. ee ___referee___
9. ee ___goalkeeper___

Which words are compound words?
11. ___sportscaster___   12. ___goalkeeper___

Analogies

Write a **list word** to complete each analogy.

1. Nimble is to lively as ___agile___ is to flexible.
2. Five is to pentathlon as ten is to ___decathlon___
3. Wrist is to hand as ___ankle___ is to foot.
4. Sedan is to car as ___kayak___ is to canoe.
5. Judge is to courtroom as ___umpire___ is to ballgame.
6. Baseball is to catcher as ___hockey___ is to goalie.
7. Basket is to basketball as target is to ___archery___
8. Movie reviewer is to film as ___sportscaster___ is to athletic event.

Word Application

Underline the **list word** in each sentence that is used incorrectly. Write the correct **list word** on the line.

1. People who take part in a contest are called referees. ___contestants___
2. The goalkeeper sprained his ankle running to the finish line. ___sprinter___
3. He trained to be an umpire in the youth soccer league. ___referee___

130   Lesson 32 • Words from Sports

LIST WORDS

acrobatics	archery	scrimmage	ankle
toboggan	umpire	decathlon	skiing
aerobics	hockey	gymnastics	kayak
Olympics	referee	goalkeeper	soccer
sportscaster	sprinter	contestant	agile

Puzzle
Unscramble the **list words** to complete the crossword puzzle.

ACROSS
3. REPALOGEKE
4. LNHACDTOE
7. LKNEA
9. CSMRIMGAE
12. LMOPCIYS
13. RPRISTNE
14. HKOYCE
17. YMSNAIGSTC
18. OCSERC
19. IGKSIN

DOWN
1. EREFERE
2. BSRAOEIC
5. ONSATTNETC
6. OOGBAGTN
7. GAILE
8. PAQRETSRSCST
10. CARBSTAIOC
11. EIUMPR
15. AKAKY
16. YCRAHER

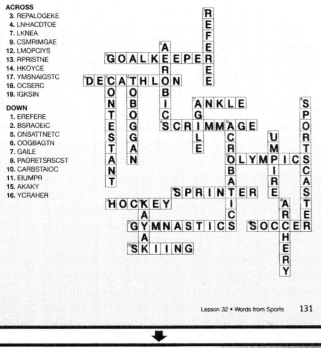

Crossword solution:
REFEREE, GOALKEEPER, DECATHLON, AEROBICS, CONTESTANT, TOBOGGAN, ANKLE, SCRIMMAGE, AGILE, ACROBATICS, OLYMPICS, UMPIRE, SPORTSCASTER, SPRINTER, HOCKEY, KAYAK, GYMNASTICS, SOCCER, SKIING, ARCHERY

Lesson 32 • Words from Sports   131

Proofreading

Use the proofreading marks to correct the mistakes in the article below. Then, write the misspelled **list words** correctly on the lines.

Proofreading Marks
◯ spelling mistake   ⋀ add comma
? add question mark   / small letter

Did you know the first modern Olympic Games were held in Athens Greece, in 1896? The athletes competed in the sports of cycling, fencing, gimnastics, tennis, shooting, swimming, track and field, weightlifting, and wrestling. One sprinter James B. Connolly of the United States, became the first modern champion of the Olimpics when he won the triple jump. Today, many more athletes compete in the games in a wide variety of sports that include skiing, hokey, basketball, and archiry.

1. gymnastics
2. sprinter
3. Olympics
4. skiing
5. hockey
6. archery

Writing a News Story

A metaphor is a comparison of two things without using the words like or as. Read these examples of metaphors.
Skiing is flying on snow.   A sprinter is a human jackrabbit.
Write a news story describing an Olympic event using three metaphors of your own. The **list words** may suggest some ideas. Use as many of them in your story as possible. After proofreading and revising, share your story with a group. Compare the images created by the metaphors.

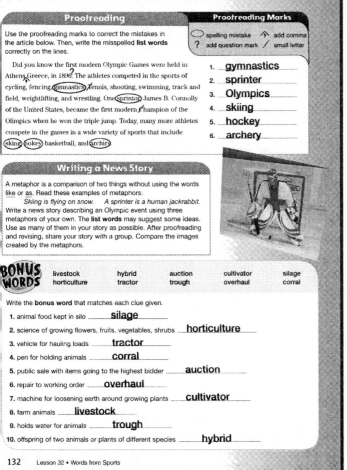

BONUS WORDS

livestock	hybrid	auction	cultivator	silage
horticulture	tractor	trough	overhaul	corral

Write the **bonus word** that matches each clue given.

1. animal food kept in silo _____ silage
2. science of growing flowers, fruits, vegetables, shrubs _____ horticulture
3. vehicle for hauling loads _____ tractor
4. pen for holding animals _____ corral
5. public sale with items going to the highest bidder _____ auction
6. repair to working order _____ overhaul
7. machine for loosening earth around growing plants _____ cultivator
8. farm animals _____ livestock
9. holds water for animals _____ trough
10. offspring of two animals or plants of different species _____ hybrid

132   Lesson 32 • Words from Sports

Puzzle Encourage students to refer to the words at the top of the page if they have difficulty remembering the spelling pattern of any word.

Spelling and Writing   Page 132

Proofreading Use this sentence to review the proofreading marks: *Wear Are Omar Ted and Bill going*

Writing a News Story Elicit the difference between a metaphor and a simile. Then, have students identify the two things being compared in the metaphors. *(skiing, flying on snow; sprinter, human jackrabbit)* Ask students to say each metaphor replacing *flying on snow* and *human jackrabbit* with ideas of their own. Urge students to discuss the metaphors in small groups.

Bonus Words   Page 132

Farming Help students define the **bonus words**. Have them use dictionaries to find the meanings of any unfamiliar words. Students in rural areas may be familiar with these words while students in urban areas may not. Provide pictures and additional reading material as needed to help students understand the importance of farming and agriculture in our society.

Bonus Words Test
1. Mr. Smith will **overhaul** the damaged plow.
2. These **hybrid** tomatoes grow to an enormous size.
3. He'll use a **cultivator** to loosen the packed soil.
4. The **livestock** on our farm includes cattle.
5. The horses that are for sale are in the **corral**.
6. The pigs drank water from a wooden **trough**.
7. Sam towed the disabled machine with the **tractor**.
8. The gardener discussed the science of **horticulture**.
9. Mrs. West will bid on a bull at the cattle **auction**.
10. **Silage** is stored in a silo to feed animals in winter.

Final Test
1. We took a **kayak** expedition on the Colorado River.
2. Jeff won an ice **hockey** scholarship to college.
3. The team captain argued with the **umpire**.
4. What a great **scrimmage** game!
5. Each **contestant** in the race was issued a number.
6. Will the **referee** explain the rules before the game?
7. They sped down the snowy hill on the **toboggan**.
8. The **sportscaster** interviewed the winning team.
9. She was **agile** and climbed easily up the rope.
10. **Gymnastics** helps build strength and flexibility.
11. He's a **sprinter** and doesn't run long distances.
12. The **goalkeeper** made a spectacular save.
13. Competing in a **decathlon** requires great stamina.
14. Is Mrs. Loo the **aerobics** instructor at the gym?
15. Ten **soccer** teams competed in the state finals.
16. Her **ankle** ached, but she completed the marathon.
17. Ted is a member of the Junior **Olympics** ski team.
18. She performed **acrobatics** on the trampoline.
19. We spent our vacation **skiing** at Mount Pleasant.
20. My school's **archery** team won three medals.

Lesson 33 — Words with Latin and Greek Prefixes

Objective
To spell words with Latin and Greek prefixes

Pretest
1. That kind of exaggeration is called **hyperbole**.
2. In stories, an **omniscient** narrator knows all things.
3. Young children are often **hyperactive**.
4. Sand is an **omnipresent** nuisance in beach houses.
5. Our **multimedia** advertising appeals to everyone.
6. Anna wore black slacks and a **multicolored** blouse.
7. The desert **panorama** was magnificent.
8. Greek myths show the belief in **polytheism**.
9. This amount of food could easily feed a **multitude**!
10. I have **multiple** sneakers, all for different sports.
11. The sun is over the equator during an **equinox**.
12. The shirt looks like silk, but it's **polyester**.
13. Do you try to spell **polysyllabic** words by syllable?
14. The center is **equidistant** from both goal posts.
15. The practice of plural marriages is called **polygamy**.
16. The people believed their ruler to be **omnipotent**.
17. An actor can tell a story through **pantomime**.
18. The scales will balance at **equilibrium**.
19. A **polygon** is a figure with many sides.
20. What **pandemonium** the apes caused at the zoo!

Spelling Strategy   Page 133
After students have read the spelling rule, discuss the meanings of the **list words**. Have students consult the rule if needed to make intelligent guesses about the meanings of unfamiliar words. Then, elicit other words students know containing these prefixes. Help students analyze the spelling of each **list word** and ways to remember it.

Vocabulary Development Remind students to think carefully about the meaning and spelling of each answer.

Dictionary Skills Review sound-spelling symbols and accent marks using the word *polysyllabic.* (päl′i si lab′ik)

Spelling Practice   Pages 134–135
Word Analysis This classifying activity will help students compare and contrast **list words** containing the prefixes *poly, pan, hyper, equi, multi,* and *omni.* To extend, have students research additional words with these prefixes.

Word Application Point out that two or three **list words** are to be substituted for the underlined words in each sentence and that each replacement word must make sense in the sentence. When finished, have volunteers read the sentences aloud, substituting their answers for the underlined words. You may wish to have students discuss whether the substitutions improve the sentences.

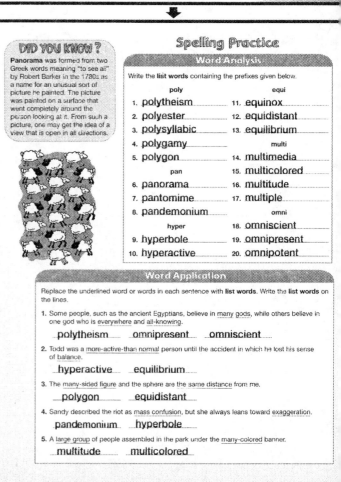

82

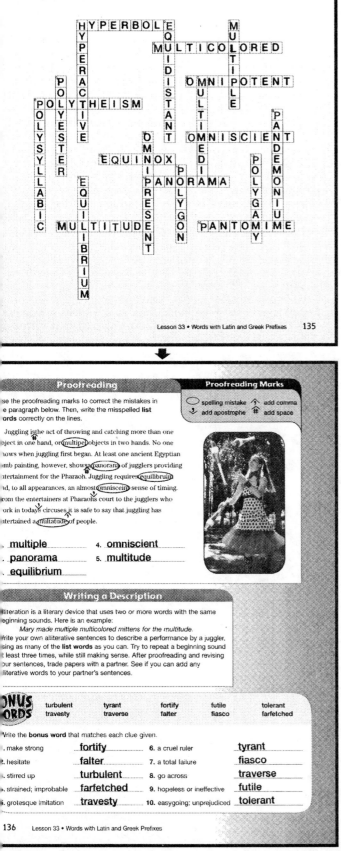

LIST WORDS

hyperbole	multicolored	multiple	equidistant
omniscient	panorama	equinox	multitude
hyperactive	polytheism	polyester	omnipotent
omnipresent	pandemonium	polygamy	pantomime
multimedia	polysyllabic	polygon	equilibrium

Puzzle
This is a crossword puzzle without clues. Use the length and the spelling of each **list word** to complete the puzzle.

Lesson 33 • Words with Latin and Greek Prefixes   135

Proofreading

Proofreading Marks

○ spelling mistake   ∧ add comma
↲ add apostrophe   # add space

Use the proofreading marks to correct the mistakes in the paragraph below. Then, write the misspelled **list words** correctly on the lines.

Juggling is the act of throwing and catching more than one object in one hand, or multiple objects in two hands. No one knows when juggling first began. At least one ancient Egyptian tomb painting, however, shows panorama of jugglers providing entertainment for the Pharaoh. Juggling requires equilibruim and, to all appearances, an almost omniscein sense of timing. From the entertainers at Pharaohs court to the jugglers who work in todays circuses it is safe to say that juggling has entertained a multatude of people.

1. multiple   4. omniscient
2. panorama   5. multitude
3. equilibrium

Writing a Description

Alliteration is a literary device that uses two or more words with the same beginning sounds. Here is an example:
   Mary made multiple multicolored mittens for the multitude.
Write your own alliterative sentences to describe a performance by a juggler. Using as many of the **list words** as you can. Try to repeat a beginning sound at least three times, while still making sense. After proofreading and revising your sentences, trade papers with a partner. See if you can add any alliterative words to your partner's sentences.

BONUS WORDS

turbulent	tyrant	fortify	futile	tolerant
travesty	traverse	falter	fiasco	farfetched

Write the **bonus word** that matches each clue given.

1. make strong   **fortify**   6. a cruel ruler   **tyrant**
2. hesitate   **falter**   7. a total failure   **fiasco**
3. stirred up   **turbulent**   8. go across   **traverse**
4. strained; improbable **farfetched** 9. hopeless or ineffective **futile**
5. grotesque imitation **travesty** 10. easygoing; unprejudiced **tolerant**

136   Lesson 33 • Words with Latin and Greek Prefixes

Puzzle Review students' strategies for solving crossword puzzles without clues.

Spelling and Writing   *Page 136*
Proofreading Use this sentence to review the proofreading marks: *Sue hav youseen Jays books?*

Writing a Description Point out to students that many tongue-twisters use alliteration, as in the example, "*She sells sea shells by the sea shore.*" Encourage students to be playful with language and to think of alliterative word combinations. As a group, you may wish to generate lists of words starting with certain letters. Then, have students write their sentences.

Bonus Words   *Page 136*
Alliteration Point out that the **bonus words** in this lesson are related by sound, not topic. Through discussion and dictionary use, help students understand the words' meanings. If possible, find and display examples of alliteration from literature or poetry. Then, have students complete the **bonus word** activity.

Bonus Words Test
1. The manufacturers **fortify** milk with vitamin D.
2. The engine started to **falter,** but then ran smoothly.
3. The **turbulent** water foamed over the rocks.
4. During the revolution, the **tyrant** was overthrown.
5. That news story was a **travesty** of television news.
6. Your idea sounds **farfetched,** but it just might work.
7. I don't want my name associated with this **fiasco**!
8. It snowed, so we can **traverse** the slopes on skis.
9. Our efforts to keep dry were **futile,** so we got wet.
10. Some people are more **tolerant** of cold than others.

Final Test
1. Sasha's bed is covered with a **multicolored** quilt.
2. What a lovely **panorama** I saw at the hilltop!
3. Their **polytheism** was expressed in their art.
4. Today you have a **multitude** of decisions to make.
5. The shop has **multiple** cages filled with birds.
6. Very young children think parents are **omnipotent**.
7. In charades, you **pantomime** different actions.
8. Can an ear infection affect a person's **equilibrium**?
9. Each figure is a **polygon**, except the circle.
10. The cat at the dog show caused **pandemonium**.
11. Do tall tales use **hyperbole** for a humorous effect?
12. Ron was unaware, not **omniscient** of the situation.
13. When I'm tired, other people seem **hyperactive**.
14. At the shore, dampness is an **omnipresent** force.
15. A **multimedia** show was planned for the event.
16. In this country, **polygamy** is against the law.
17. Let's meet at a place **equidistant** from our homes.
18. She has a **polysyllabic** name—Saltinstall.
19. I rarely have to iron this **polyester** shirt.
20. The vernal **equinox** occurs in March.

Lesson 34

Compound Words and Hyphenates

Objective
To spell compound words and hyphenated words

Pretest

1. **Throughout** her life, she worked to fight poverty.
2. The **handlebars** on Diane's new bike are too low.
3. His **motorcycle** is at the automotive repair shop.
4. That **absent-minded** boy always forgets things!
5. There are **twenty-nine** students in our math class.
6. The astronauts climbed aboard the **spacecraft**.
7. Did the police question the **eyewitness**?
8. I was able to buy the car after much **self-sacrifice**.
9. The captain was looking for **able-bodied** sailors.
10. Jesse is a **part-time** employee at the factory.
11. On hot days, we enjoy our **air-conditioned** house.
12. We tasted the purple grapes from the **vineyard**.
13. Ann keeps her recipes in a **loose-leaf** binder.
14. Lia won the race by **two-thousandths** of a second.
15. The **quarterback** threw a touchdown pass.
16. A **bookkeeper** keeps a company's financial records.
17. Does a **copyright** protect work from being copied?
18. Is this filmstrip from the **audio-visual** department?
19. The answer to the problem is **nine-hundredths**.
20. **Three-fourths** of the class went on the field trip.

Spelling Strategy
Page 137

To reinforce the spelling rule, say the following words and have students use a dictionary to identify which words are compounds and which are hyphenates: *self-control, pothole, outspoken,* and *stage-struck.* Then, have students study the **list words** and name the two words that form each **list word**. Point out that most numbers between *twenty-one* and *ninety-nine* are hyphenated. Review syllabication by having volunteers write sample **list words** on the board, and placing a dot between the syllables.

Vocabulary Development Remind students that a hyphenated word is misspelled if the hyphen is omitted.

Dictionary Skills When finished, have students find sound-spellings for additional **list words**, if desired.

Spelling Practice
Pages 138–139

Word Analysis To review analogies, have students identify the **list word** that completes this sentence:
Heated is to winter as _____ is to summer. (*air-conditioned*).

Word Application Have students make up their own riddle questions for the **list words** *vineyard, part-time, three-fourths,* and *quarterback,* and then exchange the riddles with partners to solve.

Compound Words and Hyphenates
Lesson 34

TIP
A **compound word** is a combination of two or more words.
space + craft = spacecraft
A compound word may have a hyphen between the words.
loose-leaf
Many number words are also spelled with a hyphen.
twenty-nine

Vocabulary Development
Match the words in columns A and B to form **list words**.

A		B
1. able	able-bodied	cycle
2. space	spacecraft	leaf
3. self	self-sacrifice	conditioned
4. motor	motorcycle	out
5. copy	copyright	fourths
6. loose	loose-leaf	witness
7. air	air-conditioned	bodied
8. through	throughout	sacrifice
9. eye	eyewitness	right
10. three	three-fourths	craft

LIST WORDS
1. throughout
2. handlebars
3. motorcycle
4. absent-minded
5. twenty-nine
6. spacecraft
7. eyewitness
8. self-sacrifice
9. able-bodied
10. part-time
11. air-conditioned
12. vineyard
13. loose-leaf
14. two-thousandths
15. quarterback
16. bookkeeper
17. copyright
18. audio-visual
19. nine-hundredths
20. three-fourths

Dictionary Skills
Write the **list word** that matches each sound-spelling.
1. (twen'tē nīn) **twenty-nine**
2. (han'd'l bärz) **handlebars**
3. (kwôr'tər bak) **quarterback**
4. (book'kēp'ər) **bookkeeper**
5. (ab's'nt mīn'did) **absent-minded**
6. (nīn hun'dridths) **nine-hundredths**
7. (tōō thou' z'ndths) **two-thousandths**
8. (ô'dē ō vizh'ōō wəl) **audio-visual**
9. (vin'yərd) **vineyard**
10. (pärt'tīm) **part-time**

137

DID YOU KNOW?
On a football team, the **quarterback** is the player who calls the plays and receives the ball when it is snapped back by the center. The position most likely was invented by Walter Chauncey Camp in the early days of football.

Spelling Practice
Word Analysis
Write **list words** to answer the questions below. Which **list words** complete these analogies?
1. Pitcher is to baseball as **quarterback** is to football.
2. Steering wheel is to car as **handlebars** are to bicycle.
3. Sailor is to ship as astronaut is to **spacecraft**
4. Grapes are to **vineyard** as vegetables are to farm.
What is another way to say "all the way through"?
5. **throughout**
What is another name for a motion picture presentation?
6. **audio-visual**
What **list words** do these numerals represent?
7. .09 **nine-hundredths** 9. 29 **twenty-nine**
8. 3/4 **three-fourths** 10. .002 **two-thousandths**

Word Application
Write **list words** to answer the following questions.
1. What do you call someone who is always forgetting things? **absent-minded**
2. What do you call someone who is in good health? **able-bodied**
3. What is a two-wheeled motor vehicle? **motorcycle**
4. What is another name for a rocket? **spacecraft**
5. What protects someone from stealing a story? **copyright**
6. What kind of place keeps you cool in the summer? **air-conditioned**
7. What is another name for an accountant? **bookkeeper**
8. What do you call paper that fits in a three-ring binder? **loose-leaf**
9. What do you call it when you deprive yourself of something? **self-sacrifice**
10. What kind of job would you have if you worked only ten hours weekly? **part-time**
11. What do you call someone who sees a historic event take place? **eyewitness**

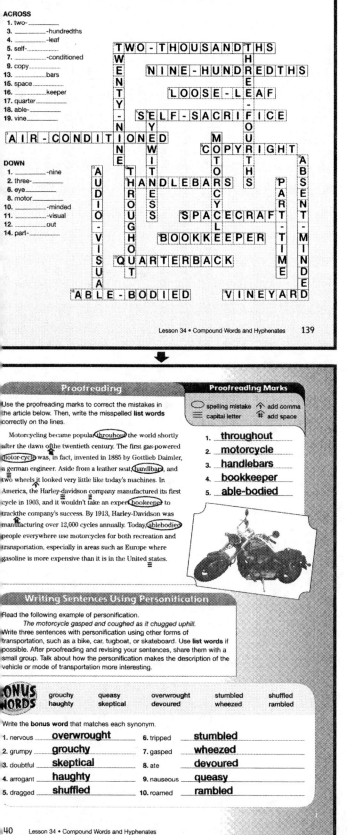

Puzzle
Fill in the puzzle by completing each word part to make compound and hyphenated **list words**. Then, write the **list words** in the puzzle. Allow one box for each hyphen.

ACROSS
1. two-_____
3. _____-hundredths
4. _____-leaf
5. self-_____
7. _____-conditioned
9. copy_____
13. _____bars
15. space_____
16. _____keeper
17. quarter_____
18. able-_____
19. vine_____

DOWN
1. _____-nine
2. three-_____
6. eye_____
8. motor_____
10. _____-minded
11. _____-visual
12. _____out
14. part-_____

Puzzle grid answers:
TWO-THOUSANDTHS
NINE-HUNDREDTHS
LOOSE-LEAF
SELF-SACRIFICE
AIR-CONDITIONED
COPYRIGHT
HANDLEBARS
SPACECRAFT
BOOKKEEPER
QUARTERBACK
ABLE-BODIED
VINEYARD
(intersecting words: TWENTY-NINE, AUDIO-VISUAL, THROUGHOUT, EYEWITNESS, MOTORCYCLE, THREE-FOURTHS, PART-TIME, ABSENT-MINDED)

Lesson 34 • Compound Words and Hyphenates   139

Proofreading
Use the proofreading marks to correct the mistakes in the article below. Then, write the misspelled **list words** correctly on the lines.

Proofreading Marks
◯ spelling mistake   ⌃ add comma
≡ capital letter   ⊔ add space

Motorcycling became popular throuhout the world shortly after the dawn of the twentieth century. The first gas-powered motor-cycle was, in fact, invented in 1885 by Gottlieb Daimler, a german engineer. Aside from a leather seat, handlbars, and two wheels it looked very little like today's machines. In America, the Harley-davidson company manufactured its first cycle in 1903, and it wouldn't take an expert bookeeper to track the company's success. By 1913, Harley-Davidson was manufacturing over 12,000 cycles annually. Today, ablebodied people everywhere use motorcycles for both recreation and transportation, especially in areas such as Europe where gasoline is more expensive than it is in the United states.

1. throughout
2. motorcycle
3. handlebars
4. bookkeeper
5. able-bodied

Writing Sentences Using Personification
Read the following example of personification.
   The motorcycle gasped and coughed as it chugged uphill.
Write three sentences with personification using other forms of transportation, such as a bike, car, tugboat, or skateboard. Use **list words** if possible. After proofreading and revising your sentences, share them with a small group. Talk about how the personification makes the description of the vehicle or mode of transportation more interesting.

BONUS WORDS

grouchy	queasy	overwrought	stumbled	shuffled
haughty	skeptical	devoured	wheezed	rambled

Write the **bonus word** that matches each synonym.

1. nervous __overwrought__
2. grumpy __grouchy__
3. doubtful __skeptical__
4. arrogant __haughty__
5. dragged __shuffled__
6. tripped __stumbled__
7. gasped __wheezed__
8. ate __devoured__
9. nauseous __queasy__
10. roamed __rambled__

40   Lesson 34 • Compound Words and Hyphenates

Puzzle Emphasize to students that if a word has a hyphen they are to write a hyphen in a box.

Spelling and Writing   Page 140
Proofreading Use this sentence to review the proofreading marks: "Let's fixa lunch" siad dad.

Writing Sentences Using Personification Ask students to name the object that is being personified and what human traits are attributed to it. (*motorcycle: gasped, coughed*) Then, have students suggest objects they might like to write about. List the ideas on the board and urge the class to think of human traits that could be applied to the different objects. Encourage students to use these ideas as they write.

Bonus Words   Page 140
Human Characteristics Ask students to define the **bonus words**, having them consult dictionaries to discover the meanings of any unfamiliar words. Encourage volunteers to use the words in oral sentences. If desired, have students use one or more of the words to write a brief character sketch of a real or fictional person.

Bonus Words Test
1. The man **rambled** around the country for years.
2. My stomach was **queasy** after the rough ferry ride.
3. Leon was so hungry he quickly **devoured** the steak.
4. Al has a **grouchy** voice, but he's really very pleasant.
5. She **wheezed** and coughed because of her allergies.
6. Pam was **skeptical** about what she read in the paper.
7. The elderly man **shuffled** up the hall in his slippers.
8. In a **haughty** tone, he ordered me to move his bags.
9. The actress **stumbled** onto the stage and fell.
10. Mom was **overwrought** with worry when I was late.

Final Test
1. The light flashed in **two-thousandths** of a second.
2. That **motorcycle** has a powerful engine!
3. Ella used **audio-visual** aids in her science project.
4. Was he an **eyewitness** to the first space launch?
5. Cassie gripped the **handlebars** of her new bike.
6. It was chilly in the **air-conditioned** theater.
7. The **spacecraft** orbited the moon for three days.
8. Tanya bought **loose-leaf** paper for her notebook.
9. The inn's **bookkeeper** totaled the day's receipts.
10. These grapes were grown in Granddad's **vineyard**.
11. Through **self-sacrifice**, she succeeded.
12. Juan has a **part-time** job two days a week.
13. The **absent-minded** woman lost her keys again.
14. Is the **copyright** date on our encyclopedia 2001?
15. Len did the job in **three-fourths** the normal time.
16. The news spread quickly **throughout** the school.
17. We need **able-bodied** people to move the piano.
18. Add three-hundredths to **nine-hundredths**.
19. The **quarterback** is going for the touchdown!
20. Maria earned **twenty-nine** dollars mowing lawns.

Challenging Words

Objective
To spell words that do not follow spelling rules

Pretest

1. The continuous rain was **beneficial** to the crops.
2. Did they **eliminate** two of the contestants?
3. We had **numerous** complaints about the service.
4. Which **restaurant** serves the best Chinese food?
5. Folk tales were passed down as an oral **tradition**.
6. A **hypocrite** says one thing and means another.
7. The price of this dress is **extravagant**!
8. He has the **privilege** of leading the holiday parade.
9. Ron's new bike is **similar** to the one that Will has.
10. Vi has a **tremendous** ability to learn new things.
11. Such harsh **criticism** of the book was unexpected.
12. Lying in bed late on Saturday mornings is a **luxury**.
13. Mrs. Lopez is a **prominent** official in the town.
14. Mieko signed her letter, "**Sincerely** yours."
15. The boys took sailing lessons at the **yacht** club.
16. The school board sets the **educational** standards.
17. Joan of Arc was a **martyr** who died for her beliefs.
18. We will **probably** go to the beach for our vacation.
19. Stacy is not **susceptible** to the influence of others.
20. Did the **suddenness** of the storm surprise you?

Spelling Strategy   *Page 141*

Discuss the spelling rule with students and stress that there are some words to which no handy spelling rules apply. Point out that the pronunciation of these challenging words helps little when spelling them. The spelling patterns of these words must be studied and practiced. Then, discuss the spelling patterns of the **list words**, helping students to recognize the spelling difficulties of each word.

Vocabulary Development When finished, you may wish to have students find antonyms for as many of the **list words** in the activity as they can.

Dictionary Skills If needed, you may wish to suggest that students consult the pronunciation key in their dictionaries to review the diacritical marks.

Spelling Practice   *Pages 142–143*

Word Analysis Tell students that saying or repeating a word to themselves may or may not help them recall the letters that are missing. Urge students to refer to the **list words** on page 143 if they are doubtful about the spelling of any word.

Word Application Have a volunteer explain the directions. If necessary, elicit from students the answers to the first item to be sure they understand the process. (*numerous, prominent*)

TIP
Some words are difficult to spell because they don't follow the usual spelling rules. The best way to become familiar with these challenging words is to study, memorize, and practice using them.

Word	"Trick"	Word	"Trick"
yacht	silent ch	luxury	x = /gzh/
hypocrite	y = /i/, silent e	susceptible	second s is silent
similar	ar = /ər/	martyr	y = /ə/

Vocabulary Development

Write the **list word** from column **B** that matches the synonym in column **A**.

A		B
1. inclined	susceptible	suddenness
2. favorable	beneficial	numerous
3. informative	educational	criticism
4. remove	eliminate	restaurant
5. many	numerous	eliminate
6. eatery	restaurant	prominent
7. review	criticism	extravagant
8. outstanding	prominent	luxury
9. lavish	extravagant	educational
10. abruptness	suddenness	susceptible
11. indulgence	luxury	beneficial

Dictionary Skills

Write the **list word** that matches each sound-spelling.

1. (luk'shə rē) luxury
2. (trə dish'ən) tradition
3. (priv''l ij) privilege
4. (hip'ə krit) hypocrite
5. (tri men'dəs) tremendous
6. (sim'ə lər) similar
7. (sin sir'lē) sincerely
8. (yät) yacht
9. (mär'tər) martyr
10. (präb'ə blē) probably

LIST WORDS
1. beneficial
2. eliminate
3. numerous
4. restaurant
5. tradition
6. hypocrite
7. extravagant
8. privilege
9. similar
10. tremendous
11. criticism
12. luxury
13. prominent
14. sincerely
15. yacht
16. educational
17. martyr
18. probably
19. susceptible
20. suddenness

141

DID YOU KNOW?
Restaurant comes from the French word meaning "restore." When we go to a restaurant to eat, we hope to have our strength and energy restored.

Spelling Practice
Word Analysis

Fill in the missing letters to form **list words**. Then, write the words on the lines.

1. trem_e_nd_o_u_s   tremendous
2. m_a_rt_y_r   martyr
3. ben_e_fic_i_al   beneficial
4. prob_a_b_ly   probably
5. educat_i_o_na_l   educational
6. sin_c_er_e_ly   sincerely
7. su_d_d_e_nn_e_s_s   suddenness
8. h_y_po_c_rite   hypocrite
9. crit_i_ci_s_m   criticism
10. su_s_c_ept_i_ble   susceptible
11. l_u_x_u_r_y   luxury
12. ya_c_h_t   yacht
13. prom_i_n_ent   prominent
14. rest_a_u_r_a_nt   restaurant
15. priv_i_l_e_g_e   privilege

Word Application

Replace the underlined words in each sentence with **list words**, and write them on the lines.

1. There have been <u>many</u> occasions on which <u>important</u> people have visited the monument.
   numerous   prominent

2. It is a <u>high honor</u> to share the <u>custom</u> of Thanksgiving with such kind people.
   privilege   tradition

3. Lack of funds will help to <u>do away with</u> all of the <u>lavish</u> frills that we once enjoyed.
   eliminate   extravagant

4. The <u>quickness</u> of the storm caught the captain of the <u>large boat</u> off guard.
   suddenness   yacht

5. Ruby's <u>eatery</u> is <u>comparable</u> to those found along major highways throughout the country.
   restaurant   similar

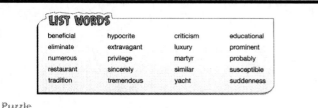

LIST WORDS

beneficial	hypocrite	criticism	educational
eliminate	extravagant	luxury	prominent
numerous	privilege	martyr	probably
restaurant	sincerely	similar	susceptible
tradition	tremendous	yacht	suddenness

Puzzle
Use the **list words** to complete the crossword puzzle.

ACROSS
1. a special right
2. very many
4. very likely; without much doubt
6. one who pretends to be virtuous
8. being of help or use
9. a place where meals are bought and eaten
13. having feelings that are easily affected
16. very large or great
17. handing down of customs
18. almost the same
19. the act of making judgments

DOWN
1. widely known; famous
3. giving instruction
5. anything that gives comfort, but is not necessary for life
7. a large boat
10. honestly; truthfully
11. spending more than one can afford
12. the quality of happening unexpectedly
14. do away with
15. one who suffers for a belief or cause

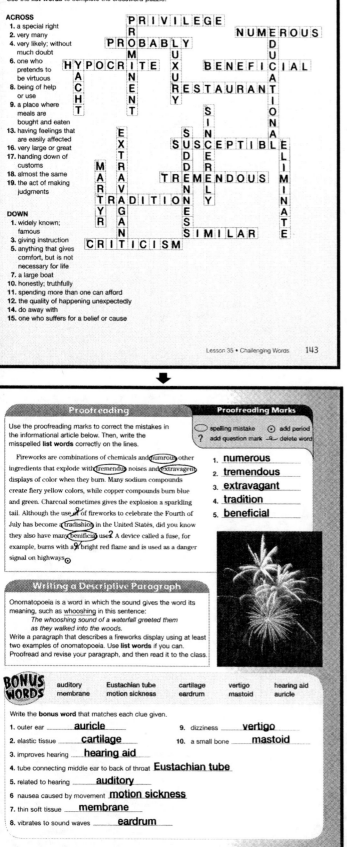

Proofreading
Use the proofreading marks to correct the mistakes in the informational article below. Then, write the misspelled **list words** correctly on the lines.

Fireworks are combinations of chemicals and numerous other ingredients that explode with tremendus noises and extravagent displays of color when they burn. Many sodium compounds create fiery yellow colors, while copper compounds burn blue and green. Charcoal sometimes gives the explosion a sparkling tail. Although the use of of fireworks to celebrate the Fourth of July has become a tradishion in the United States, did you know they also have many benificial uses? A device called a fuse, for example, burns with a bright red flame and is used as a danger signal on highways.

Proofreading Marks
⬭ spelling mistake   ⊙ add period
? add question mark   ⌿ delete word

1. numerous
2. tremendous
3. extravagant
4. tradition
5. beneficial

Writing a Descriptive Paragraph
Onomatopoeia is a word in which the sound gives the word its meaning, such as whooshing in this sentence:
The whooshing sound of a waterfall greeted them as they walked into the woods.
Write a paragraph that describes a fireworks display using at least two examples of onomatopoeia. Use **list words** if you can. Proofread and revise your paragraph, and then read it to the class.

BONUS WORDS

auditory	Eustachian tube	cartilage	vertigo	hearing aid
membrane	motion sickness	eardrum	mastoid	auricle

Write the **bonus word** that matches each clue given.

1. outer ear   auricle
2. elastic tissue   cartilage
3. improves hearing   hearing aid
4. tube connecting middle ear to back of throat   Eustachian tube
5. related to hearing   auditory
6. nausea caused by movement   motion sickness
7. thin soft tissue   membrane
8. vibrates to sound waves   eardrum
9. dizziness   vertigo
10. a small bone   mastoid

Puzzle Remind students to use capital letters and to print neatly as they fill in the puzzle.

Spelling and Writing   Page 144
Proofreading Review the proofreading marks with this sentence: *"Wat does is 'wary' mean" asked Leah*

Writing a Descriptive Paragraph Point out the spelling difficulties in the word *onomatopoeia*. Then, have students identify the example of onomatopoeia in the sentence. (*whooshing*) Before they write, urge students to make a list of three sounds describing a fireworks display. Afterward, have students read their sentences, using good oral expression.

Bonus Words
The Ear and Hearing Discuss the human ear, applying the **bonus words** to the discussion. Have students consult a dictionary or encyclopedia to find the meanings of any unfamiliar words. If possible, provide a diagram or model of the human ear, and have students point out the auditory canal, eardrum or tympanic membrane, mastoid, Eustachian tube, and auricle.

Bonus Words Test
1. The fleshy outer ear consists of skin and **cartilage**.
2. The **auricle**, or outer ear, collects sound waves.
3. The eardrum is the tympanic **membrane**.
4. Sound waves cause the **eardrum** to vibrate.
5. Sound travels through the **auditory** canal.
6. Swallow to try to open your **Eustachian tube**.
7. The **mastoid** is the bony area of the middle ear.
8. An ear infection may cause **vertigo**, or dizziness.
9. A **hearing aid** is a device that improves hearing.
10. Inner-ear problems can cause **motion sickness**.

Final Test
1. Lionel's baby is **susceptible** to ear infections.
2. It's **tradition** to eat turkey on Thanksgiving.
3. Daily exercise is **beneficial** to your health.
4. What a **privilege** it would be to meet them!
5. There are **educational** programs on television.
6. He is **sincerely** sorry that he broke the window.
7. The princess sailed into the harbor on her **yacht**.
8. The **suddenness** of his actions startled us.
9. A beaver has **prominent** teeth.
10. Did the girls buy **similar** dresses for the prom?
11. I'd be a **hypocrite** if I said I liked that hat.
12. Stricter state laws will **eliminate** litter on the roads.
13. The car was much too **extravagant** for his budget.
14. We **probably** won't be late if we leave now.
15. The **tremendous** crash of thunder scared me.
16. Debra ate dinner at the new Mexican **restaurant**.
17. A **martyr** sacrifices his or her life for a cause.
18. The editor explained her **criticism** of my story.
19. We saw **numerous** animals at the wildlife preserve.
20. They won a trip to a **luxury** hotel in Hawaii.

Objective
To review spelling words with Latin roots, prefixes, sports words, compound words, hyphenated words, and challenging words

Spelling Strategy   *Page 145*

Tell students that in this lesson they will review the skills and spelling words studied in Lessons 31–35. You may wish to have students refer to previous spelling rules to review Latin roots, prefixes, words from sports, compound words, and challenging words.

Spelling Practice   *Pages 145–147*

Lesson 31 To review the Latin roots *vor, lud, lus, viv, vit, spect, ver, temp*, write on the board and discuss: *suspect, elude, vitality, introvert, carnivore,* and *temporal*. Then, have students identify the Latin roots in the **list words**. Point out the additional write-on lines to students and encourage them to add two words from Lesson 31 that they found especially difficult, or assign words that seemed difficult for everyone. (Repeat this procedure for each lesson in the Review.)

Lesson 32 Ask students what *archery, sprinter, hockey,* and *goalkeeper* have in common. (*They are sports words.*) Elicit that the **list words** are also words from sports, and then discuss their meanings.

Lesson 33 Discuss the meanings of the Latin and Greek prefixes in these words: *hyperactive, multiple, polytheism, omnipresent, pandemonium,* and *equidistant*. Then, have students identify the prefixes in the **list words**. Point out that context clues will help students determine the answer for each sentence.

Lesson 34 Have students come to the board and draw a line between the two words that make up each of these compound words: *handlebars, motorcycle, self-sacrifice, quarterback,* and *able-bodied*. Then, have students identify the words that make up each **list word**.

Lesson 35 Ask students to spell these words: *eliminate, prominent, educational,* and *suddenness*. Remind students that these words have unexpected spellings that don't follow specific rules. Then, discuss the spellings of the **list words**. Elicit from students that they must unscramble the **list words** to complete the puzzle.

Show What You Know   *Page 148*

Point out that this review will help students know if they have mastered the words in Lessons 31–35. Have a volunteer restate the directions and tell which word in the first item should be marked. (*two-thousanths*) When students have finished, have them write their misspelled words correctly.

88

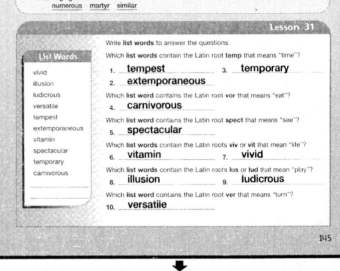

TIPS
- Recognizing and understanding Latin roots and Latin and Greek prefixes can help you spell and understand unfamiliar words. Some Latin roots and their meanings include **ver** ("turn") as in **ex**vert ("outgoing") and **viv, vit** ("live") as in re**viv**e ("return to life").
- Some Latin and Greek prefixes include **pan** ("all") as in **pan**orama ("sweeping view") and **multi** ("many") as in **multi**colored ("many colors").
- Some English words are associated with one specific topic. These words are from sports.
  acrobatics   umpire   scrimmage
- There are numerous spelling rules that can help you figure out how to spell a difficult word. When spelling a compound word, think about the way the individual words that make up the compound word are spelled. Some compound words are spelled with a hyphen dividing the two words.
  throughout   two-thousandths
- Remember to divide compound words into syllables between the words that form the compound word.
  book/keeper
- Some words do not follow ordinary spelling rules. Memorize and practice spelling these challenging words.
  numerous   martyr   similar

Lesson 31

Write **list words** to answer the questions.

List Words
vivid
illusion
ludicrous
versatile
tempest
extemporaneous
vitamin
spectacular
temporary
carnivorous

Which **list words** contain the Latin root **temp** that means "time"?
1. tempest   3. temporary
2. extemporaneous

Which **list word** contains the Latin root **vor** that means "eat"?
4. carnivorous

Which **list word** contains the Latin root **spect** that means "see"?
5. spectacular

Which **list words** contain the Latin roots **viv** or **vit** that mean "life"?
6. vitamin   7. vivid

Which **list words** contain the Latin roots **lus** or **lud** that mean "play"?
8. illusion   9. ludicrous

Which **list word** contains the Latin root **ver** that means "turn"?
10. versatile

145

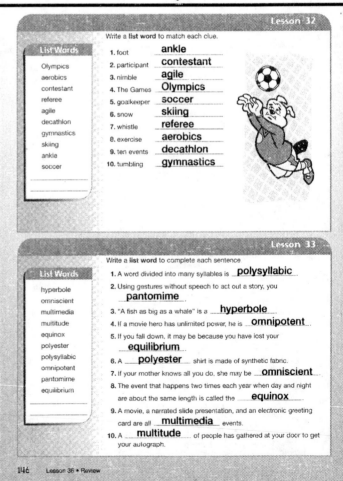

Lesson 32

Write a **list word** to match each clue.

List Words
Olympics
aerobics
contestant
referee
agile
decathlon
gymnastics
skiing
ankle
soccer

1. foot   ankle
2. participant   contestant
3. nimble   agile
4. The Games   Olympics
5. goalkeeper   soccer
6. snow   skiing
7. whistle   referee
8. exercise   aerobics
9. ten events   decathlon
10. tumbling   gymnastics

Lesson 33

Write a **list word** to complete each sentence.

List Words
hyperbole
omniscient
multimedia
multitude
equinox
polyester
polysyllabic
omnipotent
pantomime
equilibrium

1. A word divided into many syllables is polysyllabic
2. Using gestures without speech to act out a story, you pantomime
3. "A fish as big as a whale" is a hyperbole
4. If a movie hero has unlimited power, he is omnipotent
5. If you fall down, it may be because you have lost your equilibrium
6. A polyester shirt is made of synthetic fabric.
7. If your mother knows all you do, she may be omniscient
8. The event that happens two times each year when day and night are about the same length is called the equinox
9. A movie, a narrated slide presentation, and an electronic greeting card are all multimedia events.
10. A multitude of people has gathered at your door to get your autograph.

Lesson 34

List Words

absent-minded
twenty-nine
spacecraft
eyewitness
air-conditioned
part-time
vineyard
bookkeeper
copyright
audio-visual

Write the **list word** for each definition clue.

1. a number less than thirty **twenty-nine**
2. relating to both sight and sound **audio-visual**
3. not full-time **part-time**
4. a vehicle for space travel **spacecraft**
5. a garden where grapes grow **vineyard**
6. a poor memory; forgetful **absent-minded**
7. an observer; spectator **eyewitness**
8. an accountant; keeper of business records **bookkeeper**
9. the legal right to publish and sell printed materials **copyright**
10. cooled, filtered air **air-conditioned**

Lesson 35

List Words

beneficial
restaurant
hypocrite
extravagant
privilege
tremendous
criticism
yacht
probably
susceptible

Unscramble the **list words** to complete the crossword puzzle.

ACROSS
2. PETBILECUSS
7. CATHY
8. BLARBOYP
9. ARTSUENTAR
10. STROMNEEUD

DOWN
1. IMTRICISC
3. GRIEVEPILE
4. FACEBLIINE
5. TROYPHICE
6. GREATAXTANV

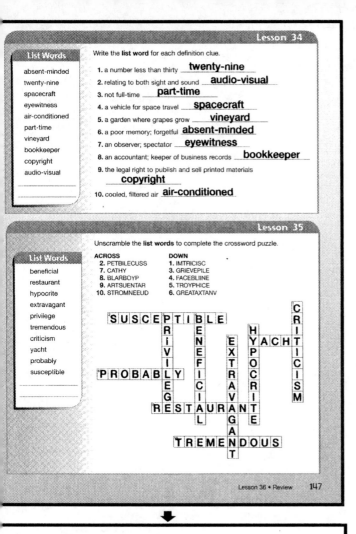

SUSCEPTIBLE
PROBABLY
RESTAURANT
TREMENDOUS
PRIVILEGE
BENEFICIAL
EXTRAVAGANT
HYPOCRITE
YACHT
CRITICISM

Lesson 36 • Review   147

Show What You Know

Lessons 31–35 • Review

One word is misspelled in each set of **list words**. Fill in the circle next to the **list word** that is spelled incorrectly.

1. ○ carnivorous ○ aerobics ● two-thousanths ○ multiple
2. ○ quarterback ○ illusion ○ equinox ● contestent
3. ○ goalkeeper ○ polyester ○ ludicrous ● bookeeper
4. ○ audio-visual ● referree ○ copyright ○ suspect
5. ○ sprinter ● polysilabic ○ nine-hundredths ○ versatile
6. ○ three-fourths ○ agile ● ellude ○ equidistant
7. ● decathelon ○ polygamy ○ beneficial ○ illusion
8. ● iliminate ○ retrospect ○ omnipotent ○ gymnastics
9. ○ tempest ● pantomine ○ numerous ○ restaurant
10. ○ equilibrium ○ vitality ○ tradition ● sking
11. ○ umpire ● hypocrit ○ extemporaneous ○ polygon
12. ● intravert ○ ankle ○ pandemonium ○ extravagant
13. ○ throughout ● priviledge ○ revive ○ scrimmage
14. ○ similar ○ kayak ● handelbars ○ temporal
15. ○ motorcycle ○ vitamin ○ soccer ● trmendous
16. ○ extrovert ● critisism ○ absent-minded ○ hockey
17. ● twentynine ○ hyperbole ○ inverse ○ luxury
18. ○ omniscient ○ spacecraft ○ prominent ● spectaculer
19. ○ temporary ○ eyewitness ○ hyperactive ● sincerly
20. ○ yacht ○ vivid ● selfsacrifice ○ part-time
21. ● abl-bodied ○ multimedia ○ acrobatics ○ educational
22. ○ multicolored ● marteyr ○ omnipresent ○ toboggan
23. ○ archery ○ panorama ● probabaly ○ vineyard
24. ● suseptible ○ Olympics ○ air-conditioned ○ polytheism
25. ○ multitude ○ loose-leaf ● suddeness ○ sportscaster

148   Lesson 36 • Review

Final Test

1. Bears eat meat, which means they're **carnivorous**.
2. They ordered tickets for the **Olympics**.
3. I used **hyperbole** when I said I could eat a horse.
4. Dan is so **absent-minded**; he loses his keys!
5. A week relaxing will be **beneficial** to your health.
6. The magician's trick was an **illusion**.
7. The **aerobics** instructor demonstrated the exercise.
8. Our **omniscient** teacher is aware of everything.
9. Are there **twenty-nine** students in Ms. Woo's class?
10. Randy got a job as a waiter in a **restaurant**.
11. The comedian wore a **ludicrous**, fruit-covered hat.
12. Amir was the first **contestant** in the diving event.
13. The **multimedia** music and laser show was fun.
14. The **spacecraft** landed after a month in space.
15. A **hypocrite** will not give you a sincere opinion.
16. Alexa is a **versatile** athlete who plays many sports.
17. The coach and **referee** argued about the penalty.
18. The king waved to the **multitude** from the balcony.
19. The **eyewitness** told the police what happened.
20. The silk blouse was an **extravagant** purchase.
21. Torrential rain accompanied the violent **tempest**.
22. The **agile** athlete moved quickly.
23. The vernal **equinox** marks the beginning of spring.
24. Is Tammy a **part-time** or full-time worker?
25. It was a **privilege** to shake the President's hand.
26. Her **extemporaneous** speech was dynamic.
27. Erki Nool won the Olympic **decathalon** in 2000.
28. The T-shirt is made from cotton and **polyester**.
29. We rode in an **air-conditioned** bus.
30. What a **tremendous** noise the explosion made!
31. His disease was caused by a lack of **vitamin** B.
32. The **gymnastics** competition was held in our gym.
33. Onomatopoeia is a **polysyllabic** word.
34. The smell of ripe grapes permeated the **vineyard**.
35. Her severe **criticism** of my song hurt my feelings.
36. Look at that **spectacular** double rainbow!
37. Tim went cross-country **skiing** in Maine last winter.
38. Ancient Greeks believed the gods were **omnipotent**.
39. Dad works as a **bookkeeper**.
40. The luxury **yacht** has five bedrooms.
41. Her job is **temporary** and will end soon.
42. Donna taped her **ankle** before she played soccer.
43. He acted out a **pantomime** of a monkey in a cage.
44. Pablo will apply for a **copyright** of his play.
45. You **probably** don't remember, but we've met.
46. Alma uses startling, **vivid** colors in her paintings.
47. Most **soccer** balls are black and white.
48. Her **equilibrium** was disturbed by the flight.
49. I returned the film to the **audio-visual** room.
50. The old dog is weak and **susceptible** to disease.

89

Review Word List

Lesson 6

Lesson 1
abdomen
actual
advancement
alien
allegiance
amateur
anniversary
approximately
association
bachelor

Lesson 2
embarrass
environment
estimate
exaggerate
hostess
lenient
medium
recollection
sterilize
tedious

Lesson 3
bulletin
capacity
cinnamon
circular
illustration
isolate
peninsula
prohibit
testimony
villain

Lesson 4
anticipation
commercial
competition
complicated
conclusion
continuous
microphone
ominous
opponent
patriotic

Lesson 5
amusement
circumference
culture
industrious
linoleum
premium
smudge
subtle
unity
vacuum

Lesson 12

Lesson 7
apparatus
apparel
appendage
appendix
appraise
appreciation
apprentice
appropriate
assault
assurance

Lesson 8
accelerate
accent
accommodate
accomplice
accurate
accustomed
acquire
affix
attitude
attraction

Lesson 9
civilization
complexion
expression
lotion
occasion
occupation
proportion
recitation
revolution
suspicion

Lesson 10
boulevard
camouflage
chauffeur
courteous
expertise
gourmet
lacquer
lieutenant
pursuit
silhouette

Lesson 11
affliction
construction
dictator
distract
fractured
historical
impact
minister
persistent
tactful

Review Word List

Lesson 18

Lesson 13
confidential
conscientious
financial
harmonious
infectious
influential
initial
provincial
spacious
unconscious

Lesson 16
attainable
available
charitable
consumable
legible
permissible
pitiable
quotable
reliable
responsible

Lesson 14
academically
annual
comically
drastically
economic
gradual
ideally
incidentally
mutual
systematic

Lesson 17
calendar
essential
fragile
gauge
league
neutral
phenomenon
sergeant
synonym
valise

Lesson 15
commission
fluctuate
fluent
fluoride
inanimate
influence
intermission
manipulate
manual
omission

Lesson 24

Lesson 19
aerial
dialect
fertile
foliage
horizontal
hurricane
irrigate
plateau
reservoir
vicinity

Lesson 22
aggressor
alliance
ghetto
inaugurate
legislature
nuclear
propaganda
rebellion
recession
referendum

Lesson 20
analyze
bacteria
contour
crucial
diagram
epidemic
evolution
frequency
sociology
specific

Lesson 23
authorize
bureau
calculator
collateral
executive
remittance
repossess
salary
signature
statistics

Lesson 21
denominator
diagonal
equation
isosceles
minimum
protractor
symmetrical
trapezoid
variable
vertical

Review Word List

Lesson 30

Lesson 25
caffeine
convenient
efficient
fiery
financier
heirloom
hierarchy
hygiene
patience
surveillance

Lesson 26
adolescence
arrogance
coincidence
correspondence
essence
obedience
occurrence
preference
significance
vengeance

Lesson 27
cyclone
cylinder
cynical
encyclopedia
paralyze
physician
python
sympathetic
synopsis
synthetic

Lesson 28
aria
fugue
maestro
pianist
podium
rhapsody
rhythm
staccato
synthesizer
xylophone

Lesson 29
adobe
cafeteria
canyon
coyote
iguana
jaguar
palomino
poinsettia
siesta
tortilla

Lesson 36

Lesson 31
carnivorous
extemporaneous
illusion
ludicrous
spectacular
tempest
temporary
versatile
vitamin
vivid

Lesson 32
aerobics
agile
ankle
contestant
decathlon
gymnastics
Olympics
referee
skiing
soccer

Lesson 33
equilibrium
equinox
hyperbole
multimedia
multitude
omnipotent
omniscient
pantomime
polyester
polysyllabic

Lesson 34
absent-minded
air-conditioned
audio-visual
bookkeeper
copyright
eyewitness
part-time
spacecraft
twenty-nine
vineyard

Lesson 35
beneficial
criticism
extravagant
hypocrite
privilege
probably
restaurant
susceptible
tremendous
yacht

Name _____

Review Test (Side A)

Read each set of words. Fill in the circle next to the word that is spelled correctly.

1. ⓐ envirement ⓒ enviroment
   ⓑ enviremint ⓓ environment

2. ⓐ onimous ⓒ omminous
   ⓑ ominus ⓓ ominous

3. ⓐ allegience ⓒ allegance
   ⓑ allegiance ⓓ alegiance

4. ⓐ cinamon ⓒ cinnamon
   ⓑ cinnoman ⓓ cinnamen

5. ⓐ commercial ⓒ comercial
   ⓑ comertial ⓓ commertial

6. ⓐ cuntinuous ⓒ continuos
   ⓑ continous ⓓ continuous

7. ⓐ tedious ⓒ tideous
   ⓑ tedeous ⓓ tidious

8. ⓐ abdoman ⓒ abdomen
   ⓑ abdemen ⓓ abdamen

9. ⓐ circumfrance ⓒ circumference
   ⓑ circumferance ⓓ circumfrence

10. ⓐ ilustration ⓒ illustrateion
    ⓑ illustration ⓓ illustrasion

11. ⓐ exxagerate ⓒ exaggarate
    ⓑ exaggerrate ⓓ exaggerate

12. ⓐ testemony ⓒ testimoney
    ⓑ testimony ⓓ testamoney

13. ⓐ amateur ⓒ ammature
    ⓑ amachure ⓓ amatuer

© Pearson Education, Inc., publishing as Modern Curriculum Press.
All rights reserved.

Lesson 6 • Review   93

Review Test (Side B)

Read each set of words. Fill in the circle next to the word that is spelled correctly.

14. (a) villen   (c) villan
    (b) villian   (d) villain

15. (a) linoluem   (c) linoleum
    (b) linolleum   (d) linnoleum

16. (a) anniversary   (c) anniversery
    (b) aniversary   (d) aniversery

17. (a) embarass   (c) emberass
    (b) embarrass   (d) embarras

18. (a) opponant   (c) oponent
    (b) oponant   (d) opponent

19. (a) premium   (c) premiem
    (b) premiem   (d) premuim

20. (a) peninsula   (c) penensula
    (b) peninsulla   (d) penninsula

21. (a) vacume   (c) vacuem
    (b) vaccum   (d) vacuum

22. (a) linient   (c) leniant
    (b) lenient   (d) leaniant

23. (a) subtle   (c) sudtle
    (b) suddle   (d) subtel

24. (a) approximately   (c) aproximatly
    (b) aproximately   (d) approximatly

25. (a) competetion   (c) compitition
    (b) competition   (d) compettition

Review Test (Side A)

Lesson 12

Read each set of phrases. Fill in the circle next to the phrase with an underlined word that is spelled correctly.

1. ⓐ his <u>tactful</u> manner
    ⓑ that <u>tacktful</u> statement
    ⓒ your <u>tackful</u> comment
    ⓓ her <u>tactfull</u> criticism

2. ⓐ his lengthy <u>recitetation</u>
    ⓑ your monotonous <u>resitasion</u>
    ⓒ her public <u>recitasion</u>
    ⓓ a dramatic <u>recitation</u>

3. ⓐ this commercial <u>bulevard</u>
    ⓑ densely populated <u>boulevard</u>
    ⓒ the tree-lined <u>boulavard</u>
    ⓓ that residential <u>bolevard</u>

4. ⓐ weight-lifting <u>apparatus</u>
    ⓑ safety <u>aparrattus</u>
    ⓒ the gymnastics <u>aparratus</u>
    ⓓ firefighting <u>apparratus</u>

5. ⓐ the famous <u>expresion</u>
    ⓑ that humorous <u>expression</u>
    ⓒ a witty <u>expreshion</u>
    ⓓ a quotable <u>expretion</u>

6. ⓐ the previous <u>dicktator</u>
    ⓑ the amiable <u>dictater</u>
    ⓒ the despised <u>dicktater</u>
    ⓓ the country's <u>dictator</u>

7. ⓐ the <u>aproppriate</u> answer
    ⓑ <u>apropriate</u> attire
    ⓒ an <u>approppriate</u> response
    ⓓ an <u>appropriate</u> amount

8. ⓐ an ambitious <u>persuit</u>
    ⓑ in <u>persuite</u> of happiness
    ⓒ in dedicated <u>pursuit</u>
    ⓓ in <u>pursuite</u> of criminals

9. ⓐ his dark <u>complexion</u>
    ⓑ her freckled <u>complection</u>
    ⓒ her fair <u>cumplection</u>
    ⓓ his clear <u>cumplexion</u>

10. ⓐ that <u>courtous</u> student
    ⓑ the <u>courteous</u> diplomat
    ⓒ his <u>curteous</u> disposition
    ⓓ a <u>corteous</u> pilot

11. ⓐ the decorated <u>lieutenant</u>
    ⓑ a first <u>lieutenent</u>
    ⓒ a female <u>leutenant</u>
    ⓓ the commanding <u>liutenant</u>

12. ⓐ <u>apreciation</u> and gratitude
    ⓑ <u>apretiation</u> and thoughtfulness
    ⓒ with sincere <u>appretiation</u>
    ⓓ with genuine <u>appreciation</u>

13. ⓐ to <u>acommodate</u> your idea
    ⓑ to <u>accommodate</u> guests
    ⓒ to <u>accomadate</u> patients
    ⓓ to <u>acomodate</u> the crowd

Review Test (Side B)

Lesson 12

Read each set of phrases. Fill in the circle next to the phrase with an underlined word that is spelled correctly.

14. (a) your positive atitude   (c) a negative attitude
    (b) this poor attittude   (d) his healthy atittude

15. (a) a likable shauffeur   (c) hired a shofer
    (b) the family chauffer   (d) an experienced chauffeur

16. (a) this church's minaster   (c) the compassionate minister
    (b) the sympathetic minisster   (d) a female minnister

17. (a) the blacksmith's apprentice   (c) an electrician's apprentiss
    (b) that mason's aprentiss   (d) a carpentry aprentice

18. (a) her lifelong ocuppation   (c) an unusual occupation
    (b) this lucrative ocuppasion   (d) a demanding occupasion

19. (a) to affix the label   (c) to affixe with glue
    (b) will afixe his signature   (d) to afix the sticker

20. (a) this hystorical city   (c) historicle fiction
    (b) a historical event   (d) hystoricle diaries

21. (a) that criminal's acompplice   (c) the smuggler's accompliss
    (b) this alleged acompliss   (d) the thief's accomplice

22. (a) a special occassion   (c) a memorable ocassion
    (b) this joyous ocasion   (d) a festive occasion

23. (a) informal apparel   (c) sleep aparrel
    (b) formal apparrel   (d) traditional apparell

24. (a) a fracksured thumb   (c) her fractured ankle
    (b) the fracktured bone   (d) his fracturred toe

25. (a) acquire a taste   (c) acquir a phone
    (b) aquire his degree   (d) acquier knowledge

Name _____

Review Test (Side A)

Read each sentence and set of words. Fill in the circle next to the word that is spelled correctly to complete the sentence.

1. This famous artist prefers to paint _____ objects.
   - ⓐ inannimate
   - ⓒ inanimate
   - ⓑ inaminate
   - ⓓ inanimmate

2. Food and water are _____ for human survival.
   - ⓐ essencial
   - ⓒ esential
   - ⓑ esencial
   - ⓓ essential

3. The _____ office could accommodate both physicians' practices.
   - ⓐ spacious
   - ⓒ spatious
   - ⓑ spacous
   - ⓓ spatous

4. The entire cast is _____ for the production's tremendous success.
   - ⓐ responsible
   - ⓒ risponsable
   - ⓑ risponsible
   - ⓓ responsable

5. A _____ was formed to investigate the alleged corruption.
   - ⓐ comission
   - ⓒ commition
   - ⓑ commision
   - ⓓ commission

6. The subway provides a _____ source of public transportation.
   - ⓐ relyable
   - ⓒ relyible
   - ⓑ reliable
   - ⓓ relible

7. The performers changed their costumes during the play's _____ .
   - ⓐ intermision
   - ⓒ intramission
   - ⓑ intermission
   - ⓓ intamission

8. _____ correspondence is filed in a locked cabinet.
   - ⓐ Confadential
   - ⓒ Confidential
   - ⓑ Confadencial
   - ⓓ Confidencial

9. The prime minister's major concern is _____ stability.
   - ⓐ econnomic
   - ⓒ ecanamic
   - ⓑ economic
   - ⓓ ecconomic

10. The man was _____ after the accident.
    - ⓐ unconscious
    - ⓒ unconscius
    - ⓑ unconcience
    - ⓓ unconscience

Review Test (Side B)

Lesson 18

Read each sentence and set of words. Fill in the circle next to the word that is spelled correctly to complete the sentence.

11. The newlyweds consulted a _____ advisor for investment advice.
  ⓐ finantiel   ⓒ financial
  ⓑ finantial   ⓓ finnancial

12. Using a _____ contributes to good time management.
  ⓐ calender   ⓒ calander
  ⓑ calandar   ⓓ calendar

13. Outerwear was _____ reduced during the winter clearance sale.
  ⓐ drastically   ⓒ drasticly
  ⓑ drasticaly   ⓓ drasticcly

14. The all-star _____ includes the best male and female players.
  ⓐ leag   ⓒ leuge
  ⓑ league   ⓓ leage

15. The elderly man was commended for his numerous _____ acts.
  ⓐ charitabal   ⓒ charitible
  ⓑ charatible   ⓓ charitable

16. Attendance at the _____ realtor's convention was larger than expected.
  ⓐ anuall   ⓒ anual
  ⓑ annule   ⓓ annual

17. The town committee voted to put _____ in the water.
  ⓐ floride   ⓒ floruid
  ⓑ fluoride   ⓓ flouride

18. My cousin is a _____ in the army.
  ⓐ sargent   ⓒ sargeant
  ⓑ seargeant   ⓓ sergeant

19. Food is a _____ commodity.
  ⓐ consumable   ⓒ consumeable
  ⓑ connsumable   ⓓ consumabel

20. I saw Mark, _____ , at the meeting.
  ⓐ insidentally ⓒ incidentaly
  ⓑ insientally   ⓓ incidentally

Review Test (Side A)

Lesson 24

Read each set of words. Fill in the circle next to the word that is spelled correctly.

1. ⓐ propaganda   ⓒ proppaganda
   ⓑ propagganda   ⓓ propganda

2. ⓐ verticle   ⓒ vurtical
   ⓑ vertical   ⓓ verticl

3. ⓐ reservoir   ⓒ reservor
   ⓑ reservore   ⓓ resurvoire

4. ⓐ allience   ⓒ alliance
   ⓑ allyance   ⓓ allianse

5. ⓐ isoseles   ⓒ isosceles
   ⓑ isoceles   ⓓ iscosceles

6. ⓐ furtile   ⓒ furtle
   ⓑ fertile   ⓓ fertle

7. ⓐ ghettoe   ⓒ getto
   ⓑ ghetto   ⓓ gettoe

8. ⓐ symmetrical   ⓒ symetrical
   ⓑ symetricale   ⓓ symmetricle

9. ⓐ irigate   ⓒ irrugate
   ⓑ irrigat   ⓓ irrigate

10. ⓐ reccession   ⓒ resession
   ⓑ ricession   ⓓ recession

11. ⓐ denominater   ⓒ denomenator
   ⓑ dinominator   ⓓ denominator

12. ⓐ huricane   ⓒ hurricane
   ⓑ huriccane   ⓓ hericane

13. ⓐ inaugurrate   ⓒ inaugurate
   ⓑ inawgurate   ⓓ inaugerate

Review Test (Side B)

Read each set of words. Fill in the circle next to the word that is spelled correctly.

14. ⓐ trapazoid   ⓒ trepazoid
    ⓑ trapezoid   ⓓ trapezoed

15. ⓐ horizontal   ⓒ horizontle
    ⓑ horizontul   ⓓ horisontal

16. ⓐ reposess   ⓒ riposess
    ⓑ reposses   ⓓ repossess

17. ⓐ analize   ⓒ analyze
    ⓑ analise   ⓓ annalyze

18. ⓐ crutial   ⓒ crucial
    ⓑ crushial   ⓓ crutiel

19. ⓐ colatteral   ⓒ colleteral
    ⓑ colateral   ⓓ collateral

20. ⓐ diagram   ⓒ diegram
    ⓑ digram   ⓓ diagrem

21. ⓐ evelution   ⓒ evolushun
    ⓑ evolution   ⓓ evoltion

22. ⓐ remitance   ⓒ remitence
    ⓑ remittance   ⓓ remmitance

23. ⓐ salery   ⓒ selery
    ⓑ salary   ⓓ salarie

24. ⓐ contuor   ⓒ conture
    ⓑ kontour   ⓓ contour

25. ⓐ autherize   ⓒ authorize
    ⓑ authorise   ⓓ autherise

Review Test (Side A)

Read each set of phrases. Fill in the circle next to the phrase with an underlined word that is spelled correctly.

1. ⓐ an unlikely correspondance   ⓒ their weekly corespondance
   ⓑ the correspondence course   ⓓ irregular coresspondance

2. ⓐ that famous peanist   ⓒ a classical pianiste
   ⓑ the solo peaniste   ⓓ an accomplished pianist

3. ⓐ that palomino mare   ⓒ a small palamino
   ⓑ the well-trained palomeno   ⓓ my old pallomino

4. ⓐ the decorative pointsettia   ⓒ household poinsetia
   ⓑ a potted pointsetia   ⓓ a bright red poinsettia

5. ⓐ the respected maestro   ⓒ an enthusiastic maistro
   ⓑ the old mastro   ⓓ an eccentric maestroe

6. ⓐ lacking rythym   ⓒ sense of rythm
   ⓑ rhythm and blues   ⓓ irregular rhythym

7. ⓐ needed a seista   ⓒ after the seesta
   ⓑ an afternoon siesta   ⓓ before the sieste

8. ⓐ the deepest canyon   ⓒ a wide canyen
   ⓑ through the kanyon   ⓓ above a kanyen

9. ⓐ lacking any perference   ⓒ your color preference
   ⓑ preferrence for seafood   ⓓ his longtime perferrence

10. ⓐ the conductor's podium   ⓒ a wooden podeum
    ⓑ a broken podiume   ⓓ the speaker's podiume

11. ⓐ a fried torteya   ⓒ a corn tortella
    ⓑ the flour tortiya   ⓓ this tortilla batter

12. ⓐ vengeance and greed   ⓒ desire for vengance
    ⓑ the victim's vengeanse   ⓓ angry venganse

13. ⓐ high-pitched arria   ⓒ a long arrea
    ⓑ a melodious aria   ⓓ the beautiful ariea

Review Test (Side B)

Read each set of phrases. Fill in the circle next to the phrase with an underlined word that is spelled correctly.

14. (a) a <u>synical</u> opportunist (c) the <u>cynical</u> comedian
    (b) <u>sinical</u> workers (d) his <u>cinical</u> assistant

15. (a) feeling of <u>arogance</u> (c) the prince's <u>arragance</u>
    (b) unequalled <u>arroganse</u> (d) <u>arrogance</u> and conceit

16. (a) <u>conveniant</u> stores (c) a <u>convenient</u> location
    (b) a <u>convinient</u> time (d) <u>conveneant</u> helpers

17. (a) the frightening <u>pythonn</u> (c) a pet <u>pithon</u>
    (b) that young <u>pithonn</u> (d) a giant <u>python</u>

18. (a) constant <u>surveilance</u> (c) careful <u>serveillence</u>
    (b) camera <u>serveilance</u> (d) under police <u>surveillance</u>

19. (a) of major <u>significance</u> (c) the hidden <u>significance</u>
    (b) misunderstood <u>significanse</u> (d) its obvious <u>signeficance</u>

20. (a) a <u>sympathetic</u> listener (c) the <u>simpathetic</u> jury
    (b) <u>sympithetic</u> friends (d) a <u>simpithetic</u> visitor

21. (a) your daily <u>hygene</u> (c) conscientious dental <u>hygiene</u>
    (b) learning about <u>hygeane</u> (d) advice about <u>higiene</u>

22. (a) without <u>pacience</u> (c) a nurse's <u>pascience</u>
    (b) requiring <u>patiense</u> (d) <u>patience</u> and tolerance

23. (a) his family <u>phisician</u> (c) a busy <u>physitian</u>
    (b) the amicable <u>physician</u> (d) an accomplished <u>phisitian</u>

24. (a) a cherished <u>heirloom</u> (c) the antique <u>airloom</u>
    (b) an unusual <u>heirloome</u> (d) this royal <u>airloome</u>

25. (a) <u>synthetec</u> vegetables (c) of <u>synthetic</u> material
    (b) with <u>sinthetic</u> fabrics (d) some <u>synthetyc</u> chemicals

Name _____

Read each sentence and set of words. Fill in the circle next to the word that is spelled correctly to complete the sentence.

1. The athlete was too tired to finish the _____ .
   - ⓐ decathalon
   - ⓑ dicathlon
   - © dekathlon
   - ⓓ decathlon

2. Ask the technicians to repair the _____ equipment.
   - ⓐ audeovisual
   - ⓑ audio-visual
   - © audio-visuel
   - ⓓ awdiovisual

3. Many _____ animals live in the wilderness.
   - ⓐ carnivorous
   - ⓑ karnivorous
   - © carniverous
   - ⓓ carniverrous

4. He has good grades, so he will _____ pass the test.
   - ⓐ probably
   - ⓑ probley
   - © probabley
   - ⓓ probebly

5. Ellen was the goalie on her _____ team.
   - ⓐ soccor
   - ⓑ socer
   - © soccer
   - ⓓ seccer

6. She thanked her hosts for the _____ of staying with them.
   - ⓐ privelege
   - ⓑ priviledge
   - © privilege
   - ⓓ privlege

7. The actors were silent when they used _____ .
   - ⓐ pantamime
   - ⓑ pantomime
   - © pantomim
   - ⓓ pantumime

8. That _____ saw the foul clearly.
   - ⓐ referee
   - ⓑ refere
   - © referree
   - ⓓ refferee

9. The financial accounts are taken care of by the _____ .
   - ⓐ bookeeper
   - ⓑ bookkeper
   - © bookeper
   - ⓓ bookkeeper

10. Long, _____ words can be difficult to spell.
   - ⓐ polysylabic
   - ⓑ polysillabic
   - © polisyllabic
   - ⓓ polysyllabic

Review Test (Side B)

Read each sentence and set of words. Fill in the circle next to the word that is spelled correctly to complete the sentence.

11. A bottle of wine from this _____ can be very expensive.
ⓐ vinyard   ⓒ vineyard
ⓑ vinyrd   ⓓ vinneyard

12. Do movie stars throw _____ parties?
ⓐ extravagent   ⓒ extravagant
ⓑ extravegant   ⓓ extrevegant

13. A _____ dream can seem real to the dreamer.
ⓐ vivvid   ⓒ vivud
ⓑ vivved   ⓓ vivid

14. The suspect didn't realize that the detective had an _____.
ⓐ eye-witness   ⓒ eyewitniss
ⓑ eyewitness   ⓓ ayewitness

15. We aren't _____, so tell us when you think you'll be late.
ⓐ omniscient   ⓒ omnicient
ⓑ omnissient   ⓓ omniscent

16. If you do _____, you will strengthen your cardiovascular system.
ⓐ airobics   ⓒ aerobics
ⓑ arobics   ⓓ erobics

17. It is _____ to believe that monkeys can drive a car.
ⓐ ludicrus   ⓒ ludicros
ⓑ ludecrus   ⓓ ludicrous

18. Wear a suit when you eat at that expensive _____.
ⓐ restaurant   ⓒ restaraunt
ⓑ restauraunt   ⓓ restrant

19. Advertisements often use _____ to sell products.
ⓐ hyperbole   ⓒ hyperbolee
ⓑ hiperbole   ⓓ hyeperbole

20. One spectacular _____ is to make a building disappear.
ⓐ illussion   ⓒ ilusion
ⓑ illusion   ⓓ ellusion

Review Test
Answer Key

Lesson 6

1. d	11. d	21. d
2. d	12. b	22. b
3. b	13. a	23. a
4. c	14. d	24. a
5. a	15. c	25. b
6. d	16. a	
7. a	17. b	
8. c	18. d	
9. c	19. a	
10. b	20. a	

Lesson 12

1. a	11. a	21. d
2. d	12. d	22. d
3. b	13. b	23. a
4. a	14. c	24. c
5. b	15. d	25. a
6. d	16. c	
7. d	17. a	
8. c	18. c	
9. a	19. a	
10. b	20. b	

Lesson 18

1. c	11. c
2. d	12. d
3. a	13. a
4. a	14. b
5. d	15. d
6. b	16. d
7. b	17. b
8. c	18. d
9. b	19. a
10. a	20. d

Lesson 24

1. a	11. d	21. b
2. b	12. c	22. b
3. a	13. c	23. b
4. c	14. b	24. d
5. c	15. a	25. c
6. b	16. d	
7. b	17. c	
8. a	18. c	
9. d	19. d	
10. d	20. a	

Lesson 30

1. b	11. d	21. c
2. d	12. a	22. d
3. a	13. b	23. b
4. d	14. c	24. a
5. a	15. d	25. c
6. b	16. c	
7. b	17. d	
8. a	18. d	
9. c	19. a	
10. a	20. a	

Lesson 36

1. d	11. c
2. b	12. c
3. a	13. d
4. a	14. b
5. c	15. a
6. c	16. c
7. b	17. d
8. a	18. a
9. d	19. a
10. d	20. b

List Words

Word	Lesson	Word	Lesson	Word	Lesson	Word	Lesson
abdomen	1	appetizer	7	bureau	23	contract	11
able-bodied	34	applaud	7	burial	13	convenient	25
absent-minded	34	appliance	7	cabana	29	conviction	9
absolute	21	appraise	7	cafeteria	29	cooperation	9
academically	14	appreciation	7	caffeine	25	copious	4
accelerate	8	apprentice	7	calculator	23	copyright	34
accent	8	appropriate	7	calendar	17	correspondence	26
access	8	approval	7	calorie	10	courteous	10
accommodate	8	approximately	1	camouflage	10	coyote	29
accompany	8	archaeology	20	campus	5	criticism	35
accomplice	8	archery	32	canyon	29	crucial	20
accord	8	arctic	17	capacity	3	crystals	27
accurate	8	aria	28	capitalist	22	culture	5
accustomed	8	armistice	22	carnivorous	31	curable	16
acquire	8	armory	4	caucus	22	currency	23
acre	19	arrogance	26	ceremonial	13	cushion	9
acrobatics	32	arsenal	22	certification	23	cycle	20
actual	1	assassin	7	chaperone	10	cyclone	27
adhesive	1	assault	7	chaplain	10	cylinder	27
administration	23	assert	7	characteristics	20	cymbals	27
adobe	29	asset	7	charitable	16	cynical	27
adolescence	26	association	1	chauffeur	10	debtor	17
advancement	1	assortment	7	cinnamon	3	decathlon	32
aerial	19	assurance	7	circular	3	decibels	28
aerobics	32	astronomy	1	circumference	5	defiance	26
affair	8	attaché	8	civilization	9	delegate	2
affection	9	attachment	8	classic	14	denominator	21
affirm	8	attainable	16	clearance	26	desist	11
affix	8	attentive	8	cockpit	4	despise	2
affliction	11	attire	3	coincidence	26	devotion	9
affront	8	attitude	8	collapse	17	diagonal	21
aggressor	22	attraction	8	collateral	23	diagram	20
agile	32	attribute	5	comically	14	dialect	19
air-conditioned	34	attune	8	commence	26	diameter	1
alfalfa	1	audio-visual	34	commercial	4	dictator	11
alien	1	auditorium	28	commission	15	diction	11
align	3	authorize	23	communicable	16	digestion	9
allegiance	1	available	16	communism	22	disposable	16
alliance	22	axis	19	compact	11	distract	11
amateur	1	bachelor	1	compass	20	district	11
ambitious	13	bacteria	20	compatible	16	dividend	23
ambulance	26	ballerina	28	competition	4	donor	4
amiable	16	barrier	3	complexion	9	dramatic	14
amusement	5	basically	14	complicated	4	drastically	14
analyze	20	basis	1	concerto	28	ecological	19
animation	15	bayou	19	conclusion	4	economic	14
animosity	15	beige	25	confidential	13	educational	35
ankle	32	beneficial	35	conflict	11	efficient	25
anniversary	1	besiege	25	congruent	21	elegance	26
annual	14	betray	2	conscientious	13	eliminate	35
anticipation	4	billion	23	consist	11	elude	31
antonym	27	blockade	4	constrict	11	emancipate	15
apparatus	7	bookkeeper	34	construction	11	embarrass	2
apparel	7	boulevard	10	consumable	16	embassy	2
appeal	7	boutique	10	contestant	32	emission	15
appease	7	brilliance	26	continent	4	emphatic	14
appendage	7	bristle	3	continuous	4	encore	28
appendix	7	bulletin	3	contour	20	encyclopedia	27

List Words

List Words

Word	Lesson	Word	Lesson	Word	Lesson	Word	Lesson
pyramid	27	senior	2	substance	5	tortilla	29
python	27	sergeant	17	substantial	14	toxic	20
quarterback	34	serum	5	subtle	5	tradition	35
quartet	28	siesta	29	suddenness	35	tragic	14
quotable	16	signature	23	suite	10	traitor	22
rebellion	22	significance	26	surveillance	25	transmission	15
receipt	25	silhouette	10	susceptible	35	transparency	1
recession	22	similar	35	suspect	31	trapezoid	21
recitation	9	sincerely	35	suspenders	5	tremendous	35
recollection	2	skew	21	suspicion	9	tremor	20
referee	32	skiing	32	symbolic	27	twenty-nine	34
referendum	22	slogan	4	symmetrical	21	two-thousandths	34
reliable	16	smudge	5	sympathetic	27	typical	27
remittance	23	soccer	32	synonym	17	umpire	32
renegade	29	socialist	22	synopsis	27	unanimous	15
repossess	23	sociology	20	synthesizer	28	unconscious	13
reprieve	25	solidify	27	synthetic	27	unity	5
reservoir	19	sombrero	29	systematic	14	uranium	5
residence	26	spacecraft	34	tactful	11	vacate	1
resistant	11	spacious	13	tamale	29	vacuum	5
resources	19	spatial	20	tangent	21	valise	17
responsible	16	specific	20	tangerine	1	vanilla	29
restaurant	35	spectacular	31	tedious	2	variable	21
restrict	11	sphere	21	tempest	31	vengeance	26
retrospect	31	sportscaster	32	temporal	31	versatile	31
revive	31	sprinter	32	temporary	31	vertical	21
revolution	9	staccato	28	tenacious	13	vicinity	19
rhapsody	28	stampede	29	tension	9	villain	3
rhythm	28	statistics	23	testify	2	vineyard	34
routine	10	stereophonic	28	testimony	3	vitality	31
sacred	2	sterilize	2	theorem	21	vitamin	31
salary	23	stethoscope	20	three-fourths	34	vivid	31
scrimmage	32	strategic	22	throughout	34	xylophone	28
self-sacrifice	34	submission	15	toboggan	32	yacht	35

Bonus Words

Word	Lesson	Word	Lesson	Word	Lesson	Word	Lesson
absurdity	5	assembly	2	boudoir	10	computation	7
acclamation	4	astute	8	breeding	25	consecutive	7
accountable	15	auction	32	broadcast	21	conservation	31
accusation	11	audible	21	Buenos Aires	26	conservative	2
aerospace	9	auditory	35	buffet	1	consolation	15
Afghanistan	19	auricle	35	Cairo	26	consommé	29
amendment	2	authentic	4	capsule	9	conversion	27
analogy	16	awareness	20	carburetor	14	corral	32
analysis	23	ballad	3	cartilage	35	couplet	3
anecdote	5	baritone	28	casserole	1	crankshaft	14
application	17	Beirut	26	chassis	14	cue	21
arbitrate	2	Belgium	19	chlorophyll	31	cultivator	32
Argentina	19	beverage	1	chromosome	25	cursor	27
artichoke	29	biodegradable	31	chronicle	21	data processing	27
asparagus	29	blacksmith	22	coalition	2	decimal	16
aspiration	17	blanch	1	colloquial	13	determined	17
assailant	11	booster	9	commentator	21	development	23

Word	Lesson	Word	Lesson	Word	Lesson	Word	Lesson
vise	23	gullible	8	octave	28	résumé	17
voured	34	haiku	3	odometer	14	rhyme	3
exterous	8	harpsichord	28	offspring	25	sanctuary	31
plomatic	2	haughty	34	omelet	29	sarcastic	5
sposition	11	hazardous	20	operetta	28	satire	5
ssatisfied	15	hearing aid	35	opportunity	17	Seoul	26
stributor	14	heroine	22	originate	23	servant	22
ocumentation	27	hilarity	5	Oslo	26	shuffled	34
ominant	25	honesty	15	Ottawa	26	silage	32
ublin	26	horticulture	32	overhaul	32	sirloin	29
lcimer	28	humble	13	overwrought	34	skeptical	34
ardrum	35	hybrid	32	oxidation	31	slapstick	5
cosystem	20	hypotenuse	7	ozone	20	soldier	22
gregious	13	imagery	3	parfait	29	sonnet	3
liptical	7	impertinent	8	percussion	28	soprano	28
nit	20	impetuous	8	perishable	1	sovereign	2
ndorsement	4	inherited	25	personable	8	speedometer	14
paulet	10	insight	23	Philadelphia	26	square root	7
pic	3	inspection	20	Philippines	19	squeamish	8
quivalent	16	integer	7	photosynthesis	31	statute	11
rroneous	15	integrity	15	pirouette	10	storage	27
spionage	10	interpret	16	piston	14	structured	27
thiopia	19	interview	17	placard	4	stumbled	34
ustachian tube	35	inventive	23	pollutant	20	Switzerland	19
xhibition	4	irony	5	potpourri	10	Sydney	26
xonerate	11	jester	22	precarious	13	tabloid	21
xperiment	23	jurisdiction	11	prediction	16	televise	21
xponent	16	knave	22	preservation	31	Thailand	19
ctor	16	laboratory	23	princess	22	throttle	14
lter	33	larceny	11	printout	27	thrust	9
milial	13	Libya	19	probability	16	tolerant	33
rcical	5	limerick	3	probation	11	tractor	32
rfetched	33	livestock	32	proficient	17	trait	25
stidious	8	lobbyist	2	promenade	10	trajectory	9
ederal	2	lucid	13	promote	4	traverse	33
elony	11	luncheon	1	propellant	9	travesty	33
asco	33	lyrical	3	proponent	2	trombone	28
llet	29	management	27	publicity	21	troubadour	28
olklore	22	marinate	1	pun	5	trough	32
ormula	23	marquee	10	purchase	4	turbulent	33
ortify	33	mastoid	35	quadrant	16	tyrant	33
ractions	16	membrane	35	quaint	13	uninhabited	31
rijoles	29	menagerie	10	qualifications	17	utensils	1
rustration	15	merchant	22	queasy	34	veal	29
urious	13	message	4	radiator	14	velocity	9
utile	33	metronome	28	radioactive	20	Venezuela	19
jarnish	1	microwave	1	ragout	10	vertices	7
jazette	21	mode	7	rambled	34	vertigo	35
jenerate	23	modem	27	ratio	7	vicarious	13
jenerator	14	motion sickness	35	recessive	25	vicious	13
jenes	25	mutation	25	reciprocal	7	vignette	10
jenetics	25	narrative	3	reentry	9	volatile	20
jenteel	8	New Delhi	26	references	17	voucher	4
jerminate	31	newscast	21	reimburse	4	waiver	11
jraphic	27	Nicaragua	19	remunerate	15	wheezed	34
jravitation	9	noxious	20	rendezvous	9	wildlife	31
jregarious	5	obligation	15	request	15	wizard	22
jrouchy	34	obnoxious	8	resignation	17	zucchini	29

Spelling Enrichment

Group Practice

Crossword Relay First, draw a large grid on the board. Then, divide the class into several teams. Teams compete against each other to form separate crossword puzzles on the board. Individuals on each team take turns racing against members of the other teams to join list words until all possibilities have been exhausted. A list word may appear on each crossword puzzle only once. The winning team is the team whose crossword puzzle contains the greatest number of correctly spelled list words or the team who finishes first.

Proofreading Relay Write two columns of misspelled list words on the board. Although the errors can differ, be sure that each list has the same number of errors. Divide the class into two teams and assign each team to a different column. Teams then compete against each other to correct their assigned lists by team members taking turns erasing and replacing an appropriate letter. Each member may correct only one letter per turn. The team that is first to correct its entire word list wins.

Detective Call on a student to be a detective. The detective must choose a spelling word from the list and think of a structural clue, definition, or synonym that will help classmates identify it. The detective then states the clue using the format, "I spy a word that. . . ." Students are called on to guess and spell the mystery word. Whoever answers correctly gets to take a turn being the detective.

Spelling Tic-Tac-Toe Draw a tic-tac-toe square on the board. Divide the class into X and O teams. Take turns dictating spelling words to members of each team. If the word is spelled correctly, allow the team member to place an X or O on the square. The first team to place three X's or O's in a row wins.

Words of Fortune Have students put their heads down while you write a spelling word on the board in large letters. Then, cover each letter with a sheet of sturdy paper. The paper can be fastened to the board with a magnet. Call on a student to guess any letter of the alphabet they think may be hidden. If that particular letter is hidden, then reveal the letter in every place where it appears in the word by removing the paper.

The student continues to guess letters until an incorrect guess is made or the word is revealed. In the event that an incorrect guess is made, a different student continues the game. Continue the game until every list word has been hidden and then revealed.

Applied Spelling

Journal Allow time each day for students to write in a journal. A spiral bound notebook can be used for this purpose. Encourage students to express their feelings about events that are happening in their lives at home or at school. Alternatively, they could write about what their plans are for the day. To get them started, you may have to provide starter phrases.

You may wish to collect the journals periodically to write comments that echo what the student has written. For example, a student's entry might read, "My brother is suceptibul to infecshuns. He will probabie need to see the doctor again today." The teacher's response could be, "People who are susceptible to infections will probably need to visit their doctors regularly to stay well." This method allows students to learn correct spelling and sentence structure without emphasizing their errors in a negative way.

Letter to the Teacher On a regular basis, have student each write a note to the teacher. At first the teacher might suggest topics or provide a starter sentence, including words from the spelling list. The teacher should write a response at the bottom of each letter that provides the student with a model of any spelling or sentence structure that evidences need of improvement.

Daily Edit Each day provide a brief writing sample on the board that contains errors in spelling, capitalization, or punctuation. Have students rewrite the sample correctly. Provide time later in the day to have the class correct the errors on the board while students self-correct their work.

Spelling Notebook Have students use the Spelling Notebook in the student book, a stenographer's notebook, or stapled-together pages of the Spelling Notebook reproducible (see page 111 in the *Teacher's Edition*) to keep a record of words they encounter difficulty spelling. Tabs could be added to some pages to separate a large notebook into sections for each letter of the alphabet. Urge students to use a dictionary or ask the teacher to help them spell words with which they are having trouble. Periodically, allow students to work in pairs to test each other on a set of words taken from their personal word list

Acrostic Poems Have students write a word from the spelling list vertically. Then, instruct them to join a word horizontally to each letter of the list word. The horizontal words must begin with the letters in the list word. They could be words that are synonyms or that describe or relate feelings about the list word. Encourage students to refer to a dictionary for help in finding appropriate words. Here is a sample acrostic poem:

    Evade
    Lose
    U-turn
    Dodge
    Escape

Poem Exchange Provide students with copies of a familiar poem. Discuss how some of the words can be exchanged for other words that have similar meanings. As students to rewrite the poem exchanging some of the words for other words.

Spelling Notebook

Level G Student Record Chart

Name _____

			Pretest	Final Test	Bonus Test
Lesson 1	Vowel **a**				
Lesson 2	Vowel **e**				
Lesson 3	Vowel **i**				
Lesson 4	Vowel **o**				
Lesson 5	Vowel **u**				
Lesson 6	Lessons 1–5 • Review		■		■
Lesson 7	Words Beginning with **ap**, **as**				
Lesson 8	Prefixes **ac**, **af**, **at**				
Lesson 9	Words Ending with **ion** or **ation**				
Lesson 10	Words with French Derivations				
Lesson 11	Latin Roots				
Lesson 12	Lessons 7–11 • Review		■		■
Lesson 13	Suffixes **ial**, **ious**				
Lesson 14	Suffixes **al**, **ally**, **ic**, **ically**, **ly**				
Lesson 15	Latin Roots				
Lesson 16	Suffixes **able**, **ible**				
Lesson 17	Challenging Words				
Lesson 18	Lessons 13–17 • Review		■		■
Lesson 19	Words from Geography				
Lesson 20	Words from Science				
Lesson 21	Words from Math				
Lesson 22	Words from History				
Lesson 23	Words from Business				
Lesson 24	Lessons 19–23 • Review		■		■
Lesson 25	Words with **ei** and **ie**				
Lesson 26	Suffixes **ance**, **ence**, **ce**				
Lesson 27	**y** as a Vowel				
Lesson 28	Words from Music				
Lesson 29	Words with Spanish Derivations				
Lesson 30	Lessons 25–29 • Review		■		■
Lesson 31	Latin Roots				
Lesson 32	Words from Sports				
Lesson 33	Words with Latin and Greek Prefixes				
Lesson 34	Compound Words and Hyphenates				
Lesson 35	Challenging Words				
Lesson 36	Lessons 31–35 • Review		■		■

Lesson	6	12	18	24	30	36
Standardized Review Test						